MEN OF METALS AND MATERIALS:
MY MEMOIRS

MEN OF METALS AND MATERIALS: MY MEMOIRS

GOPAL S. UPADHYAYA

Materials Consultant
&
Formerly, Professor at Indian Institute of Technology Kanpur

37B, Ravindrapuri
Lane 17, Varanasi 221005 India

iUniverse, Inc.
Bloomington

MEN OF METALS AND MATERIALS: MY MEMOIRS

iUniverse
1663 Liberty Drive
Bloomington, IN 47403
www.iuniverse.com
1-800-Authors (1-800-288-4677)

ISBN: 978-1-4620-1840-6 (sc)
ISBN: 978-1-4620-1843-7 (ebk)

Printed in the United States of America

iUniverse rev. date: 05/03/2011

Dedicated to my

late Parents, who
groomed me to speak truth:

Author

CONTENTS

Preface...xi

Chapter 1
My Teachers in Metallurgical Engineering...1

    Getting educated at Banaras Hindu University.......................2
    Voyage to U.K...5
    Further Studies in USSR 10

Chapter 2
My Colleagues at Varanasi, Roorkee and Kanpur.............................17

    At Banaras Hindu University...17
    At University of Roorkee 20
    At Indian Institute of Technology, Kanpur 25
    Dr. K.P. Singh 26
    Dr. E.C. Subba Rao..26
    Dr. K.P. Gupta 28
    Dr. Ahindra Ghosh 29
    Dr. G.S. Murty...30
    Dr. T.R. Ramachandran 31
    Dr. P.C. Kapur 32
    Dr. R.K. Ray 33
    Dr. Brahm Deo 34
    Other Colleagues..35

Chapter 3
Some Men of Metals and Materials from India.............................36

    Late Dr. P.L. Agrawal...36
    Late Dr. V.A. Altekar...39
    Late Dr. D.P. Antia..40

Dr. V.S. Arunachalam..43

Dr. R.D. Bhargava...47

Late Dr. S. Bhattacharjee.....................................49

Late Dr. Brahm Prakash 50

Dr. Amit Chatterjee 52

Late Professor P.R. Dhar 54

Mr. N.T. George 56

Dr. J.J. Irani 58

Professor S.K. Joshi 60

Mr. B.M. Kataria 62

Dr. R.Kumar 64

Late Mr. Y.M. Mehta...66

Dr. V.N. Misra 67

Dr. J. Mukerjee 68

Dr. M. K. Mukherjee 69

Dr. C.G.K. Nair 71

Professor K.A.Padmanabhan.....................................72

Late Mr. N.M. Pai 73

Late Dr. V.G. Paranjpe 75

Late Dr. Prabhu Nath..77

Dr. Baldev Raj 78

Professor P. Ramakrishnan.....................................80

Professor S. Ranganathan 82

Professor C.N.R. Rao 83

Late Dr. N.K. Rao...86

Dr. P.Rama Rao 88

Late Professor P. Ramachandra Rao 90

Late Dr. P. Rodriguez 92

Late Mr. P. R. Roy 94

Dr. R.G. Shah 96

Mr. R. Srinivasan 97

Late Dr. R.V. Tamhankar 99

Late Professor G.S. Tendolkar................................101

Chapter 4

Some Men of Metals and Materials from Overseas 105

Dr. L. Albano-Muller (Germany) 105

Professor R.A. Andrievski (Russia)...........................107

Late Dr. F. Benezowski (Austria)...108

Dr. Gian F. Bocchini (Italy)...110

Mr. K. J. A. Brookes (U.K.)...111

Late Professor R.F. Bunshah (USA) 112

Late Professor R.W. Cahn (U.K.) 114

Professor A. C.D. Chaklader (Canada)....................................117

Late Professor R.L. Coble (USA)..118

Late Professor Morris Cohen (USA) 119

Professoe H. Danninger (Austria)...120

Mr Edul M. Daver (USA) 121

Dr. J. Dusczyck (The Netherlands)..122

Dr. Sunil Dutta (USA) 123

Late Professor H.E. Exner (Germany) 125

Late Professor Eric Fitzer (Germany) 127

Professor R. M. German (USA)...128

Late Professor N.J. Grant (USA) 130

Late Professor H. H. Hausner (USA / Austria) 132

Professor Lai Ho-Yi (People Republic of China)...................134

Late Professor Bernard Ilschner(Germany / Switzerland) 135

Professor Shinhoo Kang (S. Korea)..136

Dr.A. Q. Khan (Pakistan)...138

Late Professor Richard Kieffer (Austria)................................140

Dr. N.C. Kothari (Australia)..142

Late Professor George Kuczynski (USA) 142

Professor Alan Lawley (USA)...144

Late Professor F.V. Lenel (USA)...145

Mr Per Lindskog (Sweden) 147

Late Dr. Sylvana Luckyx (South Africa) 148

Dr. Har Bhajan (Harb) Singh Nayar (USA).........................149

Professor R. Pampuch (Poland) 151

Dr. Henri H. Pastor (France)..152

Professor Guenter Petzow (Germany) 153

Academician Professor M.M. Ristic (Yugoslavia/Serbia) 156

Professor P.K. Rohatgi (USA) 157

Late Professor Rustom Roy (USA)..159

Professor Vinod K. Sarin (USA) 163

Late Professor W. Schatt (Germay) 165

Professor S. Somiya (Japan)..166

Professor Ken-ichi Takagi (Japan) 168
Professor A. Tholen (Denmark/Sweden)..............170
Professor F. Thummler (Germany) 171
Professor Jose M. Torralba (Spain) 173
Professor O. Van der Biest (Belgium) 174
Professor Richard Warren (Sweden).....................175

Epilogue..177
Appendix I 183
Appendix II..233

PREFACE

After getting the official retirement from the Indian Institute of Technology (IIT) at Kanpur (2001) I have been thinking to pen down some of my memoirs. I have been doing this at a rather leisure pace, when of late, I determined to finish this task quickly. There were two reaons, firstly I was afraid that my memory might be getting a bit blurred, as I am 71+, and secondly a number of my peers are gradually dying. I wanted they too read this book of mine. I may mention that I never maintained a diary and all the inputs in the book have come from my memory only.

Chapter 1 describes my Metallurgical Engineering education at the Banaras Hindu University (India), University of Birmingham (U.K.) and lastly at the Kiev Institute of Technology (Ukraine, formerly USSR). There I was lucky to have doyens like Professor Daya Swarup, Professor A.D. McQuillan and Professor G.V. Samsonov as my teachers and guide. The coverage of my last teacher ie Professor Samsonov has been comparatively more detailed,since it with him that I had by most intimate exposure as a research student. Chapter 2 covers my memoirs of colleagues at my work places ie. at BHU, University of Roorkee (now IIT, Roorkee) and IIT Kanpur. Chapter 3 and 4 cover the personal accounts of some of the men of metals and materials from India and abroad respectively with whom my interaction has been substantial. Some of the famous men from overseas are Professors Morris Cohen, Rustom Roy, Kuczynski, Hausner, Bunshah (USA), Professors Petzow, Thummler and Exner (Germany), Dr. Pastor (France), Professor Somiya (Japan) and last but not the least the notorious Dr. A.Q. Khan (Pakistan). From India some of the famous personalities are Dr. Antia, Dr. Brahm Prakash, Dr. Tamhankar, Dr. Rama Rao, Professors G.S. Tendolkar, S.K. Joshi, CNR Rao etc. Finally, 'Epologue' offers some of my own impressions on the burning issues faced in my country regarding scientific R & D, engineering education and their management.

The memoirs relate to the personalities of 20th Century and the decades mentioned like seventies, eighties etc pertain to that. I have avoided to refer each event as that of the last Century.

Finally my valuable past students, who are presently enjoying responsible positions here and abroad are also very much men of metals and materials. However, due to space limitations I could not describe them in thie book. My next book on memoires shall definitely cover them.

The book is written dispassionately withot any partisanship or prejudice. It is true that it is not that easy to write about others, but a honest attempt has been made.

March 2011   Author

1

My Teachers in Metallurgical Engineering

I was born in Varanasi (Banara+s or Kashi), the holiest city for Hindus in India in a Brahmin family of high learnings. My father was on the faculty of the Sanskrit Department of the Arts College in the famous Banaras Hindu University (BHU). Our house was in the old part of the city, made of sand stones, near the bank of Ganges. My acquaintance with metals in the childhood was foremost with brass, since our house was very near the locality of brass smiths, called 'Thatheri Bazar'. The other metal was silver in the foil form as right in our neighbourhood, the artisans used to beat and rebeat them, for uses in sweet and betel coverings. The sound of beating was always a rhythmic one. Another metal, aluminium, was considered base and was not used by our community. I came to know that the very first Aluminium company in India in Belur in the Howrah District of West Bengal State was started to produce utencils, mainly used by Hajis. Another material ceramic, was also in abundant use. The most common baked clay products were disposable drinking pots. These were quite thin walled because of the special character of Varanasi clay. The artifacts, particularly the idols of varying sizes of Hindu deities, were very decorative. Later I came to know the use of metals and their compounds in powdery form for indigenous Ayurvedic medicines. They are called 'Dhatu Bhasm', being milled in form of ultra fine powder. Practically every household using such medicines, was in possession of a mortar and pestle and used to remill the powder just before administering the medicine.

My interest with metals arose, while I was a student in standard VIII in 1950. My father was invited by a cultural society of Jamshedpur to deliver a lecture on 'Geeta'. The corresponding person Mr. N. Mishra happened to be an old student of my father. He worked in the PRO Office of Tata Steel. My father told me to accompany him. During our visit, Mr. Mishra took us for a detailed visit of the steel plant and the most exciting scene for me was the teeming of the pig iron from the blast furnace. It was so radiant and gushing that I made a point to see the operation more than once. It is irony that in my later professional years, I did not work on liquid metals, which originally attracted me towards metallurgy.

GETTING EDUCATED AT BANARAS HINDU UNIVERSITY

My whole education from schooling to Bachelors degree in metallurgical engineering was carried out at Banaras Hindu University (BHU) and its constituent school. This university was founded by social reformer and freedom fighter Madan Mohan Malviya in the year 1916. He travelled extensively across India to gather funds and donations to set up the university. In his endeavours he was supported by social activist and theosophist Ms. Annie Besant. This university was and still is the biggest in whole of Asia. Moreover, it was different than any wholly Government assisted University. The founder had a holistic philosophy both in theory and practice. It is better, if I quote here. He said: 'Education does not consist merely of book-learning and the time has come when India needs something more. The development of intellect and the building up of character must proceed hand in hand and at a time of student's life when he is most susceptible to influence . . . . We want men of constructive genius who will build up the edifice of India's moral and materials well-being.'

After schooling for many years, my affinity towards metals became dormant, till I completed my examination of B.Sc. in April, 1956. Soon there after was the summer vacation for two months and I was naturally pretty free. I was a regular visitor of the famous library of 'Nagri Pracharini Sabha', which was not far away from our house. In the meanwhile, my father informed me that the book authored by the famous metallurgist Dr. Daya Swarup of Banaras Hindu University has been published in Hindi by the former organization. I became quite curious to read the book. By that time I had read some rudimentary of metal extraction in inorganic chemistry. I presumed that the book would be a mere extension of the chemistry, but soon got amazed with the multi-facetted nature of this subject, particularly the microstructure-mechanical behaviour relationship. I reread the book and decided to learn the subject in the department, where Dr. Swarup was the Head. To be very honest, I was not too keen on the extraction side not because the subject was dry, but it was taught in a very descriptive style. The real why and how were not elaborated, as it is done now-a-days. However, the aspects of physical metallurgy were introduced very systematically. One of the best teachers was Dr. Rajendra Kumar, who took the position of a Reader in the department after a stint at Indian Institute of Technology, Kharagpur. He had done his Ph.D. in Physical Metallurgy of Steels from the famous Sheffield University, U.K. He was an excellent teacher and a fine task master.

Another teacher in Physical Metallurgy was Mr. A.K. Mallik, who after a brief stint, left for Indian Institute of Technology at Bombay. He was a good teacher, but his early half period in lectures used to be just the repetition of what he talked in the earlier lecture. This used to make us a bit bored. For Iron and Steel Making course the teacher was a British Professor G.R. Bashforth, an Unesco Professor, under whom later I worked for six months as a research scholar. Professor Bashforth was a fine gentleman, with a lot of industrial experience. At B.H.U., he built a functioning prototype of LD furnace for steel making. We the students used to watch the operation very attentively. Mr. K.N. Gupta, an alumnus of our department was the right hand of Professor Bashforth. After Professor Bashforth's stay, he moved out to join the National Metallurgical Laboratory as a scientist.

Metallurgical Analysis course was taught by Dr. H.N. Sinha, who, later, moved to IIT, Bombay and subsequently settled in Australia. Some how he was not comfortable in India with his Australian wife. His style of teaching was extempore and he never brought any teaching notes in the lecture room. Electrochemistry and corrosion was taught by Mr. D.L. Roy, who, later, shifted to IIT, Bombay. He was a kind person. The only problem with him was that he was very monotonous, while lecturing, without any raising or lowering of pitch. This used to make us a bit drowsy. There was no mechanism, then, like student reaction survey.

My other teachers at B.H.U. were R. Sharan, V.K. Agrawal, Bhanu Prakash and scores of others who had just passed out from the department. These new recruits were rather migratory in nature. Some stayed only for few months or so, before joining their new jobs in industry. The biggest industry for metallurgists was the newly founded Hindustan Steels Ltd., which had three plants at Rourkela, Bhilai and Durgapur. Some of our teachers went abroad for higher studies, notably among them were Krishan

Lal to France, Amitabh Mohanty and Bhanu Prakash to Yugoslavia. Mr. Mohanty taught us powder metallurgy. I had no prenotion that in future I shall he devoted to this branch of metallurgy. Mr. Sharan and Agrawal left for USA for their M.S. degrees at the University of Missouri and Cornell respectively. Later Mr. Sharan joined the University of Roorkee and subsequently National Institute of Foundry and Forge Technology at Ranchi. Mr. Agrawal later shifted to IIT Kanpur and subsequently to Hindustan Aluminium Co. (HINDALCO), where he did exceedingly well attaining the position of Vice-President R&D.

I shall be failing, if I do not dwell upon one of our most important teacher Dr. Daya Swarup. As such he did not teach any course completely, but rather took some special lectures. I still remember his lecture on age hardening. His look was rather an intent one, and he used to speak with some pauses. In the middle of his lecture, he used to ask questions, but never reprimanded those who did not answer correctly. The biggest contribution of Dr. Swarup was in academic administration. He brought funding in the department. He loved his past students and always took care of their professional prosperities. The department was a model in whole of Asia and when IITs started, their professors used to visit our department to study its curriculum structure and lists of laboratory experiments etc. I recall the visit of Professor Tendolkar in 1958/59, along with four Russian visiting professors of IIT Bombay. Dr. Swarup told us to explain why and how we perform our assigned experiments. Dr. Swarup was an excellent sportsman too, tennis being his favourite. It was mandatory that all students participated in sports and those who were absentees were identified and brought to the notice. Dr. Swarup instilled in us the concept of total personality. It was this attribute of his that all of his students did so well in their later lives. In the year 1962, Dr. Swarup left BHU for a still bigger mission in helping the Planning Commission, Government of Indian at New Delhi. After the end of his tenure there, he moved to his native city Kanpur and joined Thermit India Ltd. as its Technical Director. I have had a good opportunity to interact with him during my early days at IIT Kanpur.

Just after completing the B.Sc. (Met. Engg.) programme from Banaras Hindu University in June 1960, I joined Professor Bashforth's team as a research scholar. The research topic was vacuum melted creep resistant alloy steels. Under the Unesco aid, the department had obtained a small vacuum melting furnace (Mo-resistance) from Edward High Vacuum, U.K.

I was instrumental in installing the same with the help of the technician Mr. Yadav. Mr. Sukh Dev Sehgal was then working in the department as a lecturer and was also doing his part-time Ph.D. on the effect of Misch metal in stainless steels. He had just come from USA after completing his M.S. degree and was overenthusiastic in completing his research as fast as possible. One morning I found him in a bad mood. In the previous night he had heated the charge in the vacuum furnace too fast, which made the crucible to crack and the seepage of molten steel spoiling the resistor. I was more than sad and upset, since I had toiled in installing the furnace.

After six months stay at BHU, I made up my mind to move out to the University of Birmingham in U.K. Professor Bashforth was inquisitive to know which department was I joining. The Head of the Industrial Metallurgy Department at the University of Birmingham Professor E.C. Rollason was his close friend and hence Professor Bashforth suggested me to meet him. In his short period of six months at BHU, I was assigned to write a critical review on vacuum melting and casting of steels, which I completed dutifully. The review was published by me later in India. Professor Bashforth had a big collection of reprints of various papers and he offered the same as and when I was in need. He was a chain smoker and never missed a chance to book a room in the famous Clark's hotel of Varanasi every week end. Every Monday morning, he used to come as a rejuvenated man. Many of us had bought his book 'The Manufacture of Iron and Steel' (3 volumes) published by Chapamn & Hall and very fondly got it autographed by him.

VOYAGE TO U.K.

I sailed for U.K. from Bombay on 14th December, 1960 by an Italian Liner 'Flota Lauro', The ship was named 'Roma'. On the ship, there were many Indians, who mostly were proceeding in the hope of jobs. In those days there was no visa requirement for U.K. The food on the ship was not tasty and my being vegetarian was an added impediment. The Christmas was celebrated on the ship, in which may Indians took part. It was rather comic to see a Sardarji in a dressing gown, dancing in the Hall. May be he was too proud of his new gown? The captain of the ship gave the Christmas message on TV, which was translated by me in Hindi. It was the first occasion, when I saw a TV camera. On the ship, I met Professor Krishna and his wife, from Allahabad University, where he taught Physics.

He was going to MIT for further research. Van Hippel's book on Molecular Science was invariably in his hand.

All the passengers of the ship reached London by train from Genova (Italy). While crossing the English Channel, I met a young Sardarji. He suggested me to accompany him to a Gurudwara in Shepherd's bush in London. I readily accepted his offer. The Gurudwara management gave us a bed in the basement, which was pretty cold. Any way, next morning I bought a train ticket for Birmingham, which reached me around 7 PM at Snow Hill Station. It was mildly snowing. I walked to YMCA, which was very close to Railway Station. As there was no vacant room, they advised me to approach the Corporation's reception centre, which was not too far. There, I felt the real warmth in the office room, which was adequately gas heated. An Iranian student was also there in a similar need. The office staff fixed a room for us in the Selly Oak for one night only. We took a taxi and reached the locality. The land lady received us and directed to our respective rooms. I was so much tired that I immediately went into deep sleep. Next morning, I got ready, took the English breakfast in their dining room and paid the room rent to the Lady. She instructed me to keep my suitcase near the main entrance. I literally followed her instructions.

The University of Birmingham was in a walking distance from my lodge. An English lady, who happened to be a nurse in the University health centre, was passing through the main iron gate. She helped me in locating the Department of Physical Metallurgy. I climbed two floors and reached the department office. The secretary of Professor A.D. McQuillan, who was going to be my thesis supervisor, promptly escorted me to his office. He was a handsome, slim man of about 40 years age, with a nicely groomed hairs. I had earlier read his book on Titanium, coauthored by his wife Mrs. M.K. McQuillan. She was then the Director of the Titanium Division of the Imperial Metal Industries in Birmingham. Professor McQuillan greeted me and soon revealed his Irish origin. Even in the first meeting be did not hesitate to reveal that he was not too fond of Englishmen. I was a bit astonished with his open and candid statements. He called Dr. R.W. Cahn, who was a Reader in the department, to his office and introduced me to him. Later, I came to know why he did so? Dr. Cahn was very interested in Indian Culture and Philosophy. Although, a number of Indian students did study in the Industrial Metallurgy Department, I was the first one in the Physical Metallurgy Department. Professor McQuillan showed me various laboratories and took for lunch. In his research laboratory, I met Dr. D.W. Jones, who was just awarded the Ph.D. degree. He was an ICI Fellow at that time. Soon I realised that Dr. Jones is the real administrator of the laboratory and many times he used to interfere in the decision of Professor McQuillan. I could not understand the helplessness of Professor McQuillan. Anyway, I was not too much involved with Dr. Jones. Another research student was Mr. Pessal, who after his Ph.D. studies joined Westinghouse R&D in Pittsburgh. The research area of Professor McQuillan was on the nature of refractory metal alloys and their hydrides, particularly from the stand point of electronic structure. The assignment given to me was X-ray crystallography of early transition refractory metal alloys and their hydrides. The hydrides were synthesized in the laboratory with utmost precision. Prof. McQuillan ordered a pair of X-ray powder camera of Philips make, as other cameras were in the laboratory of Professor Raynor, where Rex Harris was doing Ph.D. on rare-earth alloys. I used to borrow the camera from Rex, who never hesitated in reminding me, whenever there was even a slight delay in returning it. Rex was from Wales and later joined the faculty of the department rising to the post of Headship. I must admit, that as an Indian, I was cheerfully accepted by a Welsch, than a mid-land English student.

Because of the space shortage in Professor McQuillan's laboratory, I was put up in another hall, where I was introduced to Dr. James Waber of Los Alamos Laboratory, New Mexico, U.S.A. He was on an exchange programme with Professor Raynor. His office desk was adjacent to mine. He was of the German origin and had many sons and daughters. As he was from a Nuclear Establishment, he was skeptical of others. He did have some doubt that his desk was spied. Once he enquired from me, whether I touched his materials. I consoled him and advised him to be out of the prevailing cold war syndrome. In those days India was considered more like a communist country and Americans were very skeptical. Sooner he became very friendly with me and occasionally invited me and Rex to his apartment. Later Dr. Waber became the Professor in the Materials Science Department of the North Western University at Evanston, USA.

My meeting with the Head of the Department, Professor G.V. Raynor was a formal one. He possessed a lustre in his face, with a mild smile. He spoke in measured words. I attended his lectures on alloy theory in which Dr. Waber also used to sit. Dr. R.E. Smallman, was then, a senior lecturer in the department. I attended some of his lectures. He was fond of talking about Instron machine for mechanical characterization. Soon his book 'Modern Physical Metallurgy' was published by Butterworths. The concept of materials science was creeping in USA and UK was not behind in this respect. The Birmingham metallurgical education was largely basic in nature. This made any physical metallurgist from USA to put on his intinerary Birmingham. The foundation of Physical Metallurgy Department was laid by Professor Hanson, followed by doyens like Professor Cottrell and Raynor. Dr. R.W. Cahn was married to the daughter of Professor Hanson. I used to meet this couple in Barber Hall of the University during music concerts.

Another faculty member in the department of Physical Metallurgy Dr. Eshelby could be better categorized as mathematician / physicist. He was always in thinking mode while walking and at times there was fear that he may colloid with other. He was contemporary to Dr. Bilby at Sheffield University, who also researched on similar theoretical topics.

A number of famous American professors visited our department during my stay at Birmingham. One of them was Professor Mehl from Carnegie Institute of Technology, Pittsburgh. He was a tall handsome person with extraordinary oratory. He spoke on the advent of materials science. I got introduced to him and enquired about Dr. Bunshah, an old alumnus of BHU, who completed his Ph.D. for Carnegie Institute of Technology. I shall be writing about Dr. Bunshah later. Other visitor was Professor Nix from Stanford University. These American visitors paid a lot of tribute to British physical metallurgists, a feature lacking for the German visitors.

The liberation of Goa by Indian Army was a major news during my stay at Birmingham. Many of my die hard Englishmen castigated me, but I never avoided speaking the truth. In a way they realized that India is not that weak as they had assumed.

After about one year stay of mine at Birmingham, Mr. Panchanan Tiwary, joined our department as a Commonwealth research scholar. He was from Bihar in India and a bit shy person. He researched under the supervision of Dr. S.G. Glover on stabilization of austenite. Later he was my colleague at the University of Roorkee. It is pity this bright metallurgist died prematurely because of renal ailment. His apartment in Birmingham was in an Asian-African locality. One evening we both went to watch a drama in the theatre. At the end of the show, Mr. Tiwari got badly mugged, while walking from the bus stop to his apartment. The lodging of complaint to the police did not help him in any way. I felt a bit guilty as it was I, who took the initiative to take him to the theatre.

To attend a scientific conference/seminar is a part of education. Keeping this in mind, we both myself and Mr. Tiwari attended the Annual Meeting of the Institute of Metals held at Swansea. There, we met Professor H.O. Neill, who was heading the metallurgy department of the University of Wales in Swansea. We had earlier read his book entitled 'Hardness of Metals'. Professor Hume-Rothery of the University of Oxford was also a participant. In his teens, he had completely lost the hearing capability. What a surprise? This scientist not only completed his Ph.D. at Oxford, but also laid the foundation of the world famous metallurgy department there. He always had an interpreter, who used to write a paper. Mr. R.D. Doherty was then a Ph.D. student at Oxford and he was his interpreter in the meeting. Mr. Doherty, later, became Professor at Drexel University in USA. Both myself and Doherty became close friends. During the conference, I faced a problem. The organizers during the Annual General Meeting had arranged for the gala dinner and they invited me. It was mandatory to wear the dinner jacket. As I had none, I enquired from Mr. Doherty. He had taken one on rent from Oxford and suggested me to look out one in the down town. Even with best attempt, I could not locate any shop. Anyway! I did get a sound sleep that night. I took advantage of my Swansea visit to take a tour of Mond Nickel Co. This firm was the main supplier of the metal to Rolls-Royce, which was the leader in jet engines. Dr. S.N. Anant Narayan, an alumnus of B.H.U. metallurgical engineering department, happened to be Mond Nickel's representative in India.

My stay at Bimingham University was coming to an end by December, 1962. I submitted my M.Sc. Thesis and the external examine was Dr. D.A. Robins, of English Electric Co. He was there the General Manager R&D. I had read one of his reviews in the 'Metallurgical Reviews', published periodically by the Institute of Metals. In one of its issues he had put a model of electronic concentration for elucidating the properties of refractory metals and their compounds. I did not think that essential to put that work as a reference in my thesis, and this invited the trouble for me. During the viva examination, Dr. Robins mentioned about his review. Although I replied reasonably well all the questions raised by him he was insistent that the reference of that paper must be in my thesis. Anyway, I took back all the copies of my thesis from the Registrars' office, got few pages modified and resubmitted the same. Dr. Robins readily reread and accepted the thesis. Later, Dr. Robins got shifted to the 'International Tin Research Institute'. I met him during one of the Annual Meetings of the Indian Institute of Metals held in Bombay in the year 1974. Late FAA Jasdanwala, the then President of IIM was his host.

During my stay at Bimingham two of my B.H.U. classmates V. Raghavan and Subramaniam visited me. Both were doing their Ph.D. research at the University of Sheffield. They were deeply impressed by our twin departments: Department of Physical Metallurgy and the Department of Industrial Metallurgy. Later Dr. Raghavan joined IIT Kanpur and subsequently moved to IIT, Delhi, from where he retired. Dr. Subramaniam is currently a Professor at the University of McMaster, Canada, his specialization being solidification.

After completing the M.Sc. programme by research, I wished to have some more experience. I joined Lanchester Institute of Technology at Coventry as a Research Associate and part-time lecturer. Dr. David Kirk, a graduate and Ph.D. holder from the Industrial Metallurgy Department of Birmingham University was the Head of Metallurgy Division. A research project of Alcan Industries was given to me, for which I used to visit their laboratories at Banbury, Oxfordshire. Teaching to HNC and HND students was a new experience. These boys and girls were working in industries and studying part-time in evenings.

In the middle of 1963, I decided to return to India, again by sea. This time I chose a French Liner, the ship's name was 'Vietnam'. In the ship I met my old classmate Mr. Arun Upadhye from Bombay. His father, an engineering graduate by B.H.U., had a powder metallurgy firm in Bombay, named 'Simetall'. Arun was directed by him to take sound practical training at German PM plants. He was a staunch socialist. It is surprising he permanently left India and now works in the PM plant 'Pacific Sintered Metals' in Los Angeles, U.S.A.

FURTHER STUDIES IN USSR

In October, 1966 I proceeded from Roorkee to USSR for my Ph.D. research. I was awarded the USSR Government scholarship. The advances in space technology in USSR was spectacular and this fascinated me to choose USSR for further studies. In my Air India flight from Delhi to Moscow, I met Mr. Nagarajan, whom I had previously met in the Ministry of Education in New Delhi during our interview. It was a day journey and the flight was an unusually smooth one. We were received by the USSR Ministry people at Shermetov airport and taken to a graduate student hostel is down town. The food habit had to be changed drastically. After three days of conditioning at Moscow, we two myself and Nagarajan were put in a sleeper train for Kiev, the capital of Ukraine Republic of USSR. The crossing of the bridge on Dnepre river in the morning was a real romantic scene. Kiev is also known as the city of gardens. The secretary of the Dean's Office was at the railway station to receive us. At Kiev Institute of Technology, we were lodged in one of their crowded hostel. Within few days another Indian Mr. S.K. Nag, who was teaching in Jadavpur University also joined us. We were four in a room and it was mandatory that a soviet student was also with foreign students. This soviet was an adult person is thirties and I wondered whether he was a student. The daily chores in the hostel was a difficult one. There were few toilets, but the student strength was high. The stinking atmosphere made us quite unpleasant. But, fortunately, within few months, we all were shifted in a newly constructed hostel (Hall IV) with attached toilet, bathroom and hot water facilities. It was in the Viborskaya street in the campus.

Next morning after finishing the document formalities at Dean's office, myself and Mr. Nagarajan were escorted to the Department of Heat Treatment in the Faculty of Mechanical Technology, The head of the department was Professor Permyakov, an old person with some degree of infirmity caused during the world war II. His specialization was phase transformation in steels and his laboratory was well equipped specially with magnetic measurement facilities. Mr. Nagarajan accepted to work in that department. I was still undecided. While in the University of Roorkee, I was in the mailing list of various publishers including Consultants Bureau/Plenum Press of New York, From these, I knew about some books by Professor G.V. Samsonov, who worked in Kiev. I enquired about this Professor and the Dean's office informed me that right below the laboratory of Professor Permyakov is the department (Powder Metallurgy and Rare Metals) of Professor Samsonov. I came to know that he is part-time associated with the department, but was full time associated with the Institute of Materials Problems in the Ukrainian Academy of Sciences as the Deputy-Director. On my request, the Dean Office fixed an appointment with him. As my knowledge of Russian language was zero, I requested another Indian student,Mr. Das a Chemical Engineer, to accompany me. Mr. Das had joined the Institute two years back and so he was reasonably good in Russian technical terminology. We both were sitting in the corridor, when Professor Samsonov briskly walked and entered into his office. He had a heavy weight, but this in no way hampered in his brisk steps. I could notice that he was a serious person, and was pretty busy. He asked my backgound and wanted to know in which area was I interested to research. Few days back I had purchased from the Institute bookstall the proceedings of the 'Mechanical Technology Faculty' which was an yearly publication. There I saw his review paper on transition metal refractory carbides, in which he had correlated the properties with chemical bonding. During our meeting I expressed my intention to research on refractory carbides in their homogeneity range. Professor Samsonov readily accepted my proposal and called Dr. Shluko to give me a desk. Few days later, I received a bundle of reprints related to refractory carbides. Some were in English. I started devoting part time on the technical papers, but predominantly devoting on the Russian classes. After a rigorous training of three months, I gathered enough working knowledge of the language. With passage of time the improvement was much visible.

It is opputune here if I highlight the life-sketch of this great teacher and scientist. Profesor Samsonov was born on 15th February, 1918 during the great Bolshevik upheaval in Russia in a town near Leningrad (now St. Petersburg). His whole life was spent in the communist regime of USSR. He earned his first degree at the Nonferrous Metals Institute in Moscow and had to join the Soviet Navy. At the end of the Second World War he was stationed in Austria in the Soviet occupied zone. It was here he became intimately acquainted with the extensive refractory metal and compound industries of Austria. Samsonov was fluent in German language and this helped him in mingling with Austrians at social lavel too. After cessation of war, Samsonov returned to Moscow and decided to leave the defence services and resume higher studies. In Moscow he, researched under the guidance of Professor G.A. Merson (Institute of Steel and Alloys), a noted powder metallurgist in USSR. After successful completion of his Ph.D. degree, (Kanditat), Samsonov joined the Institute of Metalkeramika (ie powder metallurgy) in the Ukrainian Academy of Sciences in Kiev as a senior scientist. The Institute was later renamed 'Institute of Materials Problems'. After few years, he defended his D.Sc. degree and was soon promoted to the Deputy Director's post in the same Institute. He was also elected Corresponding Member of the Ukrainian Academy of Sciences. He was invited to head the Powder Metallurgy Department at the Kiev Institute of Technology in capacity of a professor, which he did till his death. In the year 1968 Samsonov was awarded the Interantional Plasee Plakat instituted by late Professor Paul Schwarzkopf, the founder the metallwerk Plansee, Austra. I attended that Seminar and also presented a paper. It is pity Samsonov could not attend the seminar and the award was received by Dr. Ribalchenko of Baikov Institute of Metals Research, Moscow. It is tragedy that Professor Samsonov did not live long and died untimely at the age of 58 in December, 1975. The international scientific community was greatly bereaved. His faithfull wife Nadezhda Alexandrovna boldly faced all the trials and tribulations. The last time I met her was in the year 1977 in Kiev.

The other faculty members in the Powder Metallurgy Department of the Kiev Institute of Technology were Dr. Shluko. Dr. Bazhenova, Dr. Krushniski and others. Dr. Bazhenova was a mineral chemist with the profound knowledge of crystallography. Dr. Shluko was the Deputy Chief of the Department, with the responsibility of day to day administration. He was a clever shrewd person. One had to take him with a pinch of salt as he rarely fulfilled his promises. After initial goading, I found that with pace the things were, it will take a much longer time to complete my programme. I did not like to tell this to Professor Samonov as a complaint, but as a suggestion for speedy disposal. Professor Samsonov, other hearing me, rushed to the office of Shluko and called him to his office. In those days intercom facilities were lacking. He told him to be attentive with my requests, as I had rather limited time at my disposal. This changed the whole attitude of Dr. Shluko and hence forth, there were no major hiccups. I was given some students for their project guidance. We worked together amicably with trust. My past teaching experience was very useful on those occasions.

As Profesor Samsonov was a big shot in the Ukrainian Academy of Sciences, all the equipments of his Institute was accessible to me. The scientists, with whom I interacted were Kosolapova, Makarenko, Kovalchenko, Nemchenko and others. They were very considerate with me. The Institute's library was a useful one as numerous specialized journals were easily available. Practically all the equipments were of indigenous origin, except the electron microscope. Most of the high temperature vacuum furnaces were assembled right in the Institute's workshop. Most of the scientists used to bring their packed lunches. Professor Samsonov did not have his personal car, although financially he was well off. He always used to hire taxi, which was easily available. The maintenance of the car and a need of a driver were more of nuisance to him. On the other hand, another scientist Academician Fedordenko had his personal car. He was well connected to the high echleon of the Academy and somehow both these scientists did not pull on well each other. Professor Samsonov was of Russian origin while Fedordenko—an Ukrainian. The international reputation of former was much bigger.

One of the former students of Professor Samsonov, Dr. V.S. Neshpor was a scientist at Leningrad (now St.Petersburg). He used to visit us often. Samsonov counted him as one of his top ex-students. No wonder when he suggested me to co-write the monograph on refractory carbides, he also invited Dr. Neshpor as another coauthor. Dr. Kovalchenko was another famous scientist at the Institute of Materials Science Problems. His specialization was theory and practice of hot pressing. Dr. R.A. Andrievski, was another frequent visitor from Moscow. He is one of the best friends of mine and we exchange New Year's Greeting regularly. I shall be talking about him more in another chapter.

During my stay in Kiev, I did not loose opportunity to attend National and International Conferences mainly in Moscow, where I presented technical papers. Professor Umanskii of the Department of Metal Physics at the Moscow Institute of Steel and Alloys had organized a specialized conference on 'Refractory Compounds', in which he invited Academician Kurdjumov for inauguration. Academician Kurdjumov, after introduction with me, was keen to know as to why so many Indian scientists prefer to work in Europe/USA. It was unthinkable in USSR to take citizenship of other countries.

While I was in USSR, it was the era of President Brezhnov. It was great to see the November and May Day Parades, anywhere in USSR. The daily life of an average Soviet citizen was pretty in order. No doubt there were long queues in the department stores and restaurants, the Soviet citizens were quite accustomed to those. It is not true that the then Soviet society was completely free from evils, but these were not publicized in newspapers and we knew those only through whispers.

A mention of the Lenin Library at Moscow is worthwhile. It is one of the biggest libraries in Russia, where we can easily fetch any literature, read them and get them reproduced at nominal charges. In those days every thing was in order and no one faced any difficulty in using it. The library was open throughout 24 hours. Of course, one needs to get a special pass for the library only after getting introduced by the parent Institute/ organization. It was, therefore, mainly a reference library. My visits of the Library were fruitful for my future book writing.

In the summer of 1968, I travelled to Austria to present our research paper in the famous Plansee seminar. Professor Samsonov was to receive the prestigious Plansee Plakat in the inaugural session. He could not attend due to unknown reasons and on his behalf the award was received by Dr. Ribalchenko of Baikov Institute of Metals, Moscow, the famous USSR Academy of Sciences Institute. The carrying of scientific manuscript outside USSR was a real ordeal and full of bureaucracy. The procedure was so lengthy that I preferred to take risk, so as to participate in the conference in time. The journey was though rail and I borrowed the necessary foreign exchange from one of my past classmates Mr. P.C. Mallik, who was in Canada. The custom staff at the border were suspicious, and greedy. Their favourite query was, whether I had U.S. Dollars in cash or not. There was not much rush in the train and I was pretty alone in the coupe.

I defended my Ph.D. thesis in June 1969. The external examiner was Professor Portonoi from the Moscow Institute of Aviation Materials and the local examiner was Dr. G.N. Makarenko from the Institute of Materials Problems. In USSR, the theses defence used to be in public and notices were printed in the newspaper few weeks in advance. There thesis supervisor gives his recommendations too. It was nice to hear the praise from my supervisor Professor Samsonov in public.

Soon after getting the Ph.D. degree, I got engrossed in the book writing, which we had planed. Professor Samsonov invited me in his summer Dacha to prepare the full outline. On one Sunday I reached there by local train. At the entrance of his Dacha, I encountered his ferocious dog. Professor Samsonov calmed him down and we both enjoyed the lunch. He was alone there, or better to say he preferred to stay alone, so as to write without any disturbance.

In December 1969, I had to say good-bye to USSR. My biggest belonging was the collection of scientific books in Russian. My air-ticket was for the Aerofloat flight. The meals in the flight were not tasty, but I had no alternative. It was a great delight to reunite with my parents at Varanasi. On 1st January, 1970, I rejoined my duties at University of Roorkee, now as an Associate Professor a promotion from the earlier post held ie. Reader.

2

My Colleagues at Varanasi, Roorkee and Kanpur

I served at three places as a teacher. They were Banaras Hidu University, University of Roorkee and finally at the Indian Institute of Technology, Kanpur. At BHU the term was pretty short, only one semester, while at Roorkee it was 11 years. The longest association was at IIT Kanpur, where I achieved the ultimat fulfillment of my academic career. It was from the period 1976 to 2001. In the passages below, I have highlighted about my colleagues and their interaction with me.

At Banaras Hindu University

When I joined Banaras Hidu University (B.H.U.) after return from U.K. in September, 1963, Professor T.R. Anantharaman (TRA) was the Head of the Metallurgical Engineering Department. He was earlier with Indian Institute of Science, Bangalore as an Assistant Professor. He was not comfortable with the word 'Engineering' and he succeeded in renaming the department as mere 'Metallurgy'. Soon the university realized the follies and the old name was restored back. Other faculty members in the department were Mr. S.L. Malhotra, Mr. P. Rama Rao, Mr. P.M. Prasad, Dr. Devendra Gupta, Dr. S.S. Khanna, Dr. K.C. Tripathy, Mr. S.H. Ghude, Mr. M.L. Kapur and others. Professor TRA was the only professor and was in look out for a professor in 'Extractive Metallurgy'. Later on, this post got occupied by Professor P.K. Jena from Indian Atomic Energy. Dr. TRA was in the prime of his career. He had his Ph.D.

degree from Oxford University, followed by Post-doctoral experience at Max Planck Institute for Metals Research at Stuttgart, W. Germany. I gather, TRA was not pulling on well at IISc with Professor A.A. Krishnan, the then Head of the Department. While leaving IISc, he encouraged his final year metallurgy students to join M.Tech. Programme at BHU. In all six students joined I recollect five of them vividly : P. Ramchandra Rao, D.B. Goel, M.L. Bhatia, G.V. Shastri and V. Kutumba Rao. I taught them a course on 'Experimental Techniques in Metallurgy'. Some how, I noticed these boys were not tuned to the BHU mould. Some of them used to come in classes without even a pen. Once I was constrained to turn out a student to his hostel to bring the pen. That punishment was enough for them not to repeat the mistake. Mr. P. Ramchandra Rao had an additional degree of M.Sc. in Physics. TRA was more interested is building the strength of researches and at times it cost the undergraduate education. Mr. R.P. Wahi was doing his part-time Ph.D. in addition being a lecturer. Mr. P. Rama Rao was on the verge of defending his Ph.D. thesis in the broad area of X-ray metallurgy, to be more exact on line broadening. Once, TRA enquired the possibility of my doing Ph.D. under him. My research interest did not pertain to his topics. I politely declined his suggestion, but at the same time could feel that he did not welcome my answer. At that time he did not say anything. After few weeks, he repeated his proposal. He used to say these things in the corridor during walking. At times, I had to intentionally avoid any encounter with him in the corridor. Soon, I heard the resignation of Dr. D. Gupta, who was a Reader in the department. He was a top class metallurgist, who researched under Professor Libermann in the University of Illinois. I heard rumors about his misunderstanding with TRA on some very trivial issues. Soon Dr. Gupta resigned and joined Planning Commission under Dr. Daya Swarup. Professor Koester of Stuttgart, while returning from Japan visited our Department and gave a Seminar as well. TRA's wife was a German lady, and, naturally his relationship with German scientists were more intimate. During my stay at BHU, TRA went to CALTECH, in USA to do further research. It was there under Professor Pol Duwez, he got interested with rapid solidification. No wonder, that visit of his to USA made him initiated in this area. TRA was still not on the Senior Professor's grade, for what he was an aspirant. He knew there was a vacancy of that post at the University of Roorkee. Professor Shankar Lal, the Head of the Mechanical Engineering Department at the University did a lot of convassing to bring TRA at Roorkee. Incidentally Professor Lal's wife was an Yogoslavian. TRA was interviewed and subsequently appointed as Senior Professor. However, he used that offer to get promotion at BHU. Naturally, BHU being a Central University had a much liberal funding as compared to the University of Roorkee.

One of the habits of Professor TRA was to transfer the in-charge and staff of various laboratories too frequently, sometimes even in fortnight. This was frustrating and demoralising. Many, out of fear, could not express their displeasure. In those days, the headship of a department was not through rotation. I did hint him about this frequent transfer which he did not take well. My idea was that any person must be given enough time to show his administrative worth. I could find a restless man in TRA, although he talked much about yoga. Later, I came to know about his good personal relations in the Ministry of Education in New Delhi, which gave his department a liberal funding.

My other colleague Mr. S.L. Malhotra had still no Ph.D. degree and TRA helped him in getting admitted with financial assistance at the University of London for Ph.D. research. He was a good teacher and a good follower of TRA. It is irony that in the later stage, they developed differences.

Dr. P. Rama Rao, then lecturer, was a sober, soft spoken person with a pleasing personality. No doubt, he learnt the speech making style from TRA in injecting a lot of adjectives. I admired him then and now also. I shall be writing about him more in a later chapter.

Dr. S.S. Khanna and Dr. K.C. Tripathi were intently looking for other possible avenues and they left BHU at earliest opportunities. Dr. Khanna moved to National Institute of Foundry and Forge Technology, Ranchi, while Dr. Tripathi moved to Canada in an Aluminium R&D organisation. Mr. S.H. Ghude and M.L. Kapoor were aspiring for higher studies abroad. Mr. Ghude went to the University of Sheffield, while Mr. Kapoor joined Technical University, Berlin. There was one Mr. Y.P. Srivastava, who resigned and joined Hindalco. I had excellent relation with Mr. Ghude, who was living in a rented quarter in Lanka locality outside the B.H.U. campus. Mr. Surendra Singh was another lecturer, who later did his Ph.D. degree from Sheffield. Mr. R. Sharan, by that time, had left BHU and joined the University of Roorkee as Reader. He was still registered for his Ph.D. thesis under TRA. Later, they could not pull together and Mr. Sharan chose Professor Shankar Lal of the University of Roorkee as his guide and later was awarded Ph.D. from the same university. Professor Lal had little knowledge of metallurgy and Mr. Sharan was more or less a self guide.

AT UNIVERSITY OF ROORKEE

When I joined the University of Roorkee in May, 1964, Mr. R. Sharan and Dr. M.N. Saxena were the only faculty members. Dr. M.N. Saxena was 1949 graduate in Metallurgical Engineering from BHU. Mr. G.S. Sinha had just joined as lecturer, after getting his B.Sc. in Metallurgy from the London University. At that time, Dr. Saxena was in the University Wisconsin, Madison doing doctoral research. Mr. Sharan was the Incharge of the Metallurgical Engineering Department under the overall administrative control of Professor Kamlani and Professor Shankar Lal, who were Heads of the Department of Mechanical Engineering in sequence. Professor Lal, much later (1976), joined the Indian Institute of Technology, Kharagpur as its Director. Mr. Sharan made me the Incharge of Physical Metallurgical Laboratories and used to push me to Professor Lal for any discussions. Professor Lal was ignorant about Metallurgy and used to follow the old list of equipment supplied by the Ministry. In those days myself and Mr. G.S. Sinha were full of energy and enthusiasm. We worked painstakingly and still claim the 'Metallography Laboratory' of Roorkee as one of the best planned in India. We designed it in such a way that each student had his own optical microscope. We were against the practice of BHU and other places, where a number of students had to peep through the eyepiece on a single microscope. It was very difficult for me to convince Professor Lal about the number of microscopes we needed. Anyway we made him to get convinced on the condition that in no case we exceeded the total budget allotted to the department. All along these episodes Mr. Sharan was passive, but he gave full freedom to us. Full credit must be given to him for such a timely attitude. Later, I came to know that he was much afraid of Professor Lal in encountering him frequently. Later, Dr. Saxena, after return from USA, became the department Incharge. He also followed the practice of Mr. Sharan and made me to face the pleasure or wrath of Professor Shankar Lal. It was very educative for me to work in a new department. The critical evaluation of each quotation had to be done. The tradition of Roorkee, also taught me the style of how to write office memorandum.

The two new academic departments i.e. Metallurgical and Chemical started at the same time in 1962 and were housed in the defunct Polytechnic Building of the University. The Uttar Pradesh State Government closed the Polytechnic, as they found its Diploma holders pampered lots, who could succeed in getting all the lucrative engineering jobs in the state machinery. The Polytechnic building had to be divided into two halves and Mr. Yogesh Chandra (Lecturer, Chemical Engineering) and Mr. G.S. Sinha toiled a lot in renovating the building. With all the teaching and administrative assignments (the students by that time were in their 3rd year B.Tech. program), I had practically no time left for doing any research. I did not grumble as these experiences were equally useful. With that input, I did not face any problem in raising my laboratory later at IIT, Kanpur.

Another addition in our department was Dr. M.M. Rao, who had earned his Ph.D. from Purdue University, U.S.A. He was a CSIR Pool Officer. His stay in the university was a pretty short one, and he later moved to DMRL and then to the Indian Institute of Science, Bangalore. Dr. Rao was instrumental in framing the course content of 'Metallurgical Thermodynamics'. He was a bit fussy man and used to frown as soon as any person started speaking in Hindi. Although he had a working knowledge of the language, he was not at home in speaking.

When I joined the university, Mr. Ghananand Pandey was its Vice-Chancellor. Before that, he was with Hindustan Steel Ltd. as its chairman. He used to invite eminent metallurgists from that organisation. Dr. G.P. Chatterjee from Durgapur Steel Plant was one of them. Mr. Pandey used to visit our department frequently and was quite appreciative in nature. The first Indo-USA School for engineering teachers was held at the university in his tenure, in which many eminent engineering educator like Mr. S.C. Sen (Delhi Engineering College), Dr. R.N. Dogra, Dr. C.S. Jha (IIT, Delhi), Dr. P.K. Kelkar (Director, IIT, Kanpur) participated. The attitude of traditional Roorkee teacher and students was rather snobbish. Myself and Mr. G.S. Sinha did best to demolish that attitude. I remember a very candid remark by Mr. Sen, to clean some of the syllabi with the sacred Ganges water. This was after some remark by Professor O.P. Jain of Civil Engineering Department. Dr. Jain later became the Director of the Indian Institute of Technology, Delhi. There too his traditional attitude was intact. He used to consider metallurgy as chemistry. I disputed him vehemently.

Another faculty addition in our department was Mr. S.K. Goel. He was two years junior to me at BHU and had 2-3 years industrial training experience at German steel plants. Professor Bashforth at BHU was instrumental in fixing up this training. Mr. Goel was a tall, handsome person. He did his part-time Ph.D. at Roorkee and became a specialist in foundry and solidification.

In 1965 Dr. Saxena returned for USA and became the Incharge of the Department. Some how he and Mr. Sharan started having differences. Dr. Saxena was a difficult person to please and had problems with anyone who possessed some individuality. I, too, had differences with him. He loved docile persons. His scheme was to become a professor as soon as possible and in this he succeeded. Mr. G.S. Sinha wanted to do higher studies in U.K. He got an assistantship in the University of London and soon resigned to join it. After three years or so, he returned to India and was in search for a suitable job, but, naturally, of higher cadre. Unfortunately, he could not succeed. As his family was from as rich landlord clan of Bihar State, he did not have any objection to get engaged in business. Currently, he and his family are happily residing in Siwan (Bihar). Mr. Sinha was a trusted friend of mine. He was diplomatic and advised me to keep the temper within limits. I miss him very much.

In the July of 1965, two additions were in the Department. They were Mr. D.B. Goel and A.K. Patwardhan. Both were 1963 graduates of Indian Institute of Science, Bangalore. Mr. Goel did his M.Tech. studies from BHU, while Mr. Patwandhan from IIT, Bombay. Mr. Goel's home town was Muzaffar Nagar (not far from Roorkee), while Mr. Patwardhan had good affinity for Roorkee, as his late father was the Deputy-Director at Central Building Research Institute (CSIR) at Roorkee. Both of these colleagues were hard working. Patwardhan had completed his M.Tech. Thesis under the well known powder metallurgist Professor G.S. Tendolkar at IIT, Bombay. He also published a paper in the Transaction of the Indian Institute of Metals. After few years of teaching experience, Mr. Goel left for Stuttgart to do the doctorate research under Dr. Worlimont. At the same time, Mr. Patwardhan joined Sheffield University in U.K. under the commonwealth scholarship scheme. He was a bit casual in nature and did not suit in the typical British atmosphere. He could not submit his Ph.D. thesis in time and returned to Roorkee. He showed me some of his experimental results on transformation aspects of low alloy bainitic steels, which were quite original. Soon, he preferred to register part-time for Ph.D. under Professor M.N. Saxena. I could notice the hidden trait of rivalry between these two friends i.e. Goel and Patwandhan. Dr. Goel was much cleverer than the other and eventually obtained regular promotion. Dr. Patwardhan met a serious road accident and after prolonged illness, succumbed due to numerous complications.

In the beginning of 1966 or so, Mr. T. Varadrajan joined the Department as a lecturer. He had B.Tech. from IIT, Madras and M.Tech. from IIT, Bombay. He was very loyal to Dr. Saxena. He used to sit only when asked by Dr. Saxena to do so. He was a clever Tamilian Brahmin and got quick promotion with the blessing of Dr. Saxena. He completed his part-time Ph.D. programme under him for which Dr. TRA was the external examiner. Unfortunately, Dr. Rajan could not get lift for the post of Professor in the University. Later, he resigned and joined Malviya Regional Engineering College (now National Institute of Technology), Jaipur as Professor.

After my return from USSR, when I joined the university in January, 1970, another faculty member had already joined as Reader in Extractive Metallurgy few months back. He was Dr. Nanda (BHU-alumnus) from the University of Illinois. He was a fearless person and could not pull on well with Dr. Saxena. He resigned and joined Regional Engineering College at Rourkela (now National Institute of Technology). Unfortunately, he soon left for USA along with his medico-wife.

Some of our past undergraduates, who completed their M.Tech. programmes, mainly at BHU and IISc, joined as lecturers. They were Mr. Satya Narayan, Mr. P.S. Misra, V.S. Bhadauria and Mr. S.K. Gupta. Two ex-students of BHU Mr. S.C. Koria and Mr. Satya Prakash also joined as lecturer. Mr. V.K. Tiwary, Y. Sahai and S.K. Srivastava, who had finished their B.Tech. programme in 1968 from Roorkee, also joined as lecturers. The department was now populous. Some differences among the faculty members were visible. Dr. Saxena was authoritarian and at times capritious.

In mid-seventies Dr. M.L. Mehta, who had completed his Ph.D. degree from Swansea (U.K.) joined our department as Reader. Earlier he was with Bhabha Atomic Research Centre, as a scientist. He is an alumnus of BHU, being two years senior to me. He had seen good and bad days in BARC and was a good natured person. Dr. Saxena was bent upon not to promote me even after several interviews. Some of the experts, later, told me the episodes and the collusion of Dr. Saxena with the then Vice-Chancellor.

He always derived the prize of the loyalty from the Vice-Chancellors. After an year or so, Dr. Mehta got appointed as Professor and by his own right became the member of the University's Syndicate. The power struggle between these two professors Dr. Saxena and Dr. Mehta started soon, and I was a moot spectator. I was unhappy with the treatment meted to me. After few weeks, I decided to meet the Vice-Chancellor Dr. Jai Krishna. He listened to me and said 'Why are you so keen for Roorkee? Sky is the limit! I understood what he was hinting and soon applied for the Professor's post at IIT, Kanpur. I got interviewed and given the offer but I had to face problems in getting released from Roorkee. Anyway, I bid good-bye to the University on 10th February, 1976. Later, I was told by my colleagues at Roorkee about the fights between Dr. Saxena and Dr. Mehta.

Dr. M.L. Kapoor, whom I knew from my BHU days joined the university as Reader, more of less at the same time Dr. Mehta joined. He had completed his Dr. Ing degree from Berlin, his specialisation being Thermodynamics and Chemical Metallurgy. He was a good addition, but he was too impatient to get promoted at the University. He decided to join IIT Kanpur as Assistant Professor, but here too he wanted quick promotion. Seeing the facts of life, he once again decided to rejoin Roorkee, but now after promotion as Professor. Then onward he served the university very loyally and retired recently from the services.

It shall be fitting if I here express some of my opinions on Roorkee University. One of the major highlight of engineering education at Roorkee was that it was more industrial oriented, with the result that our students never found any problem in getting jobs in industries. Faculties were well engrossed in teaching. The research interest was not uniform among them. The lack of real academic leadership was also an impediment in some of the departments. Recently, our Central Government took over the University from the state and converted into an IIT. Mr. Pant, the Deputy Chairman, Planning Commission and Dr. M.M. Joshi, the Ex-Minister for Human Resource Development were actively instrumental in doing so. I have the opinion that any IIT must be started from the scratch, so that they maintain the originality. It would had been better if the Central Government would have converted this State University into a Central Technological University, under the control of University Grants Commission. The dilemma faced by the present faculty, whether to offer a technological education or an engineering science based education could have been avoided. It is unfortunate that the Government did not solicit opinions from past or present faculty members of the university.

AT INDIAN INSTITUTE OF TECHNOLOGY, KANPUR

My employment in IIT, Kanpur from 1976 to 2001 as a Professor facilitated me to interact with many, particularly the faculty members belonging to Physical Metallurgy and Materials Processing areas. In 1976, there were 24 faculties a number which still remain more or less the same. When I joined the Institute, most of the areas in metallurgy were covered except Powder Metallurgy.

It will be appropriate if I review few things about IIT, Kanpur. This great Institute was founded in 1960 in collaboration with U.S. Government. The first Director of the Institute was Prof. P.K. Kelkar, who admirably directed if for ten years, before joining the IIT Bombay as its Director for four more years. He rightly said that an Institute is built by its leader. Had it not been Prof. Kelkar, I doubt these two IITs would have taken the lofty position, which they enjoy today? I had a brief meeting with Professor Kelkar during his visit to the University of Roorkee in 1964. He was a man of few words. Kelkar advocated the introduction of structured science-based engineering curriculum, in which he succeeded more in IIT, Kanpur than in Bombay. He was in some sense a visionory. Last time, I met Prof. Kelkar in 1981, when He visited us to deliver the convocation address. Prof. S. Sampath was then the Director of our Institute. I would like to quote here from his speech : "The way things happened, the way diverse people were drawn into the most unusual spurt of ideas, innovation and adventure occasionally bordering on the reckless, have convinced me that the coming into being of IIT Kanpur was a historical necessity. History chose all those who were associated with IIT Kanpur in the very beginning and in the course of its subsequent development".

More details about IIT Kanpur can be had from the book authored by E.C. Subba Rao 'An Eye for Excellence', Harper Collins, New Delhi 2009. Near the end of his life Prof. Kelkar was a bit saddened man. In a letter to the 1986 IITs review committee, he made no bones about how, in his view, the IITs had allowed themselves to slide into a trough of lassitude. Prof. Kelkar died in October 1990, a full decade before the IITs fortunes and their reputation took a turn for the better.

DR. K.P. SINGH

When I joined IIT Kanpur Dr. K.P. Singh was the Head of the Department. I had known him professionally through his research work. In Canada he had done excellent research on the role of hydrogen in metals. He had a British Ph.D. degree in chemistry from the University of Durham, New Castle. Soon after joining IIT, I realised his good influence in the Institute. At times he was a bit incoherent and had the habit of name dropping. One of the common name was Dr. Narul Hasan, the then Education Minister, Government of India whom he called by the first name 'Narul'. Sooner we understood that he was not that influential as appeared to be. His wife was excellent in socialising in the Institute.

Dr. Singh taught corrosion and metallurgical thermodynamics. He was well aware of my research in Birmingham on the refractory metal hydrides. He was basically a kind person and never harmed any person. I remember in one of the department faculty meeting, some of the members were quite agitated on a trivial issue. He took it in a good stride and apologized. His laboratory was very rich in equipments and spare parts including high purity metals. One of his Ph.D. students was Mr. V.K. Sinha, who is at present a professor in the National Institute of Foundry and Forge Technology at Ranchi. His only other Ph.D. student was Mr. Subrat Ray, who is currently a professor in the University of Roorkee. His thesis topic was a theoretical one embracing solid state physics, and therefore, he was coguided by another faculty of the physics department Dr. Ramakrishna. IIT Kanpur always encouraged interdisciplinary research and the close interaction among faculty members in the coffee room was quite evident.

Dr. Singh was always nonpartisan and deplored those, who showed any favouritism. He told me something which amazed me. According to him one of the faculty members sometimes gave few days crash training to the M.Tech. applicants of his region just before their interview. I could notice some truth in it. Currently after the retirement Dr. Singh lives in Noida near Delhi along with his wife, son and daughter-in-law.

DR. E.C. SUBBA RAO

Dr. E.C. Subba Rao has been one of the undisputed academic leaders of IIT Kanpur. When I joined the Institute, he had relinquished himself from the deanship and head of the department's past, and was fully engrossed in teaching and R&D. Two of his favourite areas were ferroelectric materials and rare-earth permanent magnetic materials. Numerous researchers worked under him, one of them being Dr. Maiti ex-Director of Central Glass and Ceramic Research Institute in Kolkata. Professor Rao can be remembered as the father of Materials Science Education in India. The first ever conference on Material Science Education was organized by him at IIT Kanpur in 1966; the guest lecturers from USA were Professor Morris Cohen, Professor Dorn and Professor Azroff. Practically all players of Materials Science in India participated, including myself. My BHU classmate Dr. V. Raghavan was very much active in the conference. He was then the Assistant Professor at IIT Kanpur. Later, the proceedings of the conference was published by the Institute. The text book coauthored by Professor Subba Rao 'Experiments in Materials Science' is a good manual for every undergraduate engineering student. In those days, 'Introduction to Materials Science' was a compulsory core course for all the engineering undergraduates. Unfortunately of late, because of the insistence from few academic departments, particularly 'Computer Science and Engineering', the course has been made an optional one. I fought against this decision in the Academic Senate, but the uninspiring leadership of the then Director, could not restore the old practice.

Gradually, I could make out that a minority of the faculty members who could not be promoted under the deanship of Professor Subba Rao, were resentful to him. They were not vocal, but left no occasion in doing the whisper campaign. I found them to be wrong. Professor Rao was a man of integrity and full of fearlessness. For one of his M.Tech. students, I was one of the thesis examiners. I rather read the thesis too intently, whereas the other examiner did not do so. I asked many questions and noticed Professor Subba Rao quietly taking down some notes. In a way, he was glad that I worked on the thesis dutifully.

With the passage of time, it was probably felt by Professor Rao that he accomplished best for the Institute and it was now the time to play a still bigger role. He moved to Pune to join the newly founded Tata R,D&D Centre. Mr. J.R.D. Tata, invited him to build that centre. Soon, he organised the centre as a profit centre, with the help of freshly recruited team of scientists. One of them was Dr. Pradip, who is doing excellent. I visited his centre and presented seminar. There I met some of our past students.

Dr. Subba Rao has been a frequent visitor to USA, being invited by various US Universities. One of them is Pennsylvania State University. Few years back I met him in the IIT Kanpur campus, where he delivered the first E.C. Subba Rao Distinguished Lecture, which was instituted by an alumnus of the department, now settled in Canada. Currently, Professor Rao, after retirement from TRDD Centre, is continuing at the same place as an Emeritus Scientist.

DR. K.P. GUPTA

I knew Dr. K.P. Gupta right since 1965, when I attended the 'Materials Science Education' conference at IIT Kanpur. He was, then, the Head of the Department of Metallurgical Engineering. He was a soft spoken person, a good listener and replied in few words. He taught Physical Metallurgy, Alloy Theory and X-ray Crystallography courses. Incidentally, after a periodic review of the courses, the department found the need for a Powder Metallurgy elective course. Dr. Gupta was given the responsibility to teach that. He taught that course for a semester. This was before, I joined the Institute.

Dr. Gupta was the student of Professor Paul Beck at the University of Illinois, Urbana. There Dr. M.N. Parthasarathy and Dr. P.P. Sinha were his contemporaries. Dr. Gupta was an experimentalist par excellence. He used his own hands to do all the settings and was never dependent on technicians. He wrote a number of manuals for undergraduate students and encouraged other faculty members to do so. He was a stickler in a sense and that is why his students used to take a bit longer time to submit their theses. One of his Ph.D. students Ms. Uma Devi, was one of those. Dr. Gupta was not too fond of traveling either in India or abroad. His research publications were sound and effective. In the later part of his career at IIT Kanpur, he got interested in critical reviews of ternary phase diagrams, for which he used to take my help in translating some Russian papers. The volumes of the 'Ternary Ni-based Phase Diagram' published by the Indian Institute of Metals, are the testimony of his painstaking work. It is gratifying that he is still continuing the review work on phase diagram in Kolkata, where he has built his house.

DR. AHINDRA GHOSH

Dr. Ghosh joined IIT Kanpur some time after Dr. K.P. Gupta. He had his doctorate from MIT and did post-doctoral at Ohio State University. He was the originator of process metallurgy courses at IIT K, which contained a good blend of theory and practice. His replies to any queries are never spontaneous, as he usually takes some time to shape them with due lucidity. After Dr. K.P. Singh, he became our Head of the Department. He was very meticulous and kept all the records in tact, whether of academic or administrative type. He worked late in evenings, including the week ends. His office was just below mine. I used to take advise from him in many matters. Of late, he was given the responsibility of convening department faculty meetings, which he did with utmost impartiality. He was fearless, but did not take matters too far. He never liked any distractions from his academic pursuits. He was a regularly sought after Professor by postgraduate students in chemical metallurgy. This made the number of students working under him fairly large. Some of our colleagues were rather jealous of this fact. Once I had to put a big stop to these bickering by vehemently fighting his cause. One of his past Ph.D. students Dr. D. Bandopadhyay, who is presently a scientist at National Metallurgical Laboratory, still recalls that unsavory incident. I defended the case of this student due to the compelling reason that a gross injustice was going to be meted to him. On the occasion of Dr. Ghosh's retirement, a one-day seminar was organized in the Department. This was well attended, in what Dr. Amit Chatterjee of Tata Steel was one of the guests.

Dr. Ghosh very rarely gets annoyed. It is interesting to mention one incident. Dr. S. Ranganathan had published a paper in the Transactions of IIM on the academic activity in Metallurgy in India. He did mention about Dr. Ghosh and others, but had no mention at all of Professor K.P. Gupta. Dr. Ghosh was upset and published a letter to the editor of the Transactions, Dr. S.K. Ray. It was befitting, the editor published this in the ensuing issue of the Transactions.

It is natural here to mention about Dr. Ghosh's son 'Sudupto', who studied Metallurgical Engineering at IIT Kanpur. Initially, his interest was in Physics, and opted for metallurgy rather reluctantly. After completing the M. Tech. and Ph.D. programmes at IIT Kanpur, he is currently a faculty member in the Metallurgical Engineering Department at IIT Kharagpur.

I am glad he is near to his parents. Currently, Dr. Ghosh and his family reside in Howrah (W. Bengal). He is still very active as a consultant for Tata Steel.

DR. G.S. MURTY

Dr. G.S. Murty was a 1960 graduate from IISc, Bangalore. He completed the Ph.D. from the University of California, Berkeley in the area of superplasticity. After postdoctoral work at MIT, USA, Dr. Murty joined the faculty of IIT Kanpur as a lecturer, being subsequently promoted to the posts of Assistant Professor and Professor. When I met him first at IIT Kanpur, I found him a quiet person, with full of humility. He was pretty unassuming. His quest to the subject was deep. As a research guide, he was very much sought after person. We both guided jointly some of the M.Tech. and Ph.D. students and, thus, I came more closer to him. He used to leave the job of identifying of the research topic to the students, but still guiding them from a distance. In a way this made his students more confident, as they had to defend themselves at each and every stage. This type of approach was educative to both the student and the guide. In case of one of the Ph.D. student, Mr. P.B. Kadam, we were three guides Dr. Murty, myself and Dr. M.L. Vaidya. This was the first Ph.D. student of Dr. Vaidya and, naturally, he was very enthusiastic. Sometimes, Dr. Vaidya used to become impatient with the slow pace of the student. He wished to present some quick route, so as to save time. Dr. Murty was still on his own track and this brought some degree of disharmony. My job on these occasions was to find a middle path.

In 1995 or so, the Planning Commission, Government of India ventured on the 'Technology Development Mission'. The idea was jointly mooted by all the IITs and it was a good initiative. 'New Materials' was one of the missions, while 'Metal Matrix Composites' was one of the areas. The then Head of our Department handed this responsibility to Dr. Murty. He approached two of us : myself and Dr. Vaidya, to get associated. We readily accepted his invitation. There used to be a number of meetings in New Delhi and at IITs alternatively. There was a precondition that a matching grant had to be found, before the project was officially approved. Dr. Murty requested me to take up this assignment. After many failures, ultimately I succeeded in persuading Tata Steel to assist us. Dr. J.J. Irani, the then Managing Director, agreed to help us. By the time the project was approved, Dr. Murty took premature retirement. At the same time Dr. Vaidya too got superannuated. Thus, the job came exclusively to my shoulders, which I accomplished with good satisfaction.

Dr. Murty gave good research training to numerous students. One of them was Dr. B.P. Kashyap, who was recently the Head of the Metallurgical Engineering Department at IIT, Bombay.

To best of my knowledge, Dr. Murty was the first Indian to research on superplasticity in alloys. Later other came into picture like Dr. K.A. Padmanabhan at IIT Madras and Dr. Atul Choski at the Indian Institute of Science, Bangalore. There was an International Conference in Bangalore on superplasticity, which was attended by Dr. Murty. He was somewhat dismayed, when no mention of his contribution was made in the inaugural address. Any way, he took it as a fall out of politics prevailing in academic institutions. Dr. Murty did not join any group to further his cause. He was rather a lone person and did not seek any award or fellowship.

In the end of nineties, Dr. Murty decided to leave India and permanently moved to USA to join an Aluminium Fabrication Company in W. Virginia as its R&D Director. Unfortunately, I could not meet him during his last brief visit of IIT Kanpur, since by that time I has left IIT Kanpur. On the whole Dr. Murty seems to be a reasonably fulfilled person.

DR. T.R. RAMACHANDRAN

Dr. T.R. Ramachandran is 1960 graduate from the Indian Institute of Science and thus a classmate of Dr. G.S. Murty. After the post-graduate research work in Canada and Wales (U.K.), he joined IIT Kanpur as a lecturer and subsequently got promoted to Assistant Professor and Professor posts. His favourite research was on electron microscopy, particularly of aluminium alloys. He was instrumental in commissioning the first electron microscope at IIT Kanpur. He was an excellent teacher and was much liked by students. He also headed our department for one term. Dr. Ramachandran was a frequent visitor of McMaster University as Visiting Professor. One of his first Ph.D. students was Dr. Lahiri of Defence Metallurgical Research Laboratory (DMRL), Hyderabad. Dr. Ramachandran significantly contributed in Al-Li alloys, for which he had close collaboration with DMRL and particularly Dr. P. Rama Rao. His research contribution in Al-alloy was valued in India and the Ministry of Mines appointed him the first Director of J.L. Nehru Centre for Aluminium at Nagpur. He stayed there for a decade or so and made it one of the premier R&D organizations. It is pity that the state of affair of this centre presently is not as sound as in the time of Dr. Ramachandran. After retirement from Nagpur Dr. Ramachandran joined the Non-ferrous Metals Development Centre in Hyderabad as an Emeritus Scientist. One of his past student Dr. Balasubramaniam is the Director of this centre.

DR. P.C. KAPUR

Professor P.C. Kapur was essentially a chemical technologist, whose main specialization was Mineral Engineering. He was awarded Ph.D. from the University of California, Berkeley. His other interest was in ceramics including cements. He did pioneering research on cement based on rice husk, but could not file the patent due to Institute's bureaucracy. Dr. Kapur was an excellent teacher and speaker. His speeches in the Academic Senate were lucid, argumentative and convincing. As an outspoken man he created many adversaries, but he never bothered for that. He was one of the tutors in a core course, of which I was the instructor. I always found him very meticulous. The biggest research asset for Dr. Kapur was his excellent command in mathematics. His researches were, centered around mathematical modeling. He produced very few Ph.D. students, but they were able ones. One of them was Dr. S.P. Mehrotra, who joined the Department as faculty member, soon after receiving the Ph.D. degree. Dr. Mehrotra, later, was the Director of National Metallurgical Laboratory, Jamshedpur.

To honour Professor P.C. Kapur, the department organised an International Conference on Mineral Processing at the time of his retirement. Many well known scientists from different countries attended that conference. Dr. E.C. Subba Rao gave a very good account of Dr. Kapur's achievements. Dr. Kapur was a visiting Professor at the University of California, Berkeley more than once. In our department faculty meetings, he was a vociferous attendee. At time his deliberations used to bring quite a bit of spice. Dr. Kapur presented an invited paper in the international Conference on 'Sintering' organised by me in the year 2000 in New Delhi. He lives a retired life in Delhi, but is still active with Tata RDD Centre as its consultant.

DR. R.K. RAY

Only few years after my joining IIT Kanpur, Dr. Ray moved from Bengal Engineering College to join us as an Assistant Professor. I had already met him few years earlier at the University of Roorkee. He was there along with Professor A.K. Seal, his teacher and boss at B.E, College, to attend a National Conference on 'High Strength—High Temperature alloys'. Dr. Ray is one of the rare Indian metallurgists with two Ph.D. degrees—one from Calcutta University and the other from the University of Birmingham (U.K.). His thesis supervisor at Birmingham was Professor R.E. Smallman. Dr. Ray was much liked by students and was quite considerate with them. He developed an excellent academic cooperation with Professor Jonas of McGill University, Montreal and used to visit them on a regular basis. He wrote excellent reviews based on such collaboration. Dr. Ray's specialisation was texture studies in alloys and he founded the Society for Texture Studies in India. All along his stay at IIT Kanpur, he struggled to make the central facilities up todate. Because of the paucity of fund, most of the time he was unsuccessful. But this did not deter him. He had excellent cooperation with laboratories both in India and abroad. For some years, Dr. Ray was is Aachen (Germany) as a Humbolt Visiting Fellow. In a sense, he has more German friend than the British ones. The courses on X-ray Crystallography and Experimental Techniques in Metallurgy were frequently handled by him. One of his able Ph.D. student, Dr. S. Suwas is now a faculty member in the Indian Institute of Science. Tata steel, of late, made big changes in its R&D management. They invited Dr. Ray to be one of their consultants. Dr. Ray has been suitably recognised by IIM, which awarded him G.D. Birla Gold Medal, for his excellent research in Physical Metallurgy. Dr. Ray's trait is to create friends, both at national and international levels. He is a polished cultured person, but in case of excesses, he does not hide in expressing his out-burst. For two years, he was a part of the Institute administration, being an elected nominee of the Academic Senate on the Board of Governors. His past students, both at BE College and IIT Kanpur, have high regards for him. In June 2005, Dr. Ray retired from the services of IIT Kanpur, but he is still very active as a consultant with Tata Steel and others.

Dr. Brahm Deo

Dr. Brahm Deo joined our department in early eighties first as a Post-Doctoral Associate and then as Assistant Professor. Before that he had professional experience at Steel Authority of India's Durgapur Plant. A very striking aspect in him was a blend of industrial experience and a flare for academia. Before joining as a faculty member, Dr. Brahm Deo had research experience at the University of London. Computer application is metallurgy has been his favourite area of research. He and another faculty member Dr. Nirupam Chakravorty, who, of late, joined IIT Kharagpur, were quite compatible. Both jointly organised numerous workshops and refresher courses, which were of great value to the engineers from industry. In those days industries were not so well versed in computational techniques, and the contribution of these two faculty members has been significant.

Dr. Brahm Deo, on leave from IIT K, visited The Netherlands, where he did pioneering research in ferrous extractive metallurgy. There he wrote a book in English entitled 'Fundamentals of Steelmaking Metallurgy' along with Professor R. Boom. The book has been reviewed quite positively. Soon after his return from Netherlands, he got promoted to the Professor's post, and eventually took over the realm of the department as its Head. He was a recipient of the Best Metallurgist's award from the Ministry of Steel, Government of India. Dr. Brahm Deo had a good knack of quiet administration. He was not visible as a stickler, but at times was strict as well. Professor Tare of BHU was his M.Tech. thesis supervisor, for whom Dr. Brahm Deo has high regards. Both of us had a joint research project for an M.Tech. student, but, unfortunately, due to the departure of Dr. Brahm Deo abroad, I had to offer a new topic to the student. Dr. Brahm Deo is quite amiable with faculty members of IIT Kanpur's other departments too. He was invited by the Institute administrator to take charge of student placement centre and also of the 'Joint Entrance Examination'. His biggest love is artificial intelligence, which he proudly proclaims. In recent past, he has been the Dean of Faculty Affairs at IIT, Kanpur.

OTHER COLLEAGUES

Among other colleagues at IIT, Kanpur, who are no more alive are Dr. Raj Narayan, Dr. Sanjiv Bhargava and Dr. R. Balasubramaniam. All of these were of professor rank. Dr. Raj Narayan was an expert in corrosion and coating and wrote a book on corrosion. The latter two colleagues expired at a premature age in the year 2009. Dr. Bhargava was a completely IIT Kanpur trained person. Kanpur was his native place. Dr. Balasubramaniam was educated in B.H.U., graduating in B.Tech. (Met. Eng.) in the year 1984. He possessed a multifaceted personality. His areas of research were hydrogen in metals and corrosion. Of late he very passionately got involved in history of ancient metals and alloys available in India. Being a corrosion specialist, he did extensive field research on the corrosion aspect of Delhi iron pillar. Some of his results are published in monograph form. Only two days before his death (9th December 2009), I visited him in the hospital, while he was in a terminal stage due to oral cancer. He was mentally very alert and expressed his strong faith in undergoing his treatment through Ayurvedic medicinal system as soon as he recovers a bit. Unfortunately that day did not reach. I was invited to write the review of his book entitled 'Marvels of Indian Iron through Ages', Rupa and Co (2008), which was published in IIM Metal News (Vol. 12, No. 5, 2009, 33). It is a coincidence that the very first research students of both these colleagues Dr. Bhargava and Dr Balasubramanium worked in my laboratory under my coguidance. They are Dr. M. Sujatha now at National Aerospace Laboratory, Bangalore and Dr. Govind now at Indian Space Research Organisation, Trivandrum.

3

Some Men of Metals and Materials from India

In the present chapter an account is made of men of metals and materials from India. They belong to varying disciplines spanning from science, technology to management. I was fortunate to interact with them. Some of them are no more alive, but their contribution in shaping the metallurgical and materials development in India is quite significant. The individuals for the convenience of readers have been placed in the alphabetical order.

LATE DR. P.L. AGRAWAL

Dr. P.L. Agrawal after serving BHU as a faculty member joined Rourkela Steel Plant at the same time, I joined BHU as a metallurgy student. I had read his book in Hindi related to Industrial Fuels. He is a role model for the combination of academia with industry. During my final year programme our Head of the Department Dr. D. Swarup invited him to give few lectures. He came and delivered very lucid lectures. He had a subtle way of holding the chalk, while writing on the black board. His voice used to be at low pitch and the audience used to get concentrated because of the serious style of his speech.

Dr. Agrawal held many positions in Hindustan Steel / Steel Authority of India right from General Superintendent, General Manager to Chairman, where he continued till 1980. During his chairmanship he piloted the 3 mt. Visakhapatnam Steel Plant and set up the RDCIS (SAIL) at Ranchi. In 1980, there was a difference with the then Indira Gandhi's Government at the Centre. Her son Sanjay Gandhi was a pampered person and a great friend of a Swamiji. The Swamiji wanted steel beams at a nominal price from SAIL and this became the cause for attrition. Dr. Agrawal was a very upright person. His resignation from SAIL, became very much profitable for him as he moved to Indonesia as Technical Advisor of the steel plant PT Krakatsu Steel (1980-1986). He earned enough money there and returned to India to settle in Udaipur, his native place.

I came in contact with Dr. Agrawal from 1986 onward. He was a regular attendee of the Indian Institute of Metals Council's Meetings of which we were the members. There I noticed his managerial skill. Being from a business men caste, the techno economics was his great forte. Dr. S. Bhattacharjee was the Chairman of the IIM, Kanpur Chapter of which I was the Vice-Chairman. He had proposed to the Institution of Engineers, Kanpur Subcentre to organise Dr. Daya Swarup Memorial Lecture at Kanpur every year. Both organisations agreed this proposal immediately, as Dr. Swarup was not only a doyen but was also a citizen of Kanpur city. This memorial lecture was to be inaugurated and I suggested the name of Dr. Agrawal as the Chief Guest. Dr. Bhattacharjee instructed me to do the communication work with Dr. Agrawal.Dr. Agrawal was utmost kind and immediately accepted our invitation. Our request kindled something in him and he wanted this Memorial Lecture on a national level too. He wrote to IIM which readily accepted his proposal. He contacted major industries like TATA Steel etc. and collected many lakhs of rupees. Dr. Daya Swarup Memorial Lecture is now an annual event and the first lecture was delivered by Prof. A.K. Mallik, the then Director of IIT, Kanpur in the year 1989. By honouring Professor Mallik, Dr. Agrawal wanted to give credit to Kanpur, which had initiated the idea to honour the memory of Dr. Daya Swarup. The first Daya Swarup Memorial Lecture was held during the IIM Annual Technical Meeting held in Kolkata in November. I attended the Meeting Mrs. Daya Swarup also graced the occasion, I thanked Dr. Agrawal profusely for this noble initiative out of sheer modesty, but he gave credit to all of us.

My subsequent meeting with Dr. P.L. Agrawal was in IIM Annual Technical Meetings at Udaipur (1992) and New Delhi (1996). Mr. A.C. Wadhawan and Dr. Rodriguez were the Presidents of IIM during those occasions. In Udaipur, I met Dr. R. Kumar, Ex-Director, RRL, Bhopal, who delivered the Dr. Daya Swarup Memorial Lecture. Dr. Agrawal regarded Dr. Kumar as a very eminent metallurgist, but he did not hide that his biggest adversary was his outspokenness. As time passed, my meetings with Dr. Agrawal became infrequent. However, we were in regular correspondence. I presented him our book on 'History of Metals' in Hindi which he and his wife read with interest. He paid rich compliments to me for the book.

It is very very opportune that the Ministry of Steel, Government of India decided to honour Dr. Agrawal by awarding him the first 'Life Time Achievement Award 'in 2005.

Recently I saw the review of the book by Dr. P.L. Agrawal entitled 'Journey of a Steel Man' (2009) done by Dr. V.S. Arunachalam in Current Science. I was curious to read the book and I wrote to Dr. Agrawal as to how to purchase this book. He called me and said the book is sent as a present by the courier service. I was elated and read the book twice. Here he described in 11 Chapters (total pages 243) the whole autobiography of his. He has been consistently honest in revealing the truth, sometimes the unpleasant ones too. He has been liberal in thanking those who helped him in his testing times. Among them the most conspicuous is Mr. Mantosh Sondhi, who was the Managing Director of Bokaro Steel Plant and later the Secretary Steel and Mines. Both these technocrats jointly contributed a lot to the nation even after their retirement. One of the major contributions had been advising the Bharat Refractories Ltd. (BRL) which was incurring net losses since 1985-86 and cash losses since 1988-89. They made an in-depth study of BRL and suggested ways and means to make it viable. They submitted the Draft Report on the economic viability in 1991. According to Dr. Agrawal he did not think any follow up action was taken by BRL. I wonder, what the wastage of man power had undergone. This must have frustrated the investigators, although financially they did not miss anything from their consultancy fee. Another contributions had been in the enquiry in to Durgapur Billet Casters, auditing the performance of Visakhapatnam Steel Plant, and preparing a plan for Orissa Steel Project.

Dr. Agrawal had been candid in his appraisal. In his book he describes how the Chairman of Orissa Industries Ltd., Shri K.P. Jhunjhunwala, who had achieved excellent success in refractory production, got bogged down with the idea of starting a steel plant. Dr. Agrawal advised him against this, since steel plant was a highly capital intensive proposition. However, his friend Jhunjhunwala did not listen to him and started taking money out of the refractory plant and ultimately making it a sick unit. How many consultants of today would be so candid in their appraisal?

Dr. Agrawal was active even in the last stage of his life. He was quite regular in food habits. May be this was the secret of his long purposeful life. After brief illness Dr. Agrawal passed away on 1st September, 2010 due to lungs ailment in his native city of Udaipur. With him passed the glorious age of real 'karmayogis'.

LATE DR. V.A. ALTEKAR

Our country has not been lucky in having many extractive metallurgists. Dr. Altekar was one of the top notch extractive metallurgists. I knew Altekar, from childhood, since my father and his father were both faculty members in BHU and were good friends. Dr. Altekar did his doctorate from the famous Colorado School of Mines in USA. After graduation in metallurgical engineering he was on the faculty of BHU's metallurgical Engineering department. Dr. Altekar's greatest teaching role has been in the department of Chemical Technology at Bombay University, as professor in Metallurgical Engineering. Incidentally Bombay suited to Dr. Altekar for executing consultancy business. When offered the post of Director at National Metallurgical Laboratory (NML), Dr. Altekar accepted to join the same. His desire was to constitute it at national level in a still bigger way. His few initial years at NML were big success, but gradually he got affected by the laboratory's internal politics. The biggest handicap of Dr. Altekar was his utmost trust for his colleagues. He was a solid academician, but unfortunately was more or less surrounded by sycophants at NML. He could not distinguish between a sycophant and a real well wisher.

I visited twice NML during his tenure of directorship. Both times, was supposed to deliver invited lectures. I also met him in some meetings of IIM. He used to visit IIT, Kanpur on Faculty Selection Boards. One of the Powder Metallurgy Association of India's Annual Meeting was held in NML. Mr. Sahni of his laboratory had convened that. Dr. J.J. Irani of Tata Steel inaugurated the meeting, while I was there as the Acting President of the Association. Dr. Altekar delivered a brief but very lucid speech. His personality was very attractive. The annual budget of CSIR in those days was very limited, but within those constrains Dr. Altekar did his utmost to enhance the stature of NML.

It is pity this great metallurgist did not live longer after retirement. He died suddenly after a heart attack.

LATE DR. D.P. ANTIA

In childhood, Dr. Antia had an ambition to join Indian Military Academy at Dehradun, but due to a motorcycle accident he could not appear in the examinations. During that time a friend of his parents, who had just returned from a visit to Russia suggested Antia to study metallurgical engineering. The famous place for metallurgy was at BHU and in 1934, Dr. Antia joined the metallurgical engineering programme. At BHU, he got utmost influenced by his teacher Prof. N.P. Gandhi and Professor Iyer. The department was very much used to visual aids and Dr. Antia very much liked this way of teaching. He was a keen sportsman too who played cricket for the University and also represented U.P. twice in the Ranji Trophy tournament. He was well known throughout the University and that brought in him the leadership quality. Dr. Antia has been always beholden to his department at BHU. According to him it was the best in India and one of the few in the world, which has a reputation of good teaching with research.

After BHU education, Antia moved to MIT, where he researched on the heat treatment of steels under Dr. Morris Cohen. Both teacher and the taught were young and Dr. Cohen liked him. His research paper on the tempering studies of steel got published in the Transactions of ASM. Dr. Antia had a dream to start a Society in India on the lines of ASM. This he achieved as soon as he returned to India. To get a job in USA was not a problem for him but the patriotic zeal of Pandit Mahamana Malviya at Varanasi, which he witnessed at BHU had a very deep influence on him. He returned to India and joined the Ministry of Industry in New Delhi as Metals Development Officer. Dr. E.G. Ramchandran was his junior there. The latent management skill of Dr. Antia came to full bloom during his stay in the Ministry. After some time Dr. Antia left the Government job and got involved in industry.

His last assignment was with Union Carbide, Calcutta at the post of Managing Director. There he appointed a number of able Indian Metallurgists to assist him. One of them was Dr. P.P. Sinha, who had a Ph.D. from University of Illinois, Urbana. The battery manufacturing involves a number of materials both metallic and nonmetallic. We can, thus, certainly call Dr. Antia as the first Indian materials scientists/technologist.

Dr. Antia, while being in Calcutta, was very helpful to the IIM organisation. Being one of the founder members of IIM, he nurtured it as his baby. IIM facilities were,initially, in the Tata Steels Head Quarters in Calcutta free of cost. Dr. Antia was instrumental in managing this facility. He also edited the Transactions of IIM for which he toiled a lot. If one looks at those issues of the Transactions one can gauge the quality of review and editing of the technical papers. They were quite original and not carbon copies of elsewhere published ones. Each paper had discussion columns too. Unfortunately within the life span of Dr. Antia, the quality of the Transactions got diluted. Dr. Antia was aware of this, but expressed his helplessness to me.

Dr. Antia had a great respect for Dr. H.J. Bhabha. He was quite active in 1957 in cosponsoring the International Symposium on Rare Metals, along with Indian Atomic Energy Establishment and UNESCO. The symposium was held in Bombay and the Proceedings was published by IIM, Calcutta, the editors were Mr. R.D. Lalkaka Dr. Brahm Prakash and Dr. Jagadish Shankar. In those days I was a student at BHU, but I did purchase a copy of the Proceedings, as the topic was a novel one. Dr. Antia and Professor G.K. Ogale (Principal, Pune Engineering College) were the Vice-Presidents of IIM. What I liked in the Proceedings was the inclusion of questions /answers, which are very useful to any serious reader. Dr. Homi J. Bhabha the then Chairman of the Atomic Energy Commission inaugurated the symposium. On the dias was sitting the eminent industrialist of Bombay Mr. K.C. Mahindra, an appreciation for the industrialists. Unfortunately with passage of time the Indian private enterprises were looked down in the License Raj. It is but fitting how in the beginning of the nineties, these failings were realised by the then Prime Minister Mr. P. Narsimha Rao and a correctional measure was taken.

My first meeting with Dr. Antia was in 1963-64, while I was teaching in BHU. He came there in an annual function of the department of Metallurgical Engineering. Our meeting was brief, but very useful. My recontact with him began soon after my joining IIT Kanpur. I used to meet him in Annual Technical Meetings of IIM. He was very inquisitive about IIT, Kanpur, its faculties and the facilities. His son was in preparation of JEE Examination. of IITs and was keen to join chemical engineering branch. Dr. Antia did not object to this. As a matter of fact, he got admission at IIT, Delhi. After completion of his studies, he is more or less settled in U.S.A. After his son's admission in Delhi, Dr. Antia came in contact with Dr. V. Raghavan who was a professor in Materials Science at IIT Delhi. Dr. Raghavan became the local guardian of his son.

In IIM, the biggest contribution of Dr. Antia could be the Alloy Phase Diagrams' task. When he visited USA to receive the Fellowship of ASM he noticed a need for cooperation between Indo-US metallurgists in compiling Binary and Multi-component alloy phase diagrams. Dr. T.B. Massalskii, an old student of Professor G.V. Raynor at the University of Birmingham, and now an Emeritus-Professor at the Carnegie Mellon University, very much influenced Dr. Antia to get associated with this International Mission. Dr. Antia accepted their invitation and invited Dr. T. Mukherjee of Tata Steel to be his deputy. He more or less ordered many Indian Metallurgists to chalk out specific groups of diagrams and complete the job in time. Many of our faculty at IIT Kanpur did not find the job very exciting, except Dr. K.P. Gupta, who did volunteer. We had apprehension that Americans are using us in the name of international co-opeoration and this turned out to be the truth. I was a Council Member of IIM, when this issue came up in one of its meetings. ASM practically lifted all the work of Dr. Raghavan's ternary ferrous systems and published in multiple volumes. Probably they presented one copy to IIM Library. We resented this vociferously and could notice the inconvenience faced by Dr. Antia. He wrote a letter to Dr. T.B. Massalskii, who very kindly brought this matter, saying that in that manner one can not take out the work of even Gibbs. Now we know how much revenue the ASM made on the hard work of our Indian Metallurgists. Many big shots in Indian Metallurgy rather nominated their scientists to work full time on the project of Alloy Phase Diagrams getting their salary from their employers. The organisations were CSIR, DMRL, BARC, SAIL R&D and IIT, Delhi. Dr. Antia,later, did realise the treatment meted out to IIM, but it was too late. Now the progress in Alloy Phase Diagrams project within India is rather very sluggish.

Dr. Antia was a frequent visitor of IIT Kanpur. He was impressed by the individualism of the students and faculty here. After Dr. E.C. Subba Rao and Dr. K.P. Gupta, getting awarded the Metallurgist award, there was practically a lull for twenty years, before any of the faculty could get the award. I do not attribute fully this to Dr. Antia, but there was a strong notion that Dr. Antia was surrounded by a coterie in IIM. Dr. Antia realised this, but it was late. He told me that it was he who brought Dr.

M.N. Parthsarathy, as the then-Secretary of IIM and since then the system got skewed.

In one of his visits to IIT Kanpur Dr Antia brought a team of American Materials Scientists from Oak Ridge Lab, Pennsylvania University, University of Michigan etc. I think they were four in number. Dr. Antia was the facilitator. The idea was how best to channelise the US Government PL480 money to get some of the research work be done in India. Their attitude was a bit snobbish and we diplomatically declined to associate ourselves. Dr. Antia later guided the team to other places like Indian Institute of Science, Bangalore and probably to BARC. He apparently approved openness and blunt attitude, at times. I fail here, if I do not recount one of the incidents. It was the 50 years of IIM celebrations (1996) in New Delhi with lot of pomp and show. The IIM Headquarter or better to say the Delhi Chapter of IIM gave the job of conference arrangements to a private vendor, who was not to mark in running International Conferences. The infrastructural facilities were much below expectation. During the IIM Council Meeting in the conference, I raised this issue and demanded a cut be made on the fees payable to this private firm. Many members although agreeing with me outside the Hall, remained quiet. Dr. Minoo Dastoor was sitting beside Dr. Antia. I found him whispering into his ears. Any way, Mr. V.R. Subramanian of IIM Delhi Chapter apologized for any inconvenience caused to the delegates. At the end of the meeting Dr. Antia complimented me as a good 'Watch Dog'. In the same evening there was a gala dinner. He introduced me to his wife as an alert IIT professor. I too presented a toast for the health of the couple.

With passage of time the health of Dr. Antia got deteriorated I could notice this downfall, but he did not heed to my advice. IIM was his biggest passion. In 1997 Annual Technical Meeting of IIM held a Bangalore, he fell sick with severe paralytic attack. He was shifted to his home in Pune. His faithful wife was taking care of him practically all the time. Dr. E.C. Subbarao, who was in Pune used to see him frequently. With the death of Dr. Antia ended an important chapter of Indian Metallurgy.

DR. V.S. ARUNACHALAM

During my stay at the University of Birmingham in the year 1961 Dr. R.W. Cahn once called me in his office and said 'I have an application from India for doing Ph.D. under him. He is Mr. V.S. Arunachalam. Do you know him? 'I replied in negative, but said, I know his boss Dr. K. Tangri an alumnus of BHU. Dr. Tangri was heading the Physical Metallurgy Division at Atomic Energy Establishment in Bombay. He used to publish papers in the Journal of Nuclear Materials, of which Dr. Cahn was the editor. For a year as so Dr. Tangri worked in Fulmer Research Institute in U.K. and both he and Dr. Cahn had met each other. Dr. Cahn was on the verge of leaving Birmingham to the University of South Wales, Bangor as the first Professor in materials science. Later Mr. Arunachalam joined the team of Dr. Cahn at Bangor and completed his Ph.D. on order-disorder transformations in intermetallics. After availing the Ph.D. degree in UK, Dr. Arunachalam returned to Bombay, but soon left to join National Aeronautical Lab. (CSIR),(now National Aerospace Laboratory) in Bangalore as Assistant Director. From Roorkee, I had invited Dr. Arunachalam to present a paper in the National Seminar on High Strength High Temperature alloys organised by the Roorkee Chapter of IIM. He could not attend, as he was out in Belorussia. But he deputed his junior Dr. N. Balasubramanium to present a paper on composites. Dr.R. Krishnan of BARC was also one of the participants.

In 1970 Summer, I visited USA to attend the International Conference on Strength of Metals and Alloys organised by ASM in Asilomar, California. It was here I met Dr. Arunachalam first. As a matter of fact, the resort people had put both of us together in a room. When I exclaimed him as Dr. Arunachalam, be dismissed me and said just tell me as Arun. I started calling him Arun, but in his later life it was apparent he did not like that. I, again switched over to call him more formally as Dr. Arunachalam. In Asilomar, we both had our oral presentations. The coauthor of his paper was S.L. Mannan, who recently retired from the Indira Gandhi Centre for Atomic Research. My other BHU classmates Dr. M.C. Chaturvedi, Dr. I. Gupta and Dr. Shastri were also in the conference. There was a Banquet party in one of the evenings at the beach of Asilomar. All of us enjoyed it. The paper of Dr. Arunachalam was over by that time and so he was quite relaxed. As he was a strict vegetarian, he took course of sand witches only. But he did drink. He came in the room a bit late in night, when I was going to bed. He was so much engrossed with his technical presentation, that he periodically enquired from me about it. I told him it was excellent. But it appeared he was still not satisfied and asked the same question few more times. Anyway, he woke up early morning and left for San Francisco.

I was still asleep. In the conference I found him a good networker. He mingled with people very well. Incidentally Dr. Tangri too was in that conference. After the conference, I suppose that Dr. Arunchalem had to join the Wright-Patterson Lab. in Ohio as a visiting scientist.

The third phase of Dr. Arunachalem was in Defence R&D Organization. He joined Defence Metallurgical Lab. at Hyderabad in Director-grade under Dr. R.V. Tamhankar. The internal scientist of DMRL could not get promotion and Dr. Arunachalam was lucky in this respect. At DMRL, he worked very hard in organizing the HIP facilities and doing research on dispersion strengthened alloys. Once he invited Dr. Rishi Raj of Cornell University for some joint discussion. Soon Dr. Arunachalam rose to the position of Director and Dr. Tamhankar moved to Mishra Dhatu Nigam Ltd., just adjacent to DMRL as its Managing Director. Dr. Arunachalam was the Vice-President of Powder Metallurgy Association of India, of which Dr. Tamhankar was the President. We all could notice that Dr. Arunachalam was an ambitious man. In the Bombay Annual Meeting of PMAI in early eighties, while electing the office bearers, in the Governing Council Meeting, nominations were sought. Most of us wanted Dr. Tamhankar to continue as President. Suddently, Mr. V.R. Subramaniam of India Lead-Zinc Association, proposed the name of Dr. Arunachalam. Strangely, there was no seconder. Dr. Arunachalam got offended and gave a hidden threat that any facilities to PMAI given by DMRI shall be stripped off. He resigned from the Vice-Presidentship of PMAI. As a matter of fact, Mr. N.T. George the Honorary Secretary of PMAI faced a lot of trouble, while vacating the office of PMAI from the premises of DMRL. It is known to all that PMAI ran well even without the patronage of DMRL.

Dr. Arunachalam also served IIM as its President. He was the recipient of numerous awards from IIM including the 'Metallurgist Award' from the Ministry of Steel, Gevernment of India. I doubt whether he loves the word metallurgist as he is an ardent protagonist of Materials Science. He served numerous Government agencies including CSIR, being as the chairman of Selection Committees of NML. In one of the Council Meetings of IIM, when he was its President, he mentioned about the success of the Arjun Tank. He wanted to exhibit some brochures. His briefcase was a bit away from his chair. He told Dr. P. Rama Rao, who was then a senior scientist at DMRL to bring the brief case. Dr. Rama Rao followed his instructions. Most of us were not pleased with this imperial attitude. We know habits die hand.

Dr. Arunachalam's rise on the success ladder was unterrupted. He rose to the position of Scientific Advisor to the Minister of Defence. The President of India decorated him with many awards. He edited a book an 'Advances in Powder Metallurgy' along with a Belorussian Professor Dr. Oleg Roman. The book was published in India by Oxford Book Co. New Delhi. Dr. L.R. Vaidyanath sent a copy of it to me for its review in IIM Metal News. I took pains to read and review the same, which got published. It appears that my review was not liked by some one and a second review got published after few months I wrote to the Managing Editor Dr. Pramanik about this episode. He sincerely apologized for the duplicate review.

Apart from being ambitious, Dr. Arunachalam was a restless person. After Dr. Altekar, CSIR was in search of a new Director for NML. I was one of the applicants. The interview was organised in New Delhi Dr. Varada Rajan was then the Director-General of CSIR. Dr. S. Banerjee, Dr.V. Ramaswami (SAIL),Dr. B.K. Sarkar (ISRO), Dr. C.K. Gupta (BARC) were other external candidates. Dr. Arunachalam happened to be the chairman of the Selection Committee. He asked some questions to me,which were suitably replied. I did differ with him on the issue of identifying the research areas. It appeared he wanted only frontier areas. I emphasized that even in conventional areas we need R&D. He was a protagonist of 'leaping'. I said one need not pretend to leap all the time. I was not selected for the post and Dr. S. Banerjee soon joined the post of Director. More than two decades passed since then and it is clear to every one how much our nation has leapt forward.

After relinquishing the job at the Ministry of Defence, Dr. Arunachalam joined the Carnegie-Mellon University, Pittsburgh as a visiting Professor. He made the administration of the university to feel that he can do their technology transfer in the field of broad-band. But, finally, he could not succeed. A number of lobbyists wrote in our national newspapers about this technology transfer.

In earlier PMAI technical meetings, Dr. Arunachalam used to participate. I remember one incident during Bombay Meeting, when a paper by one of my students Dr. Haminddin was orally presented. The topic was role of Copper in sintered Fe-P alloys. Dr. Arunachalam thought that since copper is soft, their ought to be softening in the end alloy. We disputed him and convinced him that the copper does not remain there inert, but interacts and gives rise to strengthening. My student was a bit nervous before this great scientist and, therefore, I had to supplement the reply in part.

One of Dr. Arunachalam's favourite scientist at DMRL, was Dr. N. Ramakrishnan, who followed him at Carnegie-Mellon too. For few years, Dr. Ramakrishnan was Director of Regional Research Laboratory, at Bhopal and specialized in mathematical modeling.

Presently, Dr. Arunachalam is the head of Centre for Study of Science and Technology and Policy, Bangalore. We read his columns as the controversial issue of military/civilian divide of our nuclear programmes.

In July 2006, there was a hue and cry in our electronic and print media that Dr. Arunachalam was a mole for USA during the period of Mr. P.V. Narasimha Rao's Prime Ministership, which made the Americans to know all about our nuclear explosion plans. This was a mere guess in the media, which generated a lot of heat. Dr. Arunachalam got exonerated. He wrote a very interesting column in Hindustan Times Daily under the title 'My loss of honour, being branded a mole'. Spying is a common thing and is a two way affair. As we are a relatively less prosperous nation, we are more vulnerable.

DR. R.D. BHARGAVA

There are few persons who have extensively served industry, but possess the highest academic degree. Dr. R.D. Bhargava is one of them. Dr. Bhargava after completing his B.Sc. (Met. Engg.) degree from Banaras Hindu University in 1951, moved to Europe to take industrial experience. He was in Austria and Yugoslavia for a number of years and earned his Ph.D. degree from Yugoslavia. With a typical Punjabi mentality, he was an industrious person. When Mahindra group of companies started its first P/M Plant in India named 'Mahindra Sintered Products', in early sixties, they selected Dr. Bhargava to head their plant in Pune. Dr. Bhargava was then serving in UK. He accepted the job and returned to India. He was practically in know how of each and every production stage in Powder Metallurgy with due authority and competence. I met him first at Bombay IIM meeting in 1964. He was a tall, handsome person with pleasing personality. In the beginning of seventies, there was some difference with his management and he resigned and started a new company to manufacture ferrites in Pune.

The beginning of our long association started in 1973 during the meeting at Hyderabad, which Dr. R.V. Tamhankar had organised to make the foundation of 'Powder Metallurgy Association of India'. It was a small group of people of about 35 or so and the meeting lasted for two days. Captain Mahindra and Mr. B.M. Kateria of Mahindra Sintered Products were also in the meeting. As a matter of fact, Dr. Bhargava had picked up Mr. Kataria as his junior, while he was a fresh metallurgy graduate from IIT, Kharagpur. By that time, Dr. Bhargava was a reputed P/M consultant in India. Later, I was assigned the job of organizing the first ever P/M short course at the University of Roorkee under the direction of PMAI. Dr. Bhargava came to deliver some very useful lectures. Even with other preoccupations he did that job without any charges. He was so fond of me that as soon as he got settled in the university guest house, he walked to my residence to meet me. In those days, the intercom faculty in the university was negligible. Till late night we talked many things including our families, our alma mater, the Indian P/M industry and the nation's industrial health. I found him an extremely thoughtful person with a streak of humour. He even discussed with me the use of LPG gas in sintering furnaces.

Dr. Bhargava was a council member of PMAI, whose Annual Meetings he always attended religiously. This was very much appreciated. In the council meeting he praised the P/M short course organised by me. He had respect for Professor G.S. Tendolkar. As a matter of fact, he was the examiner of the Ph.D. thesis of Professor P. Ramakrishnan at IIT Bombay, whose guide was Prof. Tendolkar. In the Pune meeting of PMAI, I happened to meet his very charming wife. I was unaware that she has been diagnosed abdominal cancer. It is pity she died within few years of our meeting. Dr. Bhargava was very upset, but fortunately his son took the charge of his father at Pune.

The next phase of activity of Dr. Bhargava, started after his getting relieved from the ferrite plant. He became an International Consultant in P/M. He moved to many countries including South America. Bound Brookes UK, the parent company of MSP, gave an opportunity to him to establish a P/M plant in Mexico. At first he was a bit reluctant because of his health problem. But as a typical Punjabi, he took the challenge very seriously and built and opened the plant. It was here that he met his future wife. They got married and lived quite happily. She came to Pune and lived with him. Unfortunately, as of today I have lost contact with Dr. Bhargava. I trust he is still loyal to 'Powder Metallurgy' which he brought to India from Europe.

LATE DR. S. BHATTACHARJEE

The professional career of Dr. S. Bhattacharjee is similar to that of Dr. P.L. Agrawal. Both started their career as teacher and ended in industry. Dr. Bhattacharjee retired from Ordnance Factory Organisation as Chairman cum Managing Director. He was a BHU graduate in Metallurgical Engineering (1947) and had a Ph.D. from Manchester University, where his supervisor was Dr. H. Axon. I first met him in 1973 at B.H.U. during the Golden Jubilee Celebrations of the Metallurgical Engineering Department. He was then the Managing Director of Bokaro Steel Plant. He received the Distinguished Aluminus Award during the celebrations.

Dr. Bhattacharjee's forefathers belonged to Kanpur. His father was a famous medical practitioner in the city. His ancestral home was near General Post Office in the Civil Lines. His major contribution was in the Ordnance Factories chain, serving in various capacities. In those days the biggest metallurgical input in ordnance organisation used to be in Ishapur Ordnance Factory in 24 Paraganas (West Bengal). Dr. Bhattacharjee contributed in making gun grade steels at Ishapur. His famous metallurgical experience at Manchestor was very handy to him.

Dr. Bhattacharjee was also General Manager of Small Gun and the newly built Field Gun Factories at Kanpur. As he had a soft corner for the city he used to visit Kanpur including our IIT campus frequently. After retiring from Ordnance Factory Organisation in the beginning of eighties, he came to Kanpur to settle in his old home. His plan was to start a Management Consultancy Service. I think he succeeded quite a bit in Government Organisations, but as our economy was still not an open one, he could not make much advances in the private sector. He and his wife were very religious and they never missed to visit the Lord Hanuman Temple at Pankee every Tuesday morning. He bought a brand new Maruti 800 car, but unfortunately he developed retinal problem in one of his eyes, which made his driving difficult.

The death of Dr. Daya Swarup brought a vacuum in the set up of IIM Kanpur Chapter office bearers. We all persuaded Dr. Bhattacharjee to take over the chairmanship. As in past, I continued as the Vice-Chairman of the chapter. Dr. Bhattacharjee did bring vigour in the organisation but somehow some of the IIT Kanpur ambitious faculties did not like him. Dr. Bhattacharjee followed the Rules and Regulations as supplied by the IIM Headquarters. Some of our young faculty did not prefer to make up any genuine issue in the General Body of the IIM. With his age getting advanced, the couple wanted to settle in New Delhi, where their only son was living. He sold his parental properties at Kanpur and moved to Delhi. After his departure to Delhi, I took the charge of IIM Kanpur chapter as the Acting Chairman.

Dr. Bhattacharjee was a Bhadralok Bengalee. He never harmed any one. He attended the 1996 Golden Jubilee Celebrations of IIM held at New Delhi. The last occasion he made up was to attend the IIM Annual Meeting organized was at IIT Kanpur in 1998. Only few years after that I read in the Delhi editions of our national English daily about the sad demise of this great metallurgist. It is pity he did not receive any Government Honours, when people of for less caliber could get them. The main impediment was his self esteem which prevented him in approaching the right type of persons for furthering his cause. I wish India had many more such personalities with dedication to the profession.

LATE DR. BRAHM PRAKASH

Dr. Brahm Prakash, a doyen in Nuclear Metallurgy, was born in Punjab. He completed his M.Sc. in Chemistry from Punjab University, Lahore. Soon after he took up a job as chemist in the Western Railway's Testing Laboratory in Ajmer. He was an ambitious person like any other Punjabi, and wanted to do higher studies. He moved to MIT and completed his Sc.D. degree from Metallurgical Engineering Department under the supervision of internationally famed expert in mineral beneficiation Professor Gaudin. We the students in metallurgy had read the famous book of Gaudin published by McGraw Hill Co., N.Y.

While being a student at BHU, I heard about Dr. Brahm Prakash, who was heading the metallurgy department of Indian Institute of Science, Bangalore Soon, we came to know that he joined Atomic Energy Agency at Bombay. I first saw him in 1963, when he came to BHU as one of the experts for the faculty selection. He was a tall fair complexioned slim person with a radiance over his face. He often, smoked cigar. In any correspondence he used to write as Dr. Brahm Prakash and not Professor. May be his very short stay at IISc made him to do so?

The next meeting with Dr. Brahm Prakash was in 1970, when the Annual Meeting of IIM was held in the University of Roorkee. I was then Associate Professor and was nominated as the Convener of that event. Dr. Prakash came in taxi for Delhi and we welcomed him in the University Guest House. Next day he delivered the Presidential Address in what he talked at length about the Nuclear Fuel Complex at Hyderabad, a production unit which was his brain child. Next day, during the Annual Technical Meeting I enquired whether he could help me in getting some Ti-Mo alloy samples for our research. He readily accepted my request. After few days I heard from Mr. C.V. Sundaram of BARC about the details of the material needed. This gave me a clue as well. Whenever you wish to get hastened, better contact the top brass. One of my M.Tech. students at Roorkee Mr. M.K. Mittal did his research on the phase transformation on those alloys.

My third meeting with Dr. Brahm Prakash was in the beginning of eighties in the Annual Technical Meeting of IIM at Vadodara. Dr. Daya Swarup was also there. We interacted very extensively. My entry into Indian powder metallurgy was established by that time. Dr. Prakash was very affectionate with me. He told something very candid during the tea break. He lamented on the poor quality of new entrants in atomic energy. He said very few IIT students are joining atomic energy. The charisma of Dr. Homi Bhabha was over. I was very particular to point out that the single mode of entrance in BARC through the training school is rather an impediment to Atomic Energy. There must be two way facilities. He agreed with my argument and added that much hierarchy has entered into the organisation. He was very bold to suggest that young scientist should be groomed soon to take the leadership. If not exploited within a certain period they become infertile. In the Vadodara meeting there were two metallurgists for Atomic Energy. Dr. P. Rodriquez and Dr. Bal Deva Raj. Dr. Prakash was happy with their progress. I interrupted him and opined that proper environment and care be taken so that practically all scientists could be made fertile. His answer was yes, but in reality difficult. Always there are some dead weights in any organization, but attempt must be made to keep them in a limit.

Dr. Brahm Prakash was associated with many CSIR Laboratories on their Research Advisory Councils (RAC) as Chairman. I was one of the member of the RAC of Regional Research Laboratory, Bhopal. In most of the meetings I used to be in Bhopal. Dr. Prakash was then running the show at ISRO, Trivandrum very successfully. We used to meet closely during the dinners. He was a patient listener and used to reply in few but very lucid words. It appears some politics brought him from Atomic Energy to Space Research. As he could not get promotion for the post of Director of BARC, he was a bit unhappy. He never narrated these things in detail, but threw some hints only.

Dr. P.K. Rohatgi, the then Director of RRL was our host. He was far bolder than me, in exposing some of the follies in Indian science. It is unfortunate if Indian science comes in the control of sectarians. Dr. Brahm Prakash abhored such traits, but at the some time he was quite aware of the fact that in India you have to side with some people and make compromises. But these compromises in no way should be of disadvantage to other group of people. The death of Dr. Brahm Prakash came after his retirement from ISRO. He breathed his last in Bombay, with his loved wife,a devoted life partner, at his bed side.

DR. AMIT CHATTERJEE

When I joined BHU in 1963, as a teacher my attention was drawn to a young student, who was very dynamic and used to take part in debates. I was eager to know about him. Mr. S.H. Ghude, then a lecturer there, told me that this boy is Amit Chatterjee, son of Dr. A.B. Chatterjee of National Metallurgical Laboratory. He was different from others and this had a mark on me. After my return from USSR, I came to know that he is in UK at the University of London. Later he took assignments in a German Steel Plant. His sense of patriotism brought him back to India and his job was of a research metallurgist in Tata Steel at Jamshedpur. At Tata Steel he rose to promotions and for some time was with Tata's Sponge Iron Plant near Kharapur for producing sponge iron as the Managing Director. In 1985, IIT, Kanpur organised an International Conference in which Dr. Amit Chatterjee was invited. He is a forceful speaker with utmost clarity of thoughts. I had read his research papers in the Journal Iron and Steel Making, published by Institute of Metals, Metals and Minerals of U.K. Dr. Navin Kothari of the University of Queensland, Australia was also one of the invitees in the conference. Dr. Kothari, while talking with our students, had an air of supremacy regarding the Australian education. This irked Dr. Chatterjee. He vehemently disputed this and justified how our students are in no way inferior. As both of them were my friends, I suitably patched the matter Dr. M.C. Chaturvedi, my classmate at BHU, who is now retired from the University of Manitoba, Canada was also an invitee in the conference.

I visited Tata Steel quite a few times and on each occasion I never missed to meet Dr. Chatterjee. Our talks used to be very extensive ones, right from our BHU days, IIM and to the recent advances in steels. He is completely devoid of any regional feelings. As Amit was brought up in Jamshedpur, he was very comfortable with Hindi and even with some Bhojpuri dialect.

In 1995, IIT Kanpur initiated a major research project on sintered steels for automobile applications under the aegis of Planning Commission, Government of India, to be carried out under my direction. For this Tata Steel agreed to be the collaborator. Dr. J.J. Irani the then Managing Director of Tata Steel, asked Dr. Amit Chatterjee to attend the meting of the Steering Committee. Amit visited Kanpur along with his loving and devoted wife. He had an extensive meeting with us and our Director, Prof. R.C. Malhotra. The project was approved and got completed successfully. I was in regular contact with him in sending our R&D findings.

Dr. Chatterjee has been a regular visitor of various academic campuses on behalf of the Tata Steel to recruit graduating students. His candid comments on the syllabi, students and faculties have been very useful to our Institute. He did not shy to transmit his opinion to our Director. He still recalled the nice blend of science and technology education imparted to the Institute of Technology students at B.H.U.

My last visit at Tata Steel was in 2004. Actually it was deliberately planned by me, because of my keen desire to meet Dr. Chatterjee, whom I knew was on the verge of retirement. Actually, my main official visit was in Ranchi, not far from Jamshedpur. He immediately responded and accepted my plan of the visit. Actually he had to go at the some time to Bombay. It did not deter him from inviting me. I did visit Jamshedpur and gave a seminar in NML, where some of the research staff of Tata Steel did participate. At present Amit Chatterjee is Advisor to the Managing Director of Tata Steel. He is always an alert and jovial person with full of jest in life. After conversing with him on every occasion, I do get refreshed both academically and socially. As I live in Varanasi, I never fail to see him whenever he visits BHU. As a matter of fact at one visit in a year is quite usual for him.

Dr. Chatterjee is a prolific scientific writer as well. His book on Blast Furnace, Iron Making and of 'Sponge Iron Production by Direct Reduction of Iron Oxide' (2010) are quite famous. He also coauthored a topical book 'Iron Making and Steel Making' (2008) along with Professor Ahindra Ghosh, who was my esteemed colleague at IIT, Kanpur. The book is an excellent text book for metallurgical engineering students. The Appendix in the book covering the iron making and steel making in India is very useful, which unfortunately, is often ignored by our teachers. In addition, Dr. Chatterjee is the Chief Editor of the periodical Steel Tech published quarterly from Kolkata. The periodical is comparable to any one published in the world, both from the quality and contents viewpoint. Currently it is running in its fourth year. As a matter of fact, it has an international coverage.

LATE PROFESSOR P.R. DHAR

In my student days at BHU, we know that Prof. P.R. Dhar was the Head of the Metallurgical Engineering Department at IIT, Kharagpur. We also came to know that, essentially, he is a physicist turned into metallurgist. He had a Master's degree from Columbia University, USA. One Mr. R.A. Tiwari, a physicist, who was a research assistant at BHU had joined his group at Kharagpur. We used to jokingly say that a physicist pulls on well with another physicist. Mr. Tiwari was not that successful at BHU. I did not see Professor Dhar much in conferences and his students Mr. Tiwari, who later became a lecture and another Mr. Gupta at IIT, Kharagpur used to attend conferences and read papers. Their areas of work were mainly in physical metallurgy of steels.

During my stay in USSR, I became aware of the USSR collaboration with IIT Kharagpur. Dr. Oleg Roman a visiting professor by that time had returned back to USSR. While at the University of Roorkee (1970). I was keen to visit IIT, Kharagpur, so as to meet these Russian friends. I was well verse in Russian language and all of a sudden there was no one to speak in Russian.On the invitation of Mr. T.R. Gupta, the Managing Director of India Hard Metals, I planned to visit Calcutta. As a matter of fact, he wanted to take me as R&D Manager. I utilized that occasion to visit Kharagpur also. As I had a service contract with my University, my switching over to India Hard Metals appeared to be difficult. The adverse opinion of Dr. P.P. Sinha, who earlier served this company, also discouraged me to take further initiative. From Howrah I picked an evening train for Kharagpur. It was a sleepy town and people discouraged me to go all alone by riksha in late night. In those days the telecommunication facility was so poor that with best efforts, I could not contact Prof. Dhar of IIT, Kharagpur. Next morning, I proceeded to the campus. Most of the riksha pullers were from Andhra Pradesh. I could locate the department and found the office room of Professor Dhar in the ground floor. He welcomed me, but there was some degree of authority in him. Any person, who wished to see him, entered into his room very apologetically. Prof. Dhar used to invariably have a pipe in his mouth. He talked about my research work and enquired about new areas of research in materials. Although his research was on steels, he was a protagonist of materials science. By that time the 'Materials Science Centre' in the campus had came into existence and I could gauge there the tussle between these i.e. the department and the centre. I do not know whether Prof. Dhar was amused or annoyed with these events. After a long conversation, I wished to visit various laboratories in the department which he facilitated. He told his colleague Dr. Gutpa to escort me. Dr. Gupta, who is new serving in industry, was very helpful and showed me all the facilities. In some laboratories as soon as I was introduced to the laboratory technicians, they were very keen to khow whether I am joining their Institute. They spoke this in Bengalee, which I understood. For Dr. Gupta it was embarrassing each time to explain them that he just has come to visit the department. There I could smell the presence of the communist party of India. Even some faculties were not unaffected. The political turmoil of West Bengal did hamper the smooth progress of IIT, Kharagpur, for quite same time.

That afternoon was spent by me with the Russian experts. One of them had his wife with him who had brought souces and vodka from USSR. We all had a nice time. My Russian friends were a bit home sick. Our company even for few hours was sufficient to enjoy the Russian comradeship. I took back the evening train for Calcutta. At IIT, Kharagpur Mr. Sanjay Basu, who was scheduled soon to join the team of Professor Roman at Minsk, met me. He was a bit curious to know the state of affairs in USSR. I strongly encouraged him to proceed and he does not regret for that decision. Later Dr. Basu became the R&D Manager of the reputed cemented carbide producing firm in Pune, Sandvik Asia, and rose to the high position of Vice-President.

After retirement from IIT, Kharagpur, Professor Dhar joined a special steel production company in Calcutta as its Advisor. He also got associated very actively with the Indian Institute Metals, as the Chairman of its Examination Committee. My last meeting with him was in an Annual Technical Meeting of IIM, probably in Delhi. He was as usual with the pipe in his mouth. We exchanged pleasantries. I found in his lips a pleasing smile, which was difficult to see in earlier periods.

Like any mortal, Prof. Dhar is no more with us. His service to IIM has been substantial, but remained unrewarded.

MR. N.T. GEORGE

A native of Kerala and a devoted catholic, Mr George, after completing his education in Metallurgy from the Indian Institute of Science, Bangalore, joined various Defence Organisations right from Ordnance Factory to Defence Metallurgical Research Laboratory at Hyderabad. Dr. T.R. Anantharaman was his classmate in IISc.Many people are not aware of the fact that prior to getting established in Hyderabad, the laboratory functioned in the premises of Ishapur Ordnance Factory. Dr. N. Anjaneyulu,an alumnus of BHU with a doctorate from Germany was the Director. Dr.U.V. Bhat of BHU advised me to meet Dr. Anjaneyulu for a prospective job in DRDO. It was the summer of 1960 After travelling from Varanasi to Howrah,I reached straight to his office. It was here I met Mr. George. He was a very quiet person. I did not pay much attention to him.I did not pursue the matter further, as I had made up my mind to go abroad.Dr. Anjaneyulu told me that there was a good chance that DMRL gets established in Kanpur.As a matter of fact our Chief Minister Mr C.B. Gupta was slow in granting the land, whereas the Chief Minister of Andhra Pradesh jumped upon the proposal and gave land to DRDO free of cost.This is a glaring example how a quick decision is necessary for development of any region.Before 1960 Hyderabad used to be a sleepy city.It is only after the chain of DRDO laboratories, that its name has come in the industrial and scientific map of India.

After a long pause of 13 years, I met Mr George in DMRL.the occasion was the founding of the Powder Metallurgy Association of India, which was the brain child of Dr.R.V. Tamhankar, the then Director of DMRL.

I was specially invited from Roorkee. My boss Dr. Saxena was not willing to allow me to leave the station, but my desire to attend the meeting was so intense that I took casual leave. At DMRL I noticed Mr Acharyulu helping Mr George very obediently in conducting the meeting. I found Mr George an excellent organiser. He was a great asset to Dr. Tamhankar, who was very busy in so many other activities simultaneously. By that time I had an approved research project of DRDO on sintered aluminium alloy composites. Mr George did help me getting few of my samples examined under EPMA. During my visit of the laboratory, I was struck by the fact that all equipments were in working order. The credit for this goes to Mr George. He was a stickler and never heeded to any sort of procrastinations. He always believed that you must know your apparatus well, before you use it.

Mr George had organized an excellent powder metallurgy laboratory in DMRL. The equipments were of semi-production type. The emphasis was on cemented carbides and heavy alloys. He travelled to UK on quite some occasions to get right types of equipments. For many decades, the PM Laboratory was the prestigious place for relevant research. Profesor Tendolkar wrote me high about this from IIT, Bombay.

The bad days of Mr George started, when Dr. V.S. Arunachalam joined DMRL as Director. Mr George did not disturb any one, but at the same time he was unhappy and annoyed when he was castigated as an old fashioned metallurgist. It is an unworthy commentary when Dr. Arunachalam got many national awards based on the hard work of Mr George on aircraft sintered friction pads with no mention of Mr George in the citation. Mr George being a benevolent catholic suffered all these without any grudge.

The contribution of Mr. George as the Hon. Secretary of PMAI can be written in golden letters. He toiled and published the annual Transactions and quarterly Newsletters well in time. The papers were referred in many international publications. As soon as Dr. Arunachalam ordered him to vacate the office of PMAI from the premises of DMRL, Mr George obeyed him. He got a flat on rent in the city not far from DMRL and ran the show. As soon as I knew about this, I wrote to Dr. Tamhankar, the President of PMAI. He was helpless, as he was no more associated with DRDO. With all the virtues, one of the biggest issue before Mr. George was the financial savings in PMAI. On practically every General Body Meeting of PMAI, the balance used to be only few hundreds of Rupees. I think Mr George can not be solely blamed for that.He could have saved, but then the publications would have taken a beating, which is happening in today's PMAI.

Mr George left the Secretary's position of PMAI at the same time my term as the President lasted. It was in May 1989, when the Annual Meeting of PMAI was held in Sri Nagar. The episode was very dramatic and I shall write about this while writing on Mr P.R.Roy, the new imcumbent as PMAI President. It appears that the shadow of ghost in one form or the other was hovering over Mr. George.

Mr George made a number of International travels to promote the cause of PMAI. He was in Sweden (1979), and Canada (1984).The former was for an European PM Conference, while the latter related to MPIF International Conference on PM. Mr Kemp Roll, the Executive Director of MPIF did share with him his ups and downs in MPIF in the early stage of its formation.

My last meeting with Mr George was at the residence of Dr. Tamkankar in Hyderabad, just after the sudden death of Mr P.R. Roy. Dr. Tamhankar was not aware of this news. He immediately grabed the telephone receiver and called Mr Balaram Murthy of Nuclear Fuel Complex, Hyderabad, who was an active Council Member of PMAI. His main concern was that the Association survives.

On family side, Mr George's family is am extremely happy one.His wife is a medical doctor, while the only son after graduating in metallurgical engineering from IIT, Madras got settled in California State in USA. Of late, I have had no communication from Mr. George, but know that he is pretty frail in old age.

DR. J.J. IRANI

In the early sixties, during my stay in U.K. a name very common in the Journal of Iron and Steel Institute was of Dr. J.J. Irani.After getting M.Sc. degree in Geology from Nagpur University, Irani moved to U.K. and joned Sheffield University, where he worked under the guidance of Professor R.W.K. Honeycomb.After receiving the Ph.D. degree, he joined BISRA Laboratory (British Iron and Steel Association), where he did extensive research on physical metallurgy of steel. After few years of experience, he joined Tata Steel R&D Centre. Sooner he switched over to steelmaking side. I think he managed well this change from R & D to production.His rose to various positions like Chief Metallurgist, General Manager, President and finally Managing Director.He was very much connected to the Indian Institute of Metals, of which he was the President too. He received numerous awards from the Government and various Trade Associations.

I saw Dr. Irani first in Bombay in early seventies during the National Metallurgist Day Celebrations, where he was awarded the Metallurgist Award. He had a typical Parsee look with a well built body. His relation with Tata Group was mutual.If he delivered hard professional service, Tata Sons too gave him many facilities and groomed him to take over the top position at Tata Steel.

During his Presidentship, the Annual Technical Meeting was held in Bangalore. It was a very tumultuous period. Mrs Indira Gandhi was just assassinated few weeks back. People were doubting whether the meeting will be held or not.However due to the managerial skill of Dr. Irani the meeting ended well. Professor Honeycomb, his teacher at Sheffield, was decorated with the Honoarry Membership of IIM.

My further interaction with Dr. Irani was during IIM Council meetings, where his comments were listened very attentively.Dr. Irani always gave high regards to Dr. Dara P. Antia and Dr. Minoo N. Dastur. IIM too took Tata Steel as 'Kama Dhenu' and invariably always succeeded in getting financial support for organising their Annual Meetings.The Gala Conference Dinner was always sponsored by Tata Steel.This practice has got dampened now-a-days.

Dr. Irani wanted his worthy son to become an engineer. Living in the Steel Town his son Zubin started loving metallurgy. Incidentally after appearing in the joint entrance examination (JEE) of IITs, he joined Metallurgical Engineering Department at IIT Kanpur.His JEE rank was pretty high and he could have got admission in any branch of engineering. But he preferred metallurgical engineering. His entry into IITK brought Dr. Irani still further close to us.Zubin was a decent and polite boy and never boasted about his father. After getting his degree in Metallurgical Engineering with top rank, he joined MIT. Presently he is serving in Delhi on the top management of an US Airconditioning Company.

In mid-ninties, I had applied for a major R&D project to the Planning Commission, Government of India on 'Technology Development Mission' on new materials.The exact theme was 'Sintered Steels for Automobile Applications'.The sponsor had a precondition that every project must have an industry affiliated to it, which will give its own share both in cash and kind. The concept was a good one, but full of impediments. Some industries came forward to help in kind, but the Ministry rejected the idea. I knew that although my project would help Tata Group of Companies, it may not be of priority to Tata Steel. I reluctantly approached Dr. Irani and within a week I got a confirmatory letter. He accepted our project and deputed Dr. Amit Chatterjee to visit IIT Kanpur to formulate the exact modalities. The project ended with a success and the major credit to this goes to Tata Steel and Dr. Irani in particular.

As time passed, the moment of retirement of Dr Irani from Tata Steel approached. He sent a very affectionate letter to me thanking for all the cooperations. Tata Sons wished to take advantage of his enormous experience for the growth of their organization. At present Dr. Irani is the Director on the Board of Tata Sons.

In 2008, I met Dr. Irani in Noida during IIM Annual Technical Meeting. On that occasion, the Ministry of Steel, Government of India honourd him with the 'Lifetime Achievement Award'. Mr Ram Vilas Paswan was the then Minister. It was nice to meet Dr Irani's wife there. At Tata Steel Dr. Irani is very busy with various projects. He admits that approximately at the mid point of a career, one becomes more or less redundant in his own discipline, but gradually if he is successful in his career, his time is taken up in negotiations, maintaining public relations and decision making as then he plays the role of a leader rather than somebody, who is imparting knowledge. Actually this was the theme of his 5th Dr. Dara P. Antia Memorial Lecture delivered in January, 2010 at Pune. The title of his lecture was 'Expanding the Envelop of Corporate Responsibilty beyond the Corporate World.' The career-time engagement graph presented by him was a unique one. On innovation. Dr. Irani feels that it is not the preserve of the educated or the priviledged,. He abhors the cynicism and sarcasm of many of the Indian bosses. He started the idea of awarding the Tata Sons personnel by awards labeled as 'Dare to Try'. Such an experiment is important so as to have cross-fertilisation of ideas, to cut down hierarchy and give freedom of expression.

PROFESSOR S.K. JOSHI

After my return from USSR in Janauary 1970, I joined the University of Roorkeeas as Associat professor. After few days, there was a meeting of the Academic Senate at the University.I was an ex-officio member of the Senate.It was there during the meeting I met Professor S.K. Joshi.During my absence from the campus, he had joined the University as full Professor in physics. Prior to that he was at the University of California, Berkeley. He holds the PhD. degree from the Allahabad University. He belongs to Nainital, now in Uttarakhand State.Being a person from mountains, Dr. Joshi was a sobre and quiet person.His replies are often brief and at low pitch. At Roorkee, Dr Joshi was well aware of the internal politics of the University, but he was always a nonpartisan. He was first to enter in his department daily at sharp 8.00 AM. He guided numerous Ph.D. students in the area of condensed matter, who are spread over the country at responsible positions. I invited Dr. Joshi to examine the M.Tech thesis of one of my students, Mr. Naushad Khan, who had worked on cystral structure-electronic structure correlation of the transition metal binary alloys. Dr. Joshi asked some questions related to solid state physics, in which the student fumbled a bit.Even I would not have answered them, if I was a student.

After my departure to IIT Kanpur I missed a good sincere friend, who advised me in times of need. In one of the IITK visits, he was invited by my neighbour Prof. Gyan Mohan of Physics Departement. As soon as he knew that I am his neighbour, he walked to my door.By that time Dr. Joshi had joined the National Physical Laboratory, as its Director. The atmosphere of Delhi, which is the capital of India and the centre of power,is rather infectious. Dr. Joshi sincerely tried to remain aloof from such an influence. But we all know it is very difficult.

After the retirement of Dr. Mitra as the Director-General of the Council of Scientific and Industrial Research, Dr. Joshi was selected to that post. He did his best in reforming the CSIR, but had his own limitations.

Dr. Joshi served the Materials Research Society of India, as its President for a term.But, there he had a routine role.There was an over riding section of scientists, who had their own agenda. Prof. Joshi understood this, but many times he turned his face other way round. He was well aware as to what ails in Indian science, but he was indifferent to those.May be he did not like to get distracted?

After relinquishing his tenure at CSIR, Prof. Joshi was nominated Chaiman of the Recruitment Board of Defence Research and Development Organisation.This was a very responsible position, as any laxity in defence matter would had been detrimental in the long range. He did his job admirably well. I only wish he would had controlled the mammoth growth of DRDO and made it agile. I have seen Dr. Joshi in various annual meetings of Indian Science Congress Association. The last one was in Bangalore. He has been showered many awards from the Association.

Presently, Dr. Joshi is an Emeritus Distinguished Scientist of CSIR and is attached to his favourite National Physical Laboratory in New Delhi. I am sure he is following the old pattern of his Roorkee days. A cycle in the academic life of this scientist is getting completed with due dignity.

MR. B.M. KATARIA

Mr Kataria is a 1962 batch graduate in Metallurgical Engineering from IIT Kharagpur. Soon after graduation, he joined Mahindra Sintered Produts at Pune as a production engineer. Dr. R.D. Bhargava, General Manager of the plant was his boss, better to say teacher. He taught him every thing from A-Z of powder metallurgy. At the same time, Kataria too was a devoted trainee. I met him first in a conference at the National Metallurgical Laboratory in mid-sixties. He was a tall Punjabi with utmost dynamism. Mr Shahni of NML was engaged in copper powder production. May be that was the driving force to Mr Kataria to attend the conference? During the conference, I enquired whether he could send me some PM parts produced by his company for exhibiting to our students. He immediately agreed and did send me a big parcel.

After my return from USSR, I was suggested by the Vice-Chancellor of my University Dr. Jai Krishna to take some industrial experience during summer. I proceeded to Pune during one summer for a month for interacting with Mahindra Sintered Products. At the plant Mr Kataria was the General Manager and Captain Mahindra the Managing Director. There I missed Dr. R.D. Bhargava very much. Mr. G.M. Krishnamurthy, a metallurgy graduate of IIT Madras, was the research metallurgist. My interactions were quite productive, which not only helped me during my research but also in teaching. After the industrial experience one does get a confidence in engineering profession, not otherwise possible.

I was in a need of a good quality die set for the green compaction of metal powders. Mr Kataria was very helpful in supplying it to me per gratis, not once but twice. Here I fail in my duty if I do not mention the name of Mr. G.M. Panchal, the design engineer at MSP. He was the one of the first few Indians, who knew the art of PM tooling. In this area we metallurgical engineers are not competent.Mr Kataria, Dr. R.D Bargava and Mr. Panchal built their houses in the Mahindra Housing Colony in Pune, which I did visit once.The time was, when in capacity of President of PMAI, I was organising a workshop on 'PM in Automotive Parts'in Pune under the auspices of PMAI.Mr Kataria used to be somewhat unhappy with Mr George, the Hon. Secretary of PMAI.My former Ph.D. student Dr. P.B. Kadam was a faculty member in the Government Engineering College of Pune.We both proceeded to the MSP plant and wanted to give Mr Kataria a surprise. Mr Firodia, the then Chairman of a three wheeler company in Pune was our Chief Guest during the inauguration.

Mr Kataria held the top post of the Managing Director of MSP, which later on became a member of the Global agglomerate 'GKN Sinter Metal'. I was personally not very happy in seeing the disappearance of the word 'Mahindra'. Mr V.K. Sud, the Managing Director of Hoganas India, was a good friend of Mr. Kataria. His plant was a good source of ferrous powder to Indian PM industries. During the tenure of Mr Kataria as President pf PMAI, I attended the International Conference organised by him in New Delhi. I suppose it was in 1997. The personal acquaintance of Mr Kataria with many overseas PM industries, was very helpful in attracting a large number of international PM personalities including Mr Lindskog.

Mahindra Sintered Products' management did realise that indigenous mass production of atomized iron powder is a must for the growth of the Indian PM Industry. In 1986 Hoganas AB of Sweden eastablished its subsidiary in Ahmednagar in the Maharashtra State. Even before that Mahindra Sintered Producst began the production of atomized iron powder in Ahmednagar, Hoganas found it profitatble to purchase the plant and the deal was set in the year 1988.The Swedish Ambassador in India graced the occasion during the inauguration. It is here worth mentioning that the Hoganas Plant in Ahmednagar was the first in Asia followed by in Japan (1987) and China (1995).It is another matter that the latter companies grew much faster, and even beating the Indian production capacity.

Reverting back to my friend Kataria, I found him a person with temperament.This acted as a spice too. At times one can hear his selective abuses as well.What I liked in him was his utmost loyalty with Mahindra Group of Companies.He was an excellent fearless manager and was not at all afraid in declaring a lock out in his plant, as he could not tolerate any indiscipline.I was not aware that this energetic person is on the verge of retirement.When the news reached me, I wished him all the best.

DR. R.KUMAR

Dr. R.Kumar had been my teacher in BHU, which I have already mentioned in earlier Chapter. Here I would like to highlight some of his academic achievements. Dr. Kumar graduated in metallurgical engineering in 1950 from BHU. From the very beginning he was very fond of CSIR Laboratories and this propelled him to join Central Fuel Research Institute under CSIR. After few months of service, he proceeded to Sheffield University in UK to do the M.Met. and Ph.D. researches. His supervisor was Professor A.G. Quarrell and the topic of his thesis was on the role of hydrogen in martensitic transformation in steels.The topic was a burning one and the world's attention was drawn to his results. He was awarded the Gold Medal of Sheffield University for his research contributions.After return to India Dr. Kumar joined the Indian Institute of Technology, Kharagpur as lecturer.They had assured him of a quick promotion. With some disillusion, he decided to move to BHU as a Reader. Here in a short time Dr. Kumar made considerable contribution. He initiated the first M.Tech. program in metallurgical engineering of which Mr. V. Balasubramanium (1958 B.Tech graduate) was the first student.Later Bala did his Ph.D. from USSR and was on the faculty of IIT Bombay, before switching over to M.N.Dastur & Co.in its Bombay Branch.

At BHU, Dr. Kumar missed the promotion to professorship and Dr. Ananthraman from IISc joined as the professor. In the year 1962 Dr. Kumar joined NML as Assistant Director, the post vacated by Prof E.G. Ramchandran, who had moved to IIT Madras as a full professor. The structure and behaviour of liquid metals and alloys was the favourite research topic of Dr. Kumar.As a matter of fact he got initiated in this area right from his BHU days.My undergraduate project was on the measurement of the viscosity of lead-tin alloy melts.I was his student for two years at BHU during Bachelor's program and had opted for his elective course 'Advances in Physical Metallurgy'.

Dr. Kumar's real research output came from NML Jamshedpur.Here he developed an excellent research division and produced large number of Ph.D. students.Dr. Manjit Singh, a 1959 batch BHU graduate, was his first Ph.D. student. Dr. Singh was a very loyal associate of Dr. Kumar in his good and bad days.

Another area of research in which Dr. Kumar contributed significantly was on new grades of creep resistant steels. In those days, Indian economy was not a liberalised one and our industries had to depend on our own research outputs. In a way this was a boon. Under UNIDO scheme NML established an excellent creep laboratory. I don't know how effectively this cell is functioning now-a-days. The third area of Dr. Kumar's contribution was Al-alloys electric conductors, which was also known as PM2. These conductors were very useful in our coastal areas.

Dr. Kumar was a life member of IIM and served it in various ways. However, his relation with them was not always smooth. He narrated me an incident, which was confirmed by Dr. M.N. Parthsarathy, the then Hon. Secretary of IIM. Once his paper on liquid metal was rejected by the Institute for publication in its Transactions. This annoyed Dr. Kumar and he made an issue with IIM. He cited his other related papers, which were published in the reputed international journals. He was upset with that subjective treatment.

Rapidly solidified melt was another area of research in which Dr. Kumar's team was fascinated. In the International Conference on liquid metals held in Yugoslavia, Dr. R.W. Cahn during discussion mentioned the contribution of Dr. Kumar. Although Dr. Kumar was not personally present in that conference, such a compliment naturally made him happy.

During his NML stay Dr. Kumar wrote the seminal book entitled 'Physical Metallurgy of Steel', which got published by Asia Publishing House. The book was received very favourably. Even today, the significance of this book is undiminished.

Dr. Kumar, in mid-eighties, took sabbathical for a year and joined University of Aston in Birmingham, UK, as a visiting professor. That period, although productive for him, became a problematic too. His adversaries at NML took that occasion to their best to demolish him. But like true fighter, he came out unscathed. It was a sad commentary, when this scientist was not promoted to the Director's post at NML. Most of the time, I felt CSIR had some complex and derived a sense of false pride in inviting outsiders. This feeling of mine has a basis, since I have been in some of their selection committees. Their practice was to promote the juniors at a rather fast pace with the result that in later part of their career, many times most of these scientists became under performing. I hinted this feature many times, but it appears that the fear of trade unionism has made them not to heed to my suggestion.

The failure of Dr. Kumar to get appointed as the Director of NML made him sad.It was good that Dr. Mitra, the then Director-General of CSIR realised the mistake and ultimately the organisation made Dr. Kumar the Director of Regional Research Laboratory in Bhopal.The Powder Metallurgy Association of India had organised one of its Annual Technical Meetings at Bhopal, of which RRL was the host.Dr. R.V. Tamhankar, the then Chairman of the Research Advisory Council of the Laboratory, had also graced the occasion.I did attend that meeting and also chaired it in capacity of the Vice-Preseident of PMAI. Dr. Tamhankar seemed to be very much impressed by the academic and administrative capabilities of Dr. Kumar.

For the last 15 years, I was not in direct contact with Dr. Kumar, but I knew that he lives in Vadodara with his daughter. I got hold of his address from a scientist in RRL. Dr. Kumar was happy to receive my communication.He told me about his recent book 'Operation and Maintenance of Steam Power Boilers', published in 2008 by Allied publishers, New Delhi.The book excellently covers on the metallurgical aspects of failure analysis in boilers.I did tell him that the title needs a sub-title for a better appreciation of the book.My last meeting with him was in March, 2010 at BHU, where he had come along with his wife so as to attend the National Seminar on Environmental Management in Metallurgical Industries EMMI-2010.

LATE MR. Y.M. MEHTA

Mr. Y.M. Mehta belonged to the old generation of metallurgists, but had the modern vision.A tall slim person, Mr Mehta was always unassuming. A metallurgist turned into an industrialist, Mr Mehta started his foudry in Baroda (now Vadodara). He had a dream to make whole package of foundry equipments from testing to full production and he succeeded in that. I used to meet him during IIM Council meetings. He was very fond of speaking in Gujarati with Dr. Antia. In those days, when we did not have much indigenous foundries, the contribution of Mr Mehta has been extraordinary. It is pity he did not get any recognition from the Government of India.

Mr. Mehta rose to the position of the President of IIM. During Vadodara Annual Technical Meeting of IIM, he was our host too. There arose a controversy on an official invitation letter in which Dr. Antia was said as the 'Founder' of IIM. Many metallurgists were not happy with this misinformation. The issue was raked up by late Mr. Varshney of IIM Delhi Chapter. Anyway, the matter was resolved by naming Dr. Antia as one of the Founder Members. Dr. Antia was not very happy. He felt as if he was cheated by the sycophants, without verifying the real fact. I along with my wife did attend the ATM. Dr. Brahm Prakash and Dr. G.P. Chatterjee were notable attendees. We still remember the copious 'Srikhand' as the dessert during the lunches. Mr Vasan of Mr Mehta's Company and his charming wife did utmost to make our stay comfortable.

Mr. Mehta was a crusader. He was not happy the way IIM Divisions were giving lip service to the metal processing area. No doubt there existed an all India 'Foundrymen's Association', the metallurgical emphasis was missing there. Similar was the fate of deformation processing area. Mr Mehta advocated the cause of 'Industrial Metallurgy' Division in IIM. He wrote a lenghty letter to the IIM Headquarters and circulated it to all Council members. I replied him immediately supporting the very relevant issues raised by him. Even in the advanced age, he acknowledged my letter and removed my doubts. It is pity, few weeks after our exchange of that letter, Mr Mehta died and his mission remained unaccomplished. I wish IIM relooks the whole issue and come to a more scientific conclusion.

DR. V.N. MISRA

Dr. V.N. Misra's name can be counted among to top most mineral engineers of India. I met Dr. Misra first at the University of Roorkee in 1972 or so, where he attended the refresher course on corrosion. He was then in the faculty of Vishweshwaraiya Regional Engineering College (now a National Institute of Technology), Nagpur. Dr. Misra ia a native of Varanasi and passed out the Metallurgical Engineering program in the year 1966.

The adventurous spirit motivated Dr, Misra to migrate to Australia, where he occupied numerous responsible positions in mineral industries and universities. He has been a regular visitor of India at least once in a year. He has been an effective speaker in scientific meetings.

My enhanced interaction with Dr. Misra started after his joining the Regional Research Laboratory at Bhubaneswar as Director. Soon after his joining, he became the source of jelousy among some of the CSIR Directors. He navigated very well and did a lot of reform in his laboratory. He always furthered the cause of his scientist colleagues and did help them in getting many national awards in science and technology. I found him many times as an impatient person.My fews days stay in his laboratory made me convinced that the RRL scientists were often to be coaxed by Dr. Misra to run the show with excellence. Many times he took risks with the CSIR Headquarters. He organised one of the Annual Technical Meetings of IIM in Bhubaneswar with much pomp and show and refunded all the profits to the Headquarters.He was very dynamic in organising national seminars, at least one half-yearly. His conferences were significant by the fact that the Proceedings were invariably out before the conference. After his tenure at RRL, Dr. Misra again moved back to Australia, but I am sure the soft corner for his motherland would always benefit us in one form or the other.

DR. J. MUKERJEE

I know Dr. Mukerjee since the beginning of seventies, when he was a regular speaker in PMAI technical meetings. He was then associated with the Central Glass and Ceramic Research Institute at Kolkata. Prior to that he was a scientist at Defence Metallurgical Research Laboratory. As he wanted to settle near to his native place, he took up the assignment in Kolkata.Dr. Mukerjee had his first degree in Chemical Technology from Calcutta University, followed by a D.Sc. degree from France in the area of advanced ceramics. His birth place was Chander Nagar, a protectorate of France in India prior to independence. His desire to do higher studies in France might have been motivated by this fact. Dr. R.V. Tamhankar, the Director of DMRL, was also a degree holder from France.He persuaded Dr. Mukerjee to jon DMRL.

Dr. Mukerjee worked very productively at CGCRI, but his academic life was not without some friction.He was an honest, straight forward person and never believed in sycophancy.His research on silicon nitride was first of its kind in India and his collegues in his division were very hard working. I personally knew two of them Dr. Biswas and Dr. Das. In those days, when soliciting project fund was very difficult, Dr. Mukerjee did succeed to bring a lot of funding. His laboratory was very rich in equipments. Some of the equipments wee rather first in India. His good scientifc progress was an irritant to the scientists with less calibre. Whenever I was in Kolkata, I never missed to meet him in his laboratory and discuss scientific ideas. Dr. Mukerjee got his initial promotions timely, but he really faced injustice, when aspired to become the Director. Dr. Dipankar Chakrovorty from IIT Kanpur joined CGCRI as Director. But what a pity. Sooner he too got disillusioned and moved to Indian Association for the Cultivation of Science in Kolkata as a professor. Dr. Chakravorty was keen to live in Kolkata due to certain family reasons, although he always admired the open scientific society of IIT Kanpur. Dr. Mukerjee had to remain satisfied with the Scientist 'G' grade at CGCRI. I visited the Institute several times. What surprised me was the fact that most of its scientists were in praise of Dr. Mukerjee, but only when they were out of the Institute premises. Within the Institute there was a queer silence. Even today I could not understand the reason for such a peculiar trait.

On a personal note, Dr. Mukerjee was an excellent host. He attended all the International Conferences organised by me in New Delhi. His son Imon did his master's degree in metallurgical engineering from IIT Kanpur. He was a bright student, but did not feel happy to work in CSIR laboratories. Presently he is in a metal working industry in Andhra Pradesh.

After the retirement of Dr. Mukerjee, I revisited his Institute. I was rather unhappy to notice that most of his equipments got scattered in various laboratories and his juniors were dispersed in other Divisions.

I am pleased to see how presently after the retirement Dr. Mukerjee is engaged in social work, being engrossed in running the school founded by his grand father in Chander Nagar. I always found him a hardworking scientist. Recently he wrote the review of my edited book 'Sintering Fundamentals'. It is evident he took pains to read it elaborately. Whatever task he picks up, he does it with excellence.

DR. M. K. MUKHERJEE

Dr. Mukherjee completed his higher studies of Dr. Ing. from Stuttgart University. There he knew Professor Anantharaman quite well. He was very keen to serve his motherland. His first appointment was made in 1963 at BHU as lecturer in Metallurgical Engineering. At the same time Dr.

Vikram Sarabhai was on a global tour to recruit scientists for the Indian Space Organisation. He picked up Dr. Mukherjee from USA to lead the materials group. Thus, he did not join BHU, but accepted the offer of ISRO in Trivandrum and dedicated himself to bring India on the space map of the world. He recruited many scientists in his Group including Dr. B.K. Sarkar, Dr. P.P. Sinha, Dr. K.V. Nagarajan and others. He came in contact with Dr. R.V. Tamahankar, as both DMRL and Midhani were engaged in a number of collaborative projects with ISRO. He was one of the founder members of the Powder Metallurgy Association of India. Dr. Mukherjee was a person of encouraging type and knew very well how to pull the Group united as one team.

Dr. Mukherjee was completely nonparochial and mingled with ease with persons from all parts of India. This trait in him brought me still closer. Whenever, I invited him to either at Roorkee University or at IITK, he never declined. He invariably gave lectures in our Short Courses on PM. His lectures in seminars dealt in depth about the space mission. The mission was so time bound that there was no time left for this scientist to do basic research. One of the biggest contribution of Dr. Mukherjee can be cited the fabrication of beryllium, needed for the space program. Another area of his interest was reliability engineering.

Thee is another aspect in the life of Dr. Mukherjee. He is bachelor and is a great devotee of Ram Krishna Mission. He always preferred to stay in the dormitories of the mission rejecting the guest house facilities offered by us. Such an environment always gave him energy and enlightenment. One of my student Dr. S.K. Mukerjee was also a devotee of R.K. Mission and both of them came much nearer. Dr. Mukherjee once told me that the student wanted to become a monk, which he discouraged, as it was very hard.

With the lapse of time, the ISRO witessed changes and Dr. Mukherjee was also not unaffected by those. Gradually the day to day work was assigned to his juniors and his role became more of an advisory type. This was but natural, as with age, Dr. Mukherjee did not prefer to travel so frequesntly. He always remaind loyal to ISRO. However, I could feel that he was slowly side tracked in his organisation, which he took philosophically.

After retirement from ISRO, Dr. Mukherjee is leading a quiet life in the Ashram of R.K. Mission in Trivandrum.

Dr. C.G.K. Nair

I met Dr. Nair first in the Annual Technical Meeting of IIM in Madras in late seventies. The then Steel Minister, Government of India Mr. Biju Pattnaik was the Chief Guest. Dr. Nair after serving the Regional Engineering College (now National Institute of Technology) at Surathkal, Karnataka Pradesh, as assistant professor joined the Forge and Foundry Plant of Hindustan Aeronautical Laboratory at Bangalore. After getting the B.Tech. degree from IIT Madras in Metallurgical Engineering, he underwent his higher studies in Canada and Sheffield (UK). I think he took a right decision to leave the teaching profession. Before his joining the Forge and Foundry Plant in HAL, Dr. Ram Murthy, an old faculty of BHU and IISc, was the Chief of the Plant as well as the associated laboratory. At Bangalore, Dr. Nair worked really hard to raise the status of the laboratory by producing new prototypes, and in starting a sintered friction pad plant in HAL. I visited his Division twice, and each time I found many changes. He was very particular about the quality of his manpower and never showed any sort of favouritism.

Dr. Nair had a rare blend of competence in both science and technology and this turned out to be an asset in his career. No one could fool him, as he was always uptodate. He was not a believer in classification of metals into ferrous and nonferrous categories, which was done by IIM. However, he was nominated for the Vice-Presidentship of IIM for the Nonferrous Division. He rose to the highest post of President. I heard his deliberations in Council meetings of IIM. His contribution in preparing the status reports of nonferrous metals in India is really commendable. The dedication of Dr. Nair to HAL has been an exemplory one-right from a scientist to the rank of Chairman cum Managing Director of HAL. If one wishes to know the details of his contribution, one may read his latest book on HAL.

Even after the retirement from HAL, the academic instinct in Dr. Nair still prevails. Currently he is the Vice-Chancellor of a privately run Engineering Institute in Bangalore. He is the Honorary President of the Society of Indian Aerospace Technologies and Insustries.

PROFESSOR K.A.PADMANABHAN

Dr. Padmanabhan graduated in Metallurgical Engineering from BHU and soon went to Cambridge to do his Ph.D. His area of research was superplasticity in alloys. He returned to India and joined BHU as a lecturer. He was a fovourite student of Professor Anantharaman. His ambition was high. He later moved to IIT Madras, where he contributed maximum in metal forming area. I first met him at Vadodara Annual Technical Meeting of IIM in early eighties. He was a forceful speaker and possesed enormous clarity of thought. I found in him a spirit of oratory.

As IIT Madras was financed by the German Government, it was the favourite for German experts to visit it. At BHU during the Golden Jubilee of the Metallurgical Engineering Department (1973), Professor Anantharaman introduced Padmanabhan to Professor Ilschner.Since then the interaction of these two professors grew and fructified in form of various projects. Dr. Padmanabhan visited University of Erlangen a number of times. His placing at IIT Madras made a still more favourable interaction between him and other German Universities.The liberal German aid made the 'Metal Forming Laboratory', one of the best laboratories in any academic Institute of India. I have visited the laboratory and have been struck by a very dedicated and disciplined staff.

Dr. Padmanabhan produced a large number of students at IIT Madras.I happened to be an external examiner of one of his postgraduate students, who was deputed from HAL. Dr. Padmanabhan sees the talent of his student first and then assigns him/ her project accordingly.He had very close collaboration with ISRO and DMRL, including Indira Gandhi Center for Atomic Research, at Kalpakkam (TN). His book on superplasticity coauthored with Professor Davies is a classical book on the subject. The book has been well reviewed and appreciated in the metallurgical world.

The second and major period of my interaction with Professor Padmanabhan was after his joining IIT Kanpur as its Director. He had his own office as a Pofessor in the Advanced Centre for Materials Science, where he devoted religiously few hours with his research students. All through his stay there, he maintained a balance between academic and administrative responsibilities.The Academic Senate of IIT Kanpur, chaired by him, used to function in a very democratic style. He gave enough time to members, who wished to press some points.This was a really challenging job for him as the Senate of IIT Madras was never so vibrant in comparison to IIT Kanpur. Some lengthy discussions in Senate used to tire him at times. His unlimited trust for his Deans also brought him in trouble. A Branch change application of a student was interpreted wrongly by his Dean. The student community raised a hackle and the Senate was ceased with the issue for quite some weeks. Ultimately, the Senate gave the Chairman the power to decide. Dr. Padmanabhan turned down his earlier decision. Finally the affected student fought a litigation in the court and got the Branch change. These events did not deter Dr. Padmanabhan and he maintained his nerves in tact. But one thing he really learnt: 'Do not sign anything unless you are sure of every aspect of the case'. In some of the Senate meetings, he used to digest some cynical comments of a few members. But it did not transform into enemity with them. Dr Padmanabhan did everything with grace and dignity. Unfortunately, before the expiry of his term as Director, he resigned from the post and took up a very prestigious Pofessorship in the University of Karlsruhe, Germany at its Centre of Nanotechnology,

After about a two year stay in Germany, he returned to India and joined a private Technical University in Hyderabad as its Vice-Chancellor. His love for academia was prevailing all along. After a short stint he joined the University of Hyderabad as the first professor in Materials in the Department of Physic. He still visits IIT Kanpur and maintains contact with his counterparts. His love for his Alma Mater BHU is superb and he always recounts his good old days of the campus. I become flattered, when in good mood he addresses me 'Guru Ji'. Presently he is an adjunct professor in the School of Engineering Science and Technology at the Hyderabad University.

LATE MR. N.M. PAI

During one of my Bombay visit in 1970, I had the desire to meet Mr. Pai, the father of N.M. Pai, who was running the plant Firth Sterling Co. in Thane (Maharashtra). In those days the alloy steel making was a challenging area of work. I went straight to the Maharashtra Bank Building in Ballard Estate, where the Head Office of Mr Pai was located. As soon as I sent my visiting card and Mr Pai came to know that I am a professor, he jumped and approached to the door to welcome me. He was a warm person with a sturdy body. We talked in a relaxed atmosphere.

He narrated how he started with Tata Steel in their account's office. The man had a vision. With all the bureurocracy, he started a number of metal manufacturing companies. The other firm was 'Powder Metals and Alloys Co'. at Thane, which produced cemented carbides and tungsten based electric contact materials. The Technical Director of this firm was his son Mr. N.M. Pai. Next morning after my visit of the steel plant, the Senior Pai called his son to take care of me and show the 'Powder Metals & Alloys Co'. In look and articulation Mr N.M. Pai was very similar to his father. Since then, I and Mr N.M. Pai became fast friends. The launch of Powder Metallurgy Association of India made us to meet at least once in every year.

Mr N.M. Pai in his youth was sent by his father to take practical training in cemented carbide plant near Manchester in U.K. Both father and son had a plan to enter into engineering enterpreneurship. They had a good blend of financial management and technical expertise. In those days cemented carbide production used to be secret and in this respect the Junior Pai was lucky to get exposed to this new area in U.K. After the Indo-China War (1962) there was great demand for cemented carbides and the Government of India was very liberal to grant production licenses. The PM plant at thane was a showcase of all that stood for tungsten and its carbide. They imported the raw ore and completed the whole production cycle with utmost competence. The Pais were from Mangalore city in Karnataka, famous for the shrewd enterprising people. The Jr. Pai narrated me the whole history of how his father visited Austria a number of times to strike a collaboration with Metallwerk Plansee. He showed me the autographed portrait of famous Prof. Paul Schwarzkopf, the owner of Plansee AG.

Mr. N.M. Pai was an excellent innovator and always bubbled with enthusiasm His plant was an indigenous one in which very few parts were imported. In this respect both Pais were quite Swadeshi in spirit. With passage of time, their business enhanced and they decided to separate the tungsten powder production elsewhere in the Konkan region. Keeping this in mind a powder production plant was established in Kalwa in Ratnagiri District of Maharashtra. I visited this plant too, after attending one of the PMAI Meetings held in Goa. Mr N.M. Pai was my generous host. Whenever I visited Bombay, I never forgot to call Mr Pai. He used to rush and drive me all along from IIT Bombay to Thane. In Thane our favourite place for taking lunch/ dinner was the Boat Restaurant on the shore of a lake. During our drinks we used to discuss many things right from metallurgical personalities to the state of economy in the country. Once his son accompanied us. He was studying Chemical Engineering in Kolhapur. I could see the fine trait of enterpreneurship in this young man. After graduation, he moved to USA for higher studies.After the death of Professor Tendolakar, Pai was the saddest person. Both had excellent friendship. No wonder Professor Tendolakar willed his personal library to Mr Pai.

Mr Pai was also an expert in assembling PM Testing Units. He built sub-sieve analyser (Fischer) quite a few in number, which many laboratories in India are having.The Unit was much much cheaper as compared to the imported one.The driving force for such activities in him was not to become rich, but to show to the Indians that we too can do. I only pity that my desire to have a cold isostatic press built by him could not be accomplished, as Mr Pai died after an heart attack. Whenever I visit Mumbai, I feel being loner and miss one of my best friends and comrades.

LATE DR. V.G. PARANJPE

While I was a student at BHU, I heard the name of Dr.V.G. Paranjpe, who was very proudly mentioned as one of the best students by Dr. Daya Swarup. Dr. Paranjpe joined MIT soon after finishing his graduate program in metallurgy. Professor Morris Cohen, who happened to be the past guide of Dr. Antia, was his guide too. His research topic was again related to steel. Dr. Paranjpe could have very well stayed back in USA, but the burning patriotism in this young Maharashtrian brought him back to India. He joined R&D Centre of Tata Steel, where Mr. S. Vishwanathan and Dr. R.V. Tamahankar also worked. With much hard labour, Dr. Paranjpe selected brilliant metallurgists in his team including Dr. J.J Irani and T.Mukherjee. My first meeting with him was in 1970, when I visited Jamshedpur. He was sitting in his big meeting room along with the junior scientists. As soon as he saw me, he guessed correctly who am I and said' Hello Professor, Welcome. How are you?'His way of speaking was very assuring to me, as only on the previous day I heard from the NML people that he is rather abrasive. Our meeting was brief and he assigned one of his young scientists to show me his R & D Centre.

Dr. R.V. Tamhankar, the Director of DMRL, was the Chairman of NSCT (National Committee of Science and Technology) Task Group for 'Metals and Materials', and he requested the help of Dr. Paranjpe to visit various educational institutes to assess their capabilities in conducting R & D projects. By that time the present DST (Department of Science & Technology) structure was not existing. I was one of the members of the Assessment Committee on Powder Metallurgy subgroup, which was chaired by Dr. P. P. Sinha of Union Carbide. Dr. Paranjpe in spite of preoccupation visited various educational institutes including the University of Roorkee. In our department faculty meeting, he impressed upon the idea of integrated approach in doing research. He illustrated how for any particular steel all the aspects of processing-properties-performance-structure studies can be accomplished by a good cooperation in the team. In case some area is missing, a necessary search may be initiated to fill up that area. I was so much impressed with this philosophy of Dr. Paranjpe that I made up a point to organise my laboratory in a such a manner that many properties could be measured on the same specimens. My task was a challenging one, but I am glad to a large extent, I succeeded in this approach. Dr Paranjpe was not happy with publications of short articles or communications in journals. He always emphasized on some real contribution to the national industrial growth. I wish there were many more Paranjpes in India.

My last meeting with Dr. Paranjpe was, when I was an expert in Union Public Service Commission's selection board for a DRDO post. I had then joined my assignment at IIT Kanpur. Dr. Paranjpe was also a member of the selection board. He was glad, I left University of Roorkee As a matter of fact he was an expert in the selection for the post of professor at Roorkee, where I too gave an interview. He told me after the DRDO meeting that the great alliance of the then Vice-Chancellor of the University with the Head of the Department. Both were not keen to fill up the post. He was a bit blunt in telling them why they do the ritual of advertising the post, when their intention is not to fill up the post. After that he was never invited by the University.

Dr. Paranjpe was a man of self esteem. This brought him in trouble at Tata Steel. Of late, the Managing Director Mr Rusi Modi was not in good terms with him. They doubted that Dr. Paranjpae was doing some private consulting work in Jamshedpur. This infight resulted in the resignation of this outstanding metallurgist and eventually a loss to Tata Steel. When we met in New Delhi, Dr. Paranjpe was a freelance consultant with his office in Pune. After the meeting he invited me to the lunch in a five star hotel. While paying the bill, he blinked at me and said don't worry. This is from my company and not the personal purse. In Pune he lived in his house in Budhwar Peth. Of late, I heard that Dr. Paranjpe is no more. He died about three years back.

LATE DR. PRABHU NATH

Late Professor Prabhu Nath, who served BHU as a professor and also headed the department of Ceramic Engineering was a great friend of mine. He was a graduate in Glass Technology from BHU and obtained his Ph.D. degree from Sheffield University, U.K. We both belonged to Varanasi. I am a protagonist for both metallurgy and ceramic technology. This compelled me to frequently visit the Ceramic Engineering department. When my colleagues in the department of Metallurgical Engineering at BHU knew about this, they were rather amused. I often used to tell them that both the departments should interact to each other. In a way the discipline of ceramics is more difficult than metallurgy. The complex crystal structure of ceramics does require the extensive knowledge of crystal chemistry. Both of us used to meet in different Selection Boards quite often. His favourite question used to be on REDOX. Dr. Prabhu Nath was a master in giving different tinges in glasses and he made a fairly good business as a consultant. In that respect he appeared more like an artist, but the fact his recipes were based on hard science.

My prolonged interaction with Professor Prabhu Nath was in RRL, Bhopal. We both had been put in the same guest house for a week or so. Professor Rohatgi was, then, the Director of RRL. Dr. Shankar of the analytical chemistry division of BARC was another member of the Selection Board. Our job of interviewing the candidates was a tiring task and in the evening before dinner we all used to have a long stroll. During that occasion I noticed the real literary inclination of Dr. Nath. He had remembered all the verses of 'Shringar Shatak', the Sanskrit epic of Bhartrihari. His pronunciation of Sanskrit words was quite chaste and he also gave commentaries of the verses in English. The recitations acted as excellent appetiser before the dinners.

My later visits to his department in BHU made me feel as if he was an anguished man. There was some sort of politics in his department which made him unhappy. His son Anil was doing his Ph.D. in ceramic engineering from BHU. After completion of the higher studies he joined Central Glass and Ceramic Research Institute as a scientist and later on shifted to BHU in its faculty after the death of his father.

After retirement from BHU Dr. Nath was living in his newly built house in Varanasi with his familty.

DR. BALDEV RAJ

Dr. Baldev Raj is an ideal example, how a scientist can rise to the top position of his organisation through shear dedication. He is currently the Director of Indira Gandhi Centre for Atomic Research, Kalpakkam in Tamil Nadu State. When our planners decided to have another centre related to atomic research in addition to BARC at Trombay, they handpicked Dr. P.Rodriguez to follow Mr C.V. Sundaram. Both were given freedom to select their team and they picked up Baldev Raj as one of the scientists. Born in 1947, Dr. Raj completed his B.E. degree in Metallurgical Engineering from Ravi Shankar University in Raipur (Madhya Pradesh). May be the steel town of Bhilai, adjacent to Raipur, was the driving force for him to study metallurgy. Soon after his B.E. Program, he joined the training school of BARC and was posted under Dr. Rodriguez in its Physical Metallurgy Division. Here he worked very hard and got due promotions in succession. I first saw Dr. Raj in Vadodara IIM Technical Meeting in the early eighties. He was an over-enthusiastic young man, full of energy and stamina. I watched him from a distance in the audience and could make out that this man is bound to rise still higher. My detailed interaction with him was during my Kalpakkam visit when Dr. Rodriguez was the Director. Prior to that I had visited Kalpakkam when Mr Sundaram was the Director. Dr. Raj was taking care of the nondestructive evaluation aspect in the Centre. The area is a crucial one for any industry like atomic energy. In this Division some of my old students were also working. NDT Division at IGCAR was well maintained and a functioning one. Dr. Baldev Raj gave full freedom to his Juniors, but at the same time expected good work from them. He always looked after their genuine interests. In him I found an able administrator too. I remember once I forgot to carry the gate pass while moving out of Kalpakkam campus.On my return, I encountered difficulties to enter the Centre. But, as soon as I uttered the name of Dr. Baldev Raj, the matter could be resolved in just few minutes.

Dr. Raj was a frequent visitor of IIT Kanpur's Nuclear Enginering Division and those used to be good occasions for me to meet him. He always met me with warmth and respect. I listened his G.D. Birla Award lecture in Delhi in 1996 IIM Annual Technical Meeting. This was the Golden Jubilee Celebration Year of IIM. Being the right hand man of Dr. Rodriguez (Ex-President IIM), Dr. Raj learnt all the tid bits of IIM. He had good analytical capability, but never became any sort of critic. It was nice to see this gifted metallurgist to occupy the Presidentship of IIM (2005-2006). He is a perfect PR proficient manager. I read his messages to the members of IIM (August 2005 issue of IIM Metal News). There he cherished many dreams, but I doubt whether a short period of one year was enough to bring forth any sound reform in IIM by any President. Dr. Raj has been instrumental in introducing a position of Executive General Secretary in the IIM structure.

When I speak here about IIM, it is not inappropriate, if I mention some other basic issues too. The three Divisions of IIM are messy. Does 'Metal Science' Division cover everything related to physical and chemical science aspects of metals? If yes, then, the remaining two divisions "Ferrous' and 'Nonferrous' should cover exclusively technological aspects. While I was a Council member (two terms of three years each), I had raised this issue and, as a matter of fact, did circulate an open letter to all the Council Members. Dr. L.R. Vaidyanath was then the President of IIM and was quite agreeable to my thoughts. I had proposed another set of nomenclature and was quite opposed to divide metals into water tight compartments of ferrous and nonferrous. The better solution was to divide into subsubjects in stead of 'metal' based classification. Unfortunately, most of the Council Members thought it painstaking to bring forth any change. Another issue was related to the induction of new Council members. The Institute has some mechanism, but somehow quite a big chunk of Council Members appeared to be permanent ones. Their renominations were made probably through some undeclared quota. Third observation of mine is regarding various awards of the Institute. The 'Honorary Membership' is the highest award of the Institute, which, of late, all Presidents as a convention just after relinquishing the Presidentship invariably receive. In other Institutes/ Societies there is a provision of 'Distinguished Service Award' in which IIM is lacking. The situation becomes comic, when a Honorary Member, later gladly receives other IIM awards, much below in rank. It is a kin to a "Bharat Ratna' awardee receiving a 'Padma Award' of the Government of

India. I know, here I am risking to be called fussy. However, any vibrant Institute must not only welcome reform, but also should faithfully implement them. In this age of globalisation, many foreign Institutes have opened India Chapter, which are doing well, although one has to pay a fairly large sum as the subscription fee. The prime aim of any professional Institute, apart from the academic content, should be upgradation of the profession. The members must feel that the Institute is innovative and is sensitive in safeg-aurding the prestige of its fellow members.

To conclude about Dr. Baldev Raj, the biggest quality in him is the balance he maintains in academic and administrative duties, with which very few are bestowed. I hope our fast breeder reactor mission is substantially completed, before Dr. Raj retires. I have been a regular receipient of IGC Newsletter, with message from the Director, including the two page covering letter.

PROFESSOR P. RAMAKRISHNAN

While attending the IIM Annual Technical Meeting in Bombay in the year 1964, I listened to a paper by Mr. Ramakrishnan, who was doing his Ph.D. under the guidance of Professor G.S. Tendolkar at IIT Bombay. I knew that he did his M. Sc. in chemistry from Sagar University in Madhya Pradesh. Actually Ramakrishnan's surname is 'Menon', which most people are unaware. Professor Tendolkar appreciated his hardwork and encouraged him to attend conferences. After getting the Ph.D. degree, Dr. Ramakrishnan joined metallurgical engineering department at IIT Bombay as a lecturer. Subsequently he occupied the posts of Assistant Professor and Professor. Few years back he retired from IIT Bombay and now serves as a consultant.

Dr. Ramakrishnan trained a large number of students in powder metallurgy with whom he wrote research papers. Being from a science background, he had some intrinsic handicap in an engineering department., but this was in no way an impediment in his careeer growth. His research topics were many, some of which were not sustaining ones. For a while he initiated research on PM forging and powder injection moulding, but they were short lived. His major strength has been characterization of metal powders for which he had collaboration with the University of Iowa, USA. One of his past Ph.D. students Dr. Parmanand Singh did his research in this topic. He is presently a Professor at IIT Madras. Dr

Ramakrishnan's other student Dr. B.R. Bhagat was earlier our student at the University of Roorkee. Presently he is associated with Penn State University, USA.

Another attribute of Dr. Ramakrishnan is his enormous capability in organising conferences and editing their Proceedings. He was well liked by ASM International—India Chapter at Mumbai, to whom he contributed his best. He was also the Jt. Secretary and subsequently Vice-President, President of PMAI. He was liked by the BARC scientists as many of them registered for the Ph.D. degree of Bombay University under his external guidance. In PMAI meetings, we both were regular attendees. In the Council meetings, one can see Dr. Ramakrishnan as a very quiet man, but he used to accomplish many strategies. He knew very well, who are the fund providers for research and could succeed every time with some fund. His best qulity was not to antagonize any one and thus maximize the gain.

With passage of time, it was obvious that the relation between Dr. Ramakrishna and his past teacher Professor Tendolkar was not very cordial. Both could inject something against the other. In one of the meetings of PMAI held in BARC in the late seventies, when Professor Teldolkar was a session chairman and Dr. Ramakrishnan the paper presenter, the former profusely complimented the latter, saying that Dr. Ramakrishnan is a National Metallurgist, the honour which his teacher could not avail. Professor Tendolkar never liked churning similar papers from the same results. Such statistics become rather deceptive.

My various visits to IIT Bombay, brought us very close in many respects. I was the external examiner of one of Dr. Ramakrishnan's Ph.D. student Mr Gantaet. Dr. Ramakrishnan trained his son in the area of powder metallurgy specializing in advanced ceramics, who completed his Ph.D. from IIT Bombay. Being a typical Kerala Brahmin, Dr. Ramakrishnan used to follow many religious rituals. I would recall an incident, which happened with us. During an International Conference on Ceramics, we both were put up in the same room of the guest house of Central Power Research Institute, Bangalore. After bath, Dr. Ramakrishnan began doing his Pranayam etc, while I got engrossed in the newspaper. After the riutual, he politely commented 'What type of Brahmin you are, who does not do any ritual whatsoever.' I jokingly replied' Most of the north Indian Brahmins are freelance'. Dr. Ramakrishnan understood me.

It has been a pleasure to meet Dr. Ramakrishnan and exchange ideas. Last, I met him in February, 2008 during the Annual Technical Meeting of Powder Metallurgy Association of India held in Chennai. On that occasion the Association awarded me and my very good professional friend Mr. S.R. Sundaram, formerly at Mahindra Sintered Products as its Honorary Fellows. As usual Dr.Ramakrishnan was very active. Presently after retirement from IIT Bombay, he lives not far from the office of PMAI.

PROFESSOR S. RANGANATHAN

In early seventees during a flight from Hyderabad to Delhi, a slim agile gentleman encountered me in the aircraft and told that he has seen me in some conference. I replied: 'Then it must be at BHU'.We introduced each other. The gentleman was Dr. S. Ranganathan, who was returning to Varanasi from Madras. We talked for about 5 minutes or so. Next time I met him during one of the Annual Convocations of IITK, when his elder brother Professor S. Sampath, our the then Director had invited him. We were sitting adjacent to each other and during the long convocation period, we exchanged many news and views. He was a sharp and smart person, but I noticed that his speed of speech was a bit high. I had known about his original contribution in field ion microscopy at Cambridge University in U.K. His work has been referred in physical metallurgy text books as well. His able teacher at IISc Professor Anantharaman had also facilitated in the rise of Dr. Ranganathan.

After graduating in metallugy in the year 1962 from the Indian Institute of Science, Dr. Ranganathan spent the period 1962-65 at Cambridge, UK for the Ph.D. Degree and 1965-67 at the University of California, Berkeley on a post doctoral assignment.He joined BHU in the year 1967 as a Reader in Experimental Metallography. Dr. D. Brandon, the noted physical metallurgist of Israel was his contemporary at Cambridge. Dr. Ranganathan's contribution in metallurgy was soon recognised.With in three years of his joining BHU, he was awarded the National Metallurgist Day Award (1970). By that time only few faculties of BHU, Dr. T.R. Ananathraman and Dr P.K. Jena had received the award.

After relinquishing the Headship by Professor Anantharaman at BHU, there was some sort of serial events in the metallurgy department. Dr. Ranganathan opted professorship at IISc, while Professor P. Rama Rao joined DMRL. Their departure from BHU made Professor Anantharaman a bit loner. Professor P.M. Prasad and Dr. P. Ramachandra Rao remained loyal to him till he was at BHU,although nothing was paid back to the former. One thing was striking.Professor Ranganathan had a nostalgia for Varanasi and was a frequent visitor of the BHU campus. He has given an account of these in a very stimulating article entitled' Slowly Down the Ganges', published in the Souvenir of the Platinum Jubilee Celebrations of the metallurgical engineering department of BHU (1998).

Professor Ranganathan has been a competent administrator. He was the Secretary of the Materials Research Society of India (MRSI) for many terms and was instrumental in activating all the Divisions of the Society. He served IIM as a Council Member and occupied the offices of Vice-President and President. During his tenure, the metals Science Division of IIM, had been extremely active, not witnessed earlier. It was during his Presidentship that the IIM's Annual Technical Meeting was organised at IIT Kanpur.

Whenever I visit Bangalore, I make it a point not only to call Professor Ranganathan, but also to visit his department. No doubt some times my request had inconvenienced him, but he never turned down it. The contribution of Professor Ranganathan in the fine structure of quasicrystals has ben seminal. He very actively collaborated with Chinese and Japanese scientists in this area, and produced large number of Ph.D. aspirants including our past IIT Kanpur student Mr. Alok Singh.

After retirement from IISc, Dr. Ranganathan took up the assignment of Emeritus Professorship in the same Institute. Both he and his Institute has mutual admiration. Currently I found an interest in him towards ancient Indian Metallurgy, publication on which has been made by Tata Steel. As his personal residence is now in Bangalore, I trust the IISc shall be deriving benefit from Dr. Ranganathan for many many years to come.

PROFESSOR C.N.R. RAO

Professor CNR Rao, FRS is one of the top most materials chemist of India.The term' materials chemistry' is, of late, liked by him. Earlier he was a professor in Structural Chemistry at IISc, Bangalore. Prior to that he was a professor in Chemistry at IIT Kanpur. IIT Kanpur was not fond of too many discriminating terms and no wonder, Professor Rao did not press for any prefix, while he was in IIT Kanpur. My first meeting with

Professor Rao was in 1966 in IIT Kanpur in connection with the National Conference on Materials Science Education, organised by Professor E.C. Subbarao. I found him a very forceful speaker, but less articulate than another chemistry Professor P.T. Narasimhan. I remember Dr. S. Kumar of Central Glass and Ceramic Research Institute, Calcutta was one of the invited lecturers. Professor Rao asked him a number of questions after the lecture with his usual forceful style. The speaker was helpless and fumbled quite a lot. Next I met Professor Rao in 1971 in Hyderabad Conference 'High Temperature Materials' organized by the Atomic Energy Agency of India. Professor Rao was the Chairman of the Board of Nuclear Research, BARC in the honorary capacity.

My next meeting with Professor Rao was as a colleague, when in 1976 I joined the professor's post at IITK. He was very busy, but still gave some time to me. He was a bit upset, as he could not get the Director's promotion in the Institute and an outsider Professor A. Bhattacharjee from Jadavpur University took that position. Professor Rao more or less made up his mind to say good-bye to IITK. I could notice in the Academic Senate Meetings chaired by the then Director, that Dr. Rao was critical of some of the Director's decisions. There were other vocal teachers in the Senate including me. Since then we struck a chord of similar thinking on many issues. As Professor Rao was a dashing personality, he did not find much difficulty in his life to achieve practically all the goals which he aimed. Because of his academic excellence and position, he generated a big team of his followers, who in some way or the other are always grateful to him. In adition, he is a frequest international traveller and thus built a great team of his overseas well wishers too. In India I doubt one can succeed beyond a limit without a contact with the centre of power at New Delhi. Here too Professor Rao had a good hold. Mr Rajiv Gandhi, the then Prime Minister of India, made him his Science Advisor, which he fulfilled with much devotion.

In the beginning of eighties there was an international race in the area of high temperature oxide superconductors. Dr. Rao jumped on that and got hugh grants from the Central Government. I did review the processing and properties of such oxide superconductors in our monograph published by Trans Tech Pulications. I was skeptical about that, mainly, due to the fact such materials had poor mechanical properties and fabricability. However, my doubts were not welcomed by the then Indian scientific community. I was a protogonist of intermetallic superconductors and some

Indian physicist, natably Dr. Narlikar of National Physical Laboratory, New Delhi, were doing good work in this area. Unfortunately the lobby of oxide superconductors was much better organised and powerful, and soon the intermetallic work got stopped. It is only after the de-emphasis in USA on oxide superconductors that Indian scientists starting aping them. This is the painful saga, how a lot of financial and human resources of our country got dissipated. Japaneses on the other hand, were much smarter. They upheld their programs on intermetallics and upgraded their technology commercially.

The most productive years of Professor CNR Rao were in IISC, where he rose to the top post of the Director. His contacts in New Delhi made him successful in laying foundation of the Jawahar Lal Nehru Institute of Advanced Science, an autonomous research institute in the IISc campus, which later got shifted to a separate campus in Bangalore. He was the Founder President of this prestigious Institute. As a matter of fact, IISc loaned some land to construct the residence for the President of this new Institute. Professor Rao still resides in this house. Being an alumnus of BHU, Professor Rao remembers the old days of that great University. Recently he and his wife paid a visit to Varanasi and refreshed the old memories.

The contemporary Indian science and Professr Rao are synonym. He has been associated with Indian Science Congress Association and practically earned all its awards. In the beginning of 2004, the Annual Convention of the Association was held in Bangalore. I, too, attended the Congress. It was another opportunity to meet Professor Rao. He spoke on nanomaterials—the most burning topic of the day. He had brought a team of the young scientists to present their research work. I, as such, am not against nanomaterials, but it appears that in India, the concept has been oversold. Many researchers, who are engaged in micro-scale work do not hesitate to advertise as if they are engaged in nanomaterials. I do not wish that the Indian approach on nonomaterials comes to the similar fate as that on superconductors. One of the biggest limitation in Indian research is the lack of urgency to tackle processing aspects. This culminates in nonfulfilment of the final success in developing a product or a prototype. It is pity that the Department of Science and Technology is not aware of this urgency and is, rather, a mute onlooker.

Few years back, Professor Rao was a co-recepient of Somiya Medal, instituted by the International Union of Materials Research Societies.

Professor Rao got inspiration from the MRS (Materials Research Society) of USA to start an Indian Society in India too, known as MRSI (Materials Research Society of India). On the request of late Mr C.V. Sundaram, I too enrolled myself to a life member of this Society.

Professor Rao is a member of all the major science academies in the world including the Royal Society, London, the National Academy of Sciences, USA, the Russian Academy of Sciences, French Academy of Sciences, Japan Academy, as well as Polish, Czechoslovakian, Serbian, Slovenian, Brazil, Spanish, Korean and African Academies and the American Philosophical Society. He is a member of the Pontifical Academy of Sciences, Foreign Member of Academia European and Foreign Fellow of the Royal Society of Canada. He is on the editorial boards of several leading professional journals.

Professor Rao was also the Chairman of the Board of Governors of the Indian Institute of Technology, Kanpur, Being a top class academician he was different from the past Chairmen and contributed his best to transform the IIT into a world class institute. Professor Rao shall always be remembered for his extraordinary management skill in scientific manpower planning, formulating the national science and technology policy and above all his untiring stamina to achieve anything that stands for excellence.

LATE DR. N.K. RAO

Dr. N. Kondal Rao (1924) an alumnus of BHU and a Doctorate from Germany, has been one of the towering pillars in building the nuclear energy program of our nation. When he joined Atomic Energy, the things were at a very low key and the engineering potential of the country not at a high peak. Nuclear fuel fabrication is the most crucial part of the reactor building. The hard planning of Dr. Brahm Prakash gave birth to the beginning of the Nuclear Fuel complex at Hyderabad. They were in search for a suitable leader for that. They found none other than Dr. Kondal Rao. Dr. Rao belonged to Andhra Pradesh and he too did not mind to take this challenge. Having a training from Germany he was best suited to understand the engineering intricacies of the plant. He always remembered his BHU days, where the emphasis on workshop technology was equal to the science subjects.

My interaction with Dr. Kodal Rao began with the very foundation of PMAI (Powder Metallurgy Association of India). Dr. R.V. Tamhankar had a high regard for him. He was a founder member of PMAI as well as of the Governing Council. Subsequently he rose to the office of Presidentship. There was practically no meeting of PMAI, which he did not actively participapte till his presidentship. He was later awarded the Honoarry Membership of the PMAI. Dr. Rao was a jovial person. He took events as they came. In all the PMAI meetings, we could notice one of his favourite assistant Dr. P. Balakrishna, who did his Ph.D. from Bombay University.

Dr. N.K. Rao was a manager par excellence. He knew the art of selecting right man for a right job and never forgot the mantra of human touch. No one in his organisation hinted any dissatisfaction working under his leadership. Some of my past students of Roorkee University are working as senior engineers at NFC. They all had admiration for him. Dr. Rao had to travel quite a lot both within the country and outside during the establishment of NFC. One of his favourite country was Japan. At NFC, I found many PM equipments from Japan. The beginning of titanium and zirconium production has been a hall mark of NFC. Another area has been stainless steel tube making, to be used as nuclear structural material. The texture control in the finished products has been really a challenging job for them.

The Indian Institute of Metals rightly remembered Dr. Rao after his retirement and invited him to deliver the N.P. Gandhi Memorial Lecture. That particular Annual Technical Meeting was held in Jaipur. Other than this he was not given any major responsibility in the Institute. Dr. Rao was fully aware that it is only through the hard work that the industrial prosperity of the nation could be achieved. The present sluggishness in our nuclear power program, which has made us to lean heavily towards USA, is primarily due to the fact that our planners could not think of the right manpower management. I know how China specially took care in deputing her young scientific manpower to get the right specialised training from abroad. Even North Korea in early sixties had sent many young engineers to USSR for getting proper training in nuclear energy. I am writing this with my first hand experience during my stay in USSR. I wish our Atomic Energy Establishment would have recruited more persons like Dr. N.K. Rao, who had engineering bent of mind. A real engineer goes through a rigorous training and there is no short cut for that.

My last meeting with Dr. Rao was in NFC in early ninties, where I was invited to deliver a lecture on Nuclear Ceramic Materials. Dr. Balram Murty was then the Executive Director, just after the retirement of Dr. Kondal Rao. Two retired dignitories Dr. Kondal Rao and Dr. R.V. Tamhankar were there. Mr George had specially made that we all could meet together. During that meeting, I met my old friend Mr S.K. Mehra of BHU days. Unfortunately Mehra expired too prematurely.

Near his end Dr. Rao was confined in Hyderabad, where he had earlier built his house. On 22nd October, 2008, Dr. Rao died peacefully at his residence. His contribution to nuclear fuels for Indian reactors and other associated materials shall always be remembered.

DR. P.RAMA RAO

I have written about Dr. P. Rama Rao in an earlier Chapter. But here I shall dwell up on the scenario after the BHU period. Dr Rama Rao has contributed maximum to the metal science. While he was in DMRL, he took along with him some of his best students at BHU and gave them well designed projects. Both the leader and the young scientists worked tirelessly. Dr Rao's area of activities centered around mechanical behaviour of metals and alloys. One of his best friends was Professor Taplin of UK. He was instrumental in introducing Professor Rao to other higher ups. He brought him on the International Fracture Committee and as a matter of fact Taplin's love of India made the International sequential fracture conference to be held in New Delhi. It was around the year 1984 or so. After that there was no looking back for Dr. Rao. Dr. Rao had been instrumental in hiring good young Indian scientists from Europe and North America, notably being Dr. Sunder Rajan, Dr. Kamath, Dr. Mahajan, Dr Pandey and Dr. Prakash. I must not at the same time hide another feature of DMRL. As Dr. Rao was very busy in science, he could not make the DMRL organisation to work uniformly across the table. Some of its indifferent scientists were just overlooked. In a way it was a correct strategy, otherwise Dr Rao could not have worked as much he did.

Although Dr. Rao started his scientific research under Professor A.A. Krishnan in powder metallurgy at IISc, due to reason best known to him he did not join the PMAI as its member. In stead he helped quite a lot to Professor CNR Rao of IISc, who started Materials Research Society of India, of which I happen to be a life member. Professor CNR Rao very rightly visualized the capability of Dr. Rama Rao and made him the Honorary Secretary of MRSI, with its head office in DMRL. MRSI became a very productive association, where many members of the Indian Institute of Metals too started participating.

There was a vacancy for the Scientific Advisor to the Minister of Defence after Dr. V.S. Arunachalam's tenure, which Dr. Rao filled. He brought many changes. One thing which was noticeable, was the fact how multiple ranks in the scientists were introduced. Sometime it was very common to see many Director—grade scientists in the laboratories. We have always resisted that type of approach in our IIT system and this worked very well. I think it is better to increase the salary of the scientist, but the upgradation of rank must be done very carefully. The situation is worse, when a mediocre scientist because of his long stay in the laboratory gets upgraded. He or she becomes a dampner in the natural growth of other young colleagues.

Another quality of Dr. Rao is the humility. Very recently I received a letter from him after he received my review of the book authored by late Dr. P.L. Agrawal entitled 'Journey of a Steel man ', which was published in the periodical 'Consultancy Ahead, Vol 4, issue 3, 2010, p.76. He too had earlier reviewed this book for Business Standards. He gracefully acknowledged that my review had more detail than his write up. I doubt there are other persons who are so forthright. I would like to feature another fact which I have noticed consistently in Dr. Rama Rao. He probably likes to be exclaimed at 'Dr' rather than 'Professor'. His recent letter head did confirm this fact. Any way I still hold that once a professor, always a professor.

After the long service to MRSI as its Honorary Secretary, Dr. Rao was elected as its President. Prior to that he had been the president of IIM. The list is endless. He also graced the Presidentship of Indian Science Congress Association. Dr. Rao also served as the Secretary of the Department of Science and Technology, Government of India. His love for academia made him to join the University of Hyderabad as its Vice-Chancellor. While holding all these important national posts, Dr. Rao remained all along an humble gentleman. Last time I met Dr. Rao in METALLO 07 organised at the Indian Institute of Technology, Kanpur under the convenership of late Dr. R. Balasubramaniam. This conference was organised to celebrate the 80th Birth Anniversary of late Professor Anantharaman. I had a very warm handshake with Dr. Rao, with the same usual smile, which he possessed in old BHU days. Presently Dr. Rao is a Sarabhai Distinguished Scientist at the Advanced Centre for Powder Metallurgy and New Materials-a Department of Science and Technology sponsored centre in Hyderabad. The title of this centre has been unnecessarily lengthened by adding one more word 'International'. The centre is now emphasizing more on coatings. It is worth mentioning that the Ministry of Steel, Governmnet of India decorated Dr. Rao with the 'Lifetime Achievement Award 'in the year 2009.

LATE PROFESSOR P. RAMACHANDRA RAO

While in BHU in the year 1963, I noticed one of my M.Tech students a bit different from others. My course was titled 'Experimental Techniques in Metallurgy'. The student was none other than P. Ramachandra Rao. During his studies, he was a sobre, intelligent and thoughtful person. I used to give term papers to all my students. The students themselves selected the topics. The topic of Mr Rao was 'Nuclear Magnetic Resonance and its Application in Metallurgy', for which he presented a seminar too. Unfortunately, I could not stay for the whole semester in BHU and, therefore, could not finally examine my students. From Roorkee, I came to know that Rao topped the list. He was a favourite student of Professor Anantharaman and this may be one of the reasons that he stayed at BHU for his Ph.D. research. In the mean while, after the M.Tech. program, Dr. Anantharaman managed the post of lecturer for him. He gave Mr Rao a rather new area of research 'Rapid Solidification of Alloys'. After getting awarded the Ph.D. degree, Dr. Rao got due promotions at BHU and visited the laboratory of Professor R.W. Cahn in UK to further his research on rapid solidification.

In the beginning of eightees, while travelling from new Delhi to Varanasi by train, I met Dr. Rao in an AC coach. He was returning after attending the International Conference on rapid solidification in North America. He was not looking that perfect as he used to be. My enquiry revealed that he is sad because India could not be selected as the host for the next international meet. I solaced him and advised him not to take it very seriously. Few weeks after this I received a letter from Professor N.J.Grant of MIT expressing sympathy for the Indian bid. He was impressed by the fact that the Indian delegates did their best in the bid. It is heartening that after a gap of few sequential conferences, India did get a right place and Professor Rao's contribution was noteworthy in making the conference in India a big success.

The fever of materials science sooner got gripped in BHU too. The efforts of Professor Anantharaman got fructified in giving way for an interdisciplinary school in Materials Science and Technology. I was not happy with this decision. I even proposed that the departments of metallurgical engineering and ceramic engineering should be brought closer for such activities. The higher ups did not heed to my advice. Dr. Rao had been a Head of this School for a term. In the year 1992, I heard about the appointment of Professor Rao as the Director of National Metallurgical Laboratory (NML) at Jamshedpur. I sent promptly my greetings to him. Before his joning NML, the laboratory was in a fracturered state. The emphssis of the earlier Director was more on the renovation of the laboratory building, rather than the academic pursuit. Most of the old instruments even in working condition were written off in the garb of modernity. Dr. Rao improved upon the situation. He worked tirelessly even in his somewhat bad health. I visited his laboratory twice in his tenure and found many welcome changes. Rapid solidified Nd-Fe-B magnetic material was one of his favourite research topics. I was amazed how Dr. Rao became so flexible to write papers on topics like recycling, energy conservation, nonferrous extraction, so on and so forth. In a way he gave a nonpartisan emphasis on various research projects. He even promoted a new subdivision on Bio-materials.

After the expiry of his term at National Metallurgical Laboratory Professor Rao joined Banaras Hindu University as its Vice-Chancellor in 2002. Here he was solely engrossed in administration and finished his tenure without any major hiccup. I was hoping that under his leadership the Intitute of Technology at BHU would be converted into one of the 'Indian Institute of Technology'. But my hope remained as hope. Dr. Rao joined the Ministry of Defence's Institute of Armament Technology at Pune in 2004 as its first Vice-Chancellor. After the end of his term at Pune, Dr. Rao joined Advanced Centre for Powder Meatallurgy and New materials in Hyderabad as DAE Raja Ramanna Fellow. Last time I met him in November 2008 in Greater Noida during the Annual Technical Meeting of IIM I was there to deliver 'Dr. Daya Swarup Memorial Lecture'. Dr. Rao met his tragic death on 10th January, 2010 in Madurai in Tamil Nadu State after a massive heart attack.

Dr. Rao was a Fellow of all the science academies in India as well as a Fellow of the Academy of Sciences for the Developing World (TWAS). He won most of the major awards in engineering science including the S.S. Bhatnagar Prize and was also recognized with the Distinguished Alumnus Award of the Indian Institute of Science. He was President of the Indian Institute of Metals, Vice-President of the Materials Research Society of India and Vice-President of the Indian National Science Academy.

LATE DR. P. RODRIGUEZ

Dr. Rodriguez belonged to 1960 batch of Indian Atomic Energy Esatblishmnet trainees, who joined the establishmnet just after finishing his B.E. Program from IISc. As my class mates of BHU were also co-trainees, I had a chance to meet him during my Bombay visits. I got impressed by his manners and also dedication with which he accomplished one success after another. He served the physical metallurgy section of Metallurgy Division of BARC, before he was selected by the authority to get shifted to Kalpakkam's new centre for atomic energy, now named after Indira Gandhi. Mr. C.V. Sundaram of BARC was his leader. Mr Baldev Raj then a young metallurgist, who is presently the Director of the Centre was junior to him.

The very first paper of Dr. Rodriguez which I heard was delivered in the National Seminar on 'High Temperature Materials' under the auspices of BARC in 1971 at Hyderabad. My paper was next to his. I could notice the style of his speech, which was well coordinated. Professor E.G. Ramchandran, Head of the Metallurgical Engineering Department, IIT Madras was chairing the session. Professor Vasu of IISc was also there. From him I came to know that Mr Rodriguez was registered to IISc for his Ph.D. degree under him. Prior to that he had visited USA for getting experience in their atomic energy laboratories.He had a Master's degree from USA.

Dr. Rodriguez's major emphasis at Kalpakkam was to initiate a well coordinated research on nuclear structural materials, particularly stainless steels. His goal was to establish a materials engineering approach in knowing all about the austenitic stainless steel-right from solidification, working, joining to properties characterisation. Nondestructive testing was another area very vital for nuclear industry. He assigned this task to Dr Baldev Raj who outstandingly managed the program. Dr. Rodriguez purposefully remained at the interface of basic and applied metallurgy and that is the reason why he had been so successful as compared to other counterparts in BARC. It is not true that his Institute invariavbly undertook long range projects, but sometimes some of the projects were very shortlived. As an example I can cite the fabrication aspect of oxide superconductors. When I once visited their laboratory, I had my own doubts on some random sketchy experiments. It is good, they later stopped emphasizing on that any more.

One of the most valuable sequential seminars at Kalpakkam is 'Creep-Fatigue Interaction', which is novel in whole of Asia. Kalpakkam has been famous for many more international gatherings. My old BHU classmate Professor M.C. Chaturvedi, formerly at Manitoba Univesity, Canada is a regular attendee.

At Kalpakkam, I met another very distinguished scientist Dr Krishan Lal, who was heading the Materials Science Division. He was a product of my own Institute IIT Kanpur and did his Ph.D. from UK. This man was an individualist in nature and somehow could not very well fit into the Kalpakkam culture. It is pity he died at a rather an early age.

My debate with Dr. Rodriguez used to be on the selection of austenitic steel in place of ferritic one for nuclear applications. Ferritic steels undergo less radiation damage and have better choice. No doubt ferritic stainless steels in some ways are not that forgiving and that may be one of the reasons for the discouragement. In the recent Presidential Address of IIM by Dr. Baldev Raj a positive mention has been made for ODS ferritic steels. One of my Ph.D. students Dr S.K. Mukherjee (1983) did research on ODS 434L ferritic stainless steel. Incidentally, his external examiner was late Dr. Huet, who did outstanding research in this area in Belgium's Atomic Energy Centre at Mol.

On a personal note, I found Dr Rodriguez a very cosmopolitan personality.He did not suffer from any sort of narrowness. Even after retirement, he had enormous capacity to work and think.

It shall be appropriate, if I express here some of my thoughts on the research programs's identification in the Indian Atomic Energy Establishments. My opinion is that they are more open ended and lack that mission spirit as it is in other Governement Agencies, for example Space Organisation. I have already talked about 316L austenitic stainless steel earlier. According to my thinking, basic researches should be entrusted to the Universities and Institutes like IITs and IISc. Another example may be shape memory alloys. This topic preferably be tackled by organisations like National Aerospace Laboratory (CSIR) or DRDO. Research on fuel cells should have been taken with full steam by say Bharat Heavy Electricals R & D Centre or Central Electrochemical Research Institute, Karaikudi (Tamil Nadu). On the other hand, atomic enery people should have actively ventured researches on next generation nuclear materials,for example thorium. I am glad that the immediate past Chairman of Atomic Energy Dr. Kakodkar injected the concept of close collaboration with educational institutes. A transparency in scientific discussions, including the identification of R & D strategy is a must. It is high time our atomic energy organisation corrects the past negligences.

Dr. Rodriguez served IGCAR till October 2000. Soon after, he served as the Chairman of the Recruitment and Assessment Centre of DRDO in New Delhi.till October, 2003. He played important leadership role in the professional societies. He served as President of the Indian Institute of Metals, Indian Institute of Welding and Indiian Nuclear Society.He also served as Honorary Secretary as well as the Vice-President of the Indian Academy of Engineering. He was extremely happy that the Golden Jubillee Celebrations.of IIM was held under his Presidentship.

Dr. Rodriguez passed away on 31st August, 2008 at Chennai.He is survived by his wife, and two children. It is pity that the obituary of this eminent metallurgist was not published in many periodicals, as done for other metallurgists.

LATE MR. P. R. ROY

Mr. P. R. Roy was the 1958 batch Metallurgical Engineering graduate from Bengal Engineering College, Shibpur (W. Bangal). Professor Ahindra Ghosh of my department at IITK was his classmate. Just after graduation Mr. Roy joined the Atomic Energy training School in Bombay. From the Junior rank, he rose to the rank of Director, Materials Group of BARC. I had read his papers published in the Journal of Nuclear Materials, edited by Professor R.W. Cahn. He is undoubtedly the father of Indian Plutonium Projest. The President of the Republic of India rightly honoured him for his contributions by awarding him 'Padma Shri'.

Soon after joining IIT Kanpur as a professor in 1976, I attended the Annual Technical Meeting of IIM held in Pune. Mr Roy was in the audience, during my paper presentation. After the end of the Technical

Session, I approached him and engaged in conversation. I found him a sobre and well cultured person. Since then our cooperation began to grow. I was, then, not aware that he is very much interested in powder metallurgy.

A year after out first meteing, Mr P. R. Roy attended he PMAI Annual Technical Meeting, He did not present any paper, but was just a keen observer. Prior to him only Dr. Kondal Rao and his team from NFC were the regular attendees of PMAI meetings. Soon after his initiation with the PMAI Meeting, Mr. Roy became a regular participant and, and also joined the Association as a member. In the Jamshedpur Annual Meeting of PMAI in early eighties, Mr. Roy was elected the Vice-President of PMAI. Soon he started deputing more and more scientists from his organisation to attend the Annual Meetings. His subordinates were Dr. C. Ganguly, Mr Mazumdar, Mr Kamath, Dr. R.S. Mehrotra and others. Dr. Ganguly was his most favourite scientist and his boss Mr. Roy invariably promoted him on all possible occasions.

Since I am writing here about BARC, it is not inopportune,if I narrate one incidence. One of the instrument technologist of BARC was registered for Ph.D. in Bombay University as an external candidate. Dr. M.K. Asundi of Metallurgy Division was his thesis supervisor.The topic was on erosion of steels and the results were supposed to be interpreted with microstructure. The candidate, unfortunately, had no basic education / training in physical metallurgy and this brought him into trouble. I happened to be the external examiner of this candidate. I submitted my report asking few major rewritings. After the resubmission of this thesis, the oral examination was arranged by the University in its campus. As soon as I approached the entrance gate of the Registrar's office in the gound floor, few gentlemen were standing near the gate. I could recognize one of them, who held a senior position in BARC. I could smell their purpose of coming right from Anu Shakti Nagar to down town. A Metallurgical Engineering professor from IIT Bombay was another external examiner. I askd my acquaintance from BARC to accompany me during the oral examination. He too happily agreed to do so. He was sitting there merely as an observer. My aim was to demonstrate this gentleman the correctness of the points raised by me in the report. Dr. Asundi was all along indifferent, although I knew from the heart of the heart he wanted to salvage the candidate. After the viva examination, the BARC group took me for the lunch in a nearby restaurant.There I jokingly exclaimed them as 'Sarkari Scientists' meaninbg 'Government Scientists'.They were amused,but at the same time they all understood my hint. After seeing this episode, it is very clear now why BARC was so particular in opening an autonomous Institute to give Ph.D. degrees, probably to avoid such embarrassing situations. The question is why it is limited to their scientific staff only ?

In 1988, when I joined the PMAI as its President, Mr. R.R. Roy was the seniormost Vice-Preseident. In that year the Annual Technical Meeting of PMAI was held in New Delhi. Professor Tendolkar, who was attached with Modi Sons, Bombay as its Technical Advisor, also attended the meeting. Professor Sampath, the then Chairman of the Recruitment and Assessment Board of DRDO delivered the inaugural addresss. In the plenary session, there was an address by Mr. P.R.Roy too. I don't know why he was critical on the progress in PMAI. Many of the audience felt that a group of persons in DRDO, who were averse to Mr. George (Hon. Secretary) might have provoked Mr Roy to speak in that tone. I felt sorry for Mr Roy. Perhaps, their strategy was to oust Mr George, which they succeeded in the next year. Mr Roy was then the Director of the Materials Group of BARC.

In the year 1991, Mr Roy organised an International Conference on Advanced Ceramics at BARC. I also attended that meeting. Many eminent scientists were there. Professor Chaklader from Canada, Dr. Sunil Datta and Professor Spriggs from USA. graced the occasion. Mr P.R. Roy was then at the prime of his career.

It was a shocking news to hear about the very sad death of Mr. Roy due to massive heart attack, while playing lawn tennis on one fine Sunday. I suppose it was the year 1992.The whole nation, and those related to Indian Atomic Energy could not fill the gap generated by this sad departure for quite some time.

DR. R.G. SHAH

During the Annual Technical Meetings of Indian Ceramic Society, I used to notice an energetic person of approximately my age, who was very much involved in the deliberations. He was Dr. R.G. Shah of Graphite India R & D Centre, Bangalore. Dr. Shah completed his ceramic engineering education from Osmania University, Hyderabad. I found Dr. Shah a well read man. You talk anything from whiteware to advanced ceramics, Dr. Shah is competent in all. In early seventies, we were in great need of highly dense and strong graphite rods to be used in hot presses. Dr. Shah was very handy as he had developed that material.

Dr. Shah is a great believer in academia / industry interaction. As a matter of fact, he wanted to have some sort of sabbathical at IIT, Kanpur. It is pity due to some impediments, one being the housing problem, I could not succeed in facilitating those. Notwithstanding that, we were in regular communication I found in Dr. Shah, somewhat similar what I found in my good friend Mr. N.M. Pai from PM industry.

Dr. Shah managed the Bangalore Chapter of the Indian Ceramic Society with utmost devotion. He was the Chapter Chairman more than one term. He was also skeptical of the way the Indian Ceramic Society was run. It had the great influence of the CSIR laboratory 'Central Glass and Ceramic Research Institute', which had housed the Society.

I had a long standing invitation from Dr. Shah to deliver a lecture in Indian Ceramic Society, Bangalore Chapter. While attending the Indian Science Congress in the year 2003, I wanted to coincide that event. Everything was arranged properly but due to some misunderstanding of the timing the meeting had to be called off. However,I could fulfil my promise only later in November, 2004. The meeting was a well attended one and I was impressed by the full strength of the students of the Polytechnic Institute. They were quite inquisitive. What they required was a good guidance. I am sure Dr. Shah is doing that in Bangalore.

Dr. Shah is leading a happy retired life in Bangalore but still doing consultancy. No day passes without his being in the badminton court. A good dose of sport activity keeps him agile and alert. I am pleased that,of late, Indian Ceramic Society awarded him the Honorary Membership.

MR. R. SRINIVASAN

After laying the foundation of PMAI, we were active in holding its meetings in various regions so as to enrol more and more members,.One of the early meetings was in Calcutta in the late seventees. I specially went from Kanpur to attend that. There I first met Mr. Srinivasan, who was associated with Widia (India), Bangalore. He had a slim body, with utmost agility. What ever he uttered was with clarity and force. He was competent in commerce as well in technology. Having done his Master's degree in mechanical engineering from Germany, he was most suited for the job in Widia (India). Whenever the account sheets were on the agenda of PMAI

Governing Council Meeting, one could witness the critical queries of Mr Srinivasan. He used to attend all the technical sessions With passage of time, Mr Srinivasan rose to high position ending in the chain of Managing Director. At every stage he was ready to help research in kinds. Many times the help in kinds is far far significant as compared to the grant in cash. The first Managing Director of Widia, Bangalore was a German Dr Roettger, but the company management became so confident about Mr Srinivasan that there was no need for any German Managing Director.

Dr. R.V. Tamhankar, the president of PMAI could recognize the significance of Mr Srinivasan and he proposed his name for the Vice-President. Mr Srinivasan accepted our invitation with due humility. Whenever I was in Bangalore, I never forgot to visit Mr. Srinivasan in his factory and to know what new they are doing or planning. Although Widia (India) was a German concern, the management felt so sure of Mr. Srinivasan, that they never interfered in his decisions. The biggest skill of his was to marry the foreign technology with the available Indian manpower. He never jumped to buy a foreign equipment but preferred to assemble them in his plant. In that respect, he was very Swadeshi in spirit. There was another major cemented carbide producer in India, namely Sandvik Asia at Pune, but the philosophy of Mr Srinivasan was just the opposite of theirs. Sandvik was bigger in capacity but they were lacking in the product mixes, what Widia used to produce. In conferences Sandvik never preferred to present any technical paper, but the Widia management did encourage their young engineers to do so. My two former M.Tech students Mr Debabrat Basu and Mr S. Mazagi served in the plant of Widia. Mr Srinivasan was proud of my students. Unfortunely, Mr. Basu, later, wanted to be in West Bengal and the latter moved to Drexel University, USA to do his Ph.D. When later these young engineers met me at IIT Kanpur, I found them to possess versatile qualities. The credt to make them so matured goes entirely to Widia management and Mr Srinivasan, in particular.

With globalisation of Indian economy, there had been some changes in Widia (India) too. The musical chair game of buying and selling of plants began. Widia (India) was affected by that. Their parent company at Essen (Germany) was taken over by Kannametal of USA and they started making drastic changes in management. Mr Srinivasan had his own strategy for the growth of Widia (India). As he found difficulties in convincing his overseas bosses, he peferred to resign and start consultancy work.

Presently, Mr Srinivasan has again switched over to active technology management. He is currently the Managing Director of a cemented carbide company in Bangalore, which has the significant control from South Korea. Originally, the plant was Indicarb situated in Hosur (Tamil Nadu). I gather, the company is doing excellent under the leadership of my friend Mr R. Srinivasan

LATE DR. R.V. TAMHANKAR

During my summer industrial training in the year 1959 at Tata Steel, I was browsing the second hand books on the road side of the city market. There I purchased few old issues of TISCO Journal.The articles and reviews were exclusively written by the scientists / engineers of Tata Steel. In one of the issues, I read a paper by Mr. R.V. Tamhankar. At the end of each issue the author's brief bio-data were published. From that I knew that Mr. Tamhankar was essentially a M.Sc. (Physics) degree holder from Bombay University. He was very much involved in characterizing steels used in transformers. He had a good hand on instrumentation too. Many belonging to those days, may be aware that Professor Crussard of IRSID, France, was the Director of our National Metallurgical Laboratory and Dr. Tamhankar got encouraged by him to proceed to Paris for higher studies. After getting awarded the D.Sc. degree from Paris, he took up a job at IRSID. They were equally impressed by the name of Tata Steel in India. Dr. Tamhankar's heart was in India and was in a look out for a suitable placement. Ultimately, the chance came of his joining DMRL, Hyderabad as its Director in the year 1963. Mr R. K. Mahapatra, after completing his B Tech (1961) and MSc (1963) from Banaras Hindu University joined DMRL as a scientist and through him, we came to know more about Dr. Tamhankar.I first saw him in the Annual Technical Meeting of IIM organised in Bombay in 1964.He wore a well tailored three piece suit with gold cuff pins and a golden wrist watch.

My next meeting with Dr. Tamhankar was in 1971-72 durng the conference on high temperature materials, organised by BARC in Hyderabad. It was a well attended conference, but Dr. Tamhankar was only in the inaugural session. My third meeting was in the year 1973, when he wanted to launch two societies, Powder Metallurgy Association of India and the Magnetics Society of India. I travelled from Roorkee to Hyderabad by train and there our deep interaction began. I found him an extremely different person compared to what I thought. Within a year of the foundation of PMAI, I was deputed by my university to supervise its entarance examination at Hyderabad Exmination Centre. I was staying in the Institution of Engieeers (India) premises. I called Dr. Tamhankar and he sent me a rather big army vehicle to pick up. Although he was an extremely busy person, he gave me sufficient time. I raised the issue of the timely publication of the Transactions PMAI and the PMAI Newsletters. He instructed his Secretary to call Mr N.T. George (Hon. Secretary PMAI), who was in the post of the Deputy Director. He instructed Mr. George to complete the publication work soon. Mr George took me to his office, where I spent few hours with him. He also showed me the different laboratories at good length. I got an impression that Dr. Tamhankar was a stickler. He abhorred laziness. No wonder, during my visit of DMRL, I did not find a single equipment, which was out of order. Dr. Tamhankar knew how to harmonise the task with his collegues.He wsa sympathetic to genuine grievances, but he also knew which are the genuine ones. No one could fool him.

Dr. Tamhankar had tremendous stamina.He wanted India to be self dependent for the defence material's view point. This propelled him to plan Mishra Dhatu Nigam (MIDHANI), the superally complex near the premises of DMRL. Dr. Tamhankar had a good rapport with Mrs Indira Gandhi, the then Prime Minister of India. She realised the significance of special alloys production in India and instructed various ministries to cooperate with Dr. Tamhankar. In that connection, he had to frequently visit Delhi. He was a big mover. I think person here in India with a dream must have the role model of Dr. Tamhankar.

Dr.Tamhankar successfully managed the show of both DMRL and MIDHANI. Such a joint activity was helpful for a quick growth of MIDHANI as most of the testing facilities of DMRL were used. All of a sudden, I heard the news that Dr. Tamhankar was henceforth solely deputed to MIDHANI as the Managing Director and Dr. V.S. Arunachalam took over the Directorship of DMRL. No doubt DMRL and MIDHANI were Dr. Tamhankar's babies, being a research oriented person he had the greater weakness for the former. After his tenure at MIDHANI, Professor CNR Rao of Indian Institute of Science, persuaded Dr. Tamhankar to join his Institute as a visiting professor. He was given a residence inside the campus. Unfortunalely he met a mild paralytic attack there, but recovered soon. Subsequently, Dr. Tamhankar moved to his native place Sangli, a relatively small town in Maharashtra State. Some how this town did not suit him or his wife and they both decided to shift to Hyderabad Once I visited them in Hyderabad along with Mr N.T. George. Dr. Tamhankar couple was quite hospitable, although he was relatively weak due to old age. His flat in Vinaya Nagar was in the ground floor, so as to avoid any physical inconvenience.

On the family front, Dr. Tamhankar did have some misfortune. His first wife was bed ridden due to cronic desease. He took care of her very well, but the fatigue was visible at his face. His wife could not last long and died.After the gap of few years, Dr. Tamhankar remarried with a French lady, whom he was knowing from his IRSID days.When he remarried, he had no family responsibilities. All his wards were leading their own independent life. I first met Dr. Tamhankar couple during the inauguration of the International Symposium at Hyderabad on 'Tungsten and Molybdenum' organised by MIDHANI. His wife was quite slim and petit. She knew English reasonably well. My next meeting with them was during PMAI Annual Meeting in May, 1989 in Sri Nagar in Jammu and Kashmir State. Both had young spirit and did not mind to climb the staircase of Shankaracharya temple. Dr. Tamhankar with a stick could succeed in reaching the top. His wife and I gave helping hand. Both of them enjoyed their Sri Nagar trip. The year 1989 was the beginning of the cross border terrorist attacks in Kashmir. We read in the newspaper about the shooting and death of a terrorist.

Near the fag end of his life, Dr. Tamhankar stopped corresponding in general. His faithful wife always stood at his side. It is sad commentary, that he like Professor Tendolkar, did not get any major national recognition. The transparency with which Dr. Tamhankar steered the PMAI is worth emulating by any other professional Societies. When I heard the sad demise of Dr. Tamhankar (16 June, 1993) at the age of 76, many thoughts came to my mind-his sense of discipline, his humour, his dedication, his patriotism, his team spirit and above all the faith of a dedicated husband.

LATE PROFESSOR G.S. TENDOLKAR

During my 1959 BHU days, while busy in a laboratory class in one afternoon, we noticed a group of Russians along with an Indian Gentleman passing through the laboratory. Professor Daya Swaup, our college principal, was showing them our laboratories. This Indian Gentleman was Professor Tendolkar of IIT, Bomaby, who was escorting the team of Russian professors. They wanted to know the first hand details about our syllabii and teaching methods. Profesor Tendolkar had a middle height, with fair complexion and a pretty bald head. He had teaching experience at the department of chemical technology of Bombay University followed by a short stint at Indian Atomic Energy, Bombay. Somehow his devotion to teaching profession prevailed over pure research. In addition, I also heard that the other reason of his disenchantment with Atomic Energy was that there he was superceded by other in the hierarchy.

My first intimate meeting with Professor Tendolkar was in 1966 at IIT Kanpur, where an Indo-US Conference on Materials Science Education was organised. Professor T.R. Anantharaman and G.S. Tendolkar were there. Dr. Ramakrishnan, who was on the faculty of the Metallurgical Engineering department at IIT Bombay also participated. Myself and Professor Tendolkar mingled very well and I was impressed by his love for Indian classical music. Sometimes he muttered few words and requested me to complete the couplet.He was very jovial, but at times quite sarcastic as well.

My second meeting with Professor Tendolkar was in Ashoka Hotel during the Silver Jubilee Celebrations of IIM (1971). I went there specially from Roorkee. Professor Tendolkar by that time had read my papers. He had a singular approach for diffusion model for sintering. I could not attend the IIM Meeting fully, but could meet Professor Morris Cohen of MIT and Dr, Krishna Tangri of Manitoba University, Canada. Dr.Tangri was earlier in the Indian Atomic Energy Establishment.

My third meeting with Professor Tendolkar was in his office at IIT Bombay in the mid-seventies. I was in Bombay to ateend the Annual Technical Meting of IIM held at Taj Hotel. I was a bit amazed not to find Professor Tendolkar in the audience. After my asking about this absence, he shot back saying he was against the five star culture of the Institute. He had desired the meeting with a moderate registration fee and at a modest place eg. in an academic Institute. Unfortunately, IIM did not heed to this. Dr. V. Balasubramaniam, an alumnus of BHU Metallurgical Engineering Department, and then the ex-faculty of IIT Bombay, was also present in our meeting.We discussed many things right from the science to the national economic mismanagement. On the black board opposite to his chair, Dr.

Tendolkar used to write important engagements. On his desk, there were some very thoughtful quotations. He talked about his participation in the IISS (International Institute for the Science of Sintering) World Round Table Meeting in Yugoslavia. There he had presented a paper with the coauthorship of one of his post graduate students Mr, Sheikh.

Professor Tendolkar, once, read a book review written by me on a powder metallurgy book published by Italian Powder Metallury Association. This was in one of the issues of PMAI Newsletter. He requested me a photocopy of the book. I photocopied the same and gave it at his residence during my next Bombay visit. His residence was in East Goregaon lacality of Bombay. On that occasion I also gave him a tin box of Pan Parag, the famous chewing tobacco of Kanpur make. He had specially requested me for this item. He smiled and accepted the same. He and his wife had arranged a working dinner for all of us. His wife was teaching mathematics in Khalsa College, Bombay. She was a jovial lady. Unfortunately she died after few years. Thereafter, Professor Tendolkar became a loner. He and his loyal pet were in the house. From Goregaon local railway station to his residence, I used to walk, since the transport facility was not that ideal in those days. The eastern side of Bombay local stations is always like that as compared to the Western counterpart. However, I liked the location of his house. It gave a feeling of living in a small town, but at the same time in a metropolis.

Throughout my professional career, Professor Tendolkar was in regular correspondance with me. I received the copy of his letter sent to Mr George, Honorary Secretary of PMAI There he advocated that the Secretariat of PMAI should be shifted to IIT Bombay. I agreed with him but emphasised that it must be independent, and not be an appendix of other organisation, like IIT or BARC. Ultimately, the same happened which I feared. The secretariat moved from Hyderabad to BARC, Bombay at the insistence of the then President Mr. P.R. Roy. From that day onward the complexion of PMAI changed drastically. I am pleased that the management, of late, decided to shift the office in a rented flat near IIT Bombay campus.

With further passage of time, my meetings with Professor Tendolkar was frequent, as I used to visit IIT Bombay to deliver PM lectures in the short courses organised by PMAI. In one of my lectures, Professor Tendolkar too attended, which showed his keenness to know, whatever is new. At times he was a bit abrasive and blunt and was comfortable with persons of his qualities. He never liked any cunning person.

Recognising the contributions of Professor Tendolkar, PMAI honoured him as Honorary Member in 1980 in the Annual Technical Meeting organised in Bangalore. Professor K.P. Abraham of Indian Institute of Science delivered the welcome address. Professor Tendolkar was the second powder metallurgist after Professor H.H. Hausner to be elected to Honorary Membership.

In the PMAI Annual Technical meeting held in 1981 in Bombay, Professor Tendolkar was a participant. There I saw Mr Modi of Modi Sons, who were in business of electric contact materials. Mr Modi was in search for a technical advisor (full time) for his firm. He invited Professor Tandolkar for the same, which he accepted with some reservation.

Professor Tendolkar had strong opinion on many things, whether social, political or scientific. His candid statements were at times not properly understood even by his close colleagues. His criticism sometimes lacked alternative propositions., which used to frustrate him as well. Professor Tendolkar was liked by his students immensely. It is worthwhile to quote from his Professor N.P. Gandhi Memorial Lecture delivered at Rourkela in November 1982 under the auspices of the IIM:' My gratitude goes very much to my innumerable students who were really ahead of me with their knowledge of modern physics and mathematics and later the inevitable computer, and who constantly questioned me and thus compelled me to study my subject in depth and always kept me on my toes. They were really the equivalents of Young Scientist in Hume-Rothery's book.'

On 15th July, 1990 after a brief illness came the sad demise of Professor Tendolkar. During my subsequent visit of Bombay, I met Mr. N.M. Pai, the Technical Director of 'Powder Metals and Allloys' to know the full details. He told me that Professor Tendolkar died due gastro-intestinal complications. He was pretty weak and died all alone in night., with his dog on the bed side. He had willed his body for medical research and his personal library to Mr. N.M. Pai. Incidentally his doctor son also lives in Bombay. The whole life of Professor Tendolkar signifies his strong personality. He never followed any dogma, but only individualism.

4

Some Men of Metals and
Materials from Overseas

The present chapter describes the men (I include women also) of metals and materials with whom I have interacted both in short to long range periods. In all there are 45 personalities spread over 21 nations from all over the continents. Countrywise break down is as follows: Australia (1), Austria (3), Belgium (1), Canada (1), Denmark (1), France (1), Germany (7), Italy (1), Japan (2), Pakistan (1), People Republic of China (1), Poland (1), Russia (1), Serbia (1), South Africa (1), South Korea (1), Spain (1), Sweden (2), The Netherlands (1), U.K. (2), and USA (14).

DR. L. ALBANO-MULLER (GERMANY)

Dr. Albano-Muller is the son of a German industrialist, whose interest arose in powder metallurgy. He studied at the University of Karlsruhe under the world famous powder metallurgist Professor Thummler. I had read his research papers on sintered steels and was eager to meet him. The opportunity came in the year 1979 during my European visit. He is a man of middle height and slim built with a chiselled face. I and my wife were put up in their plant's (Sintermetal Krebsoge) guest house, not far from the main office of the firm. As soon as Dr. Muller came to know about our arrival, he rushed to welcome us. I had not yet taken bath and was in a bit untidy shape. The introductory meeting was very brief. Later, after breakfast when I reached his office, he took me to Professor Zapf, the forefront powder metallurgist of world repute. He was no more the Managing Director of the firm but was an adviser, While Dr. Muller was the Managing Director. Professor Zapf was also a part time visiting professor at the University of Karlsruhe, where he drove twice a week. He was a real busy man, who disposed off many work during the drive. Dr. Muller also introduced me Dr. Huppman, who was the Director of R&D of the company. A young engineer was assigned to me for the whole duration of our stay in Krebsoge. I visited various plants of this biggest PM Group in Germany. The most interesting part was the hot forging of PM autoparts and sintered Al-alloys. Other activities were similar to our Indian PM plants. I also gave a seminar in one of the afternoons, where I met my old acquaintance Mr Kirit Dalal and Dr. Beiss, who is just retired as a Professor in the Technical Universty, Aachen. My talk was on the master ferroalloy added sintered steels. an area in which Professor Zapf had done considerable research. Dr. Huppman was in the chair and in the concluding remarks said that my system did not achieve as it should have done. They were in the know how of all the details, but did not reveal them. I too did not press upon further. I was aware of the limitation of our sintering atmosphere.

I and my wife had opportunity to interact with the family of Dr. Muller. He invited us in his hugh house, where he made a point to invite his sister-in-law also. She is a noble and well educated Indian Tamilian Brahmin Lady, a graduate of BHU followed by higher studies in Oxford University, UK. She fell in love with the elder brother of Dr. Muller, who was also studying at Oxford. Even after being in Germany for some decades, she was a tea-totaller and pure vegetarian. It was a very pleasant evening. We appreciated that every family in the world has similar problems irrespective of the modern gadgetry.

My later meetings with Dr. Muller was in the year 1984 in Toronto, and in the 1986 PM meeting in Dusseldorf. He was very active in European Powder Metallurgy Association of which he became the President. As usual he was a warm person. His keynote lectures on European PM Status were very revealing. Dr. Muller had a vision for European PM. Their products were much denser and stronger than the American counterparts, but were costlier. They were not so much worried from the Japanese competitors, but from the American ones. In the year 1987, MAAG Gear Wheel & Machine Co. Ltd, Zurich, Switzerland purchased a majority interest of the company. No wonder the onset of globalisation also effected his plant, which was later sold to GKN of UK and subsequently to Sinter

Metal, USA. The history of Krebsoge plant must be studied by any PM businessman. This will be educative for him.

Presently Dr. Albano-Muller is no more associated with Krebsoge plant. Many of their powder metallurgista whom I knew left the organisation, except one Dr. Volker Arnhold, who is currently the Vice-President of R&D of GKN Sinter Metal at Krebsoge.

PROFESSOR R.A. ANDRIEVSKI (RUSSIA)

I first saw Dr. Andrievski during my research student days in Kiev, when he ws there to deliver a seminar. Unfortunately, we were not formally introduced, although he knew very well who I was. Those days were tough for Russians to mingle with foreigners. By that time I had read his Russian textbook on powder metallurgy coauthored with Academician Fedorchenko. At that time he was a faculty member in Nonferrous Metals Institute in Moscow. Professor Andrievski was liked by all and had no adversaries. My book on Refractory Carbides coauthored with Samsonov and Neshpor was full length reviewed by him, for the Journal 'Inorganic Materials' (USSR Academy of Sciences, Moscow). His review was an objective one and he did not hide the criticism. I met him in 1979 in Poland during Sintering Summer School. Also, there were Professor Skorokhod and Professor Kisly from Kiev, Ukraine. Professor Andrievski researched on many areas of refractory compounds right from thermodynamics to the superplastic behaviour. Of late, he got interested in nanosize crystalline materials at the Institute of Chemical Technology, Academy of Sciences, Chernogalovka near Moscow. I had a chance to visit this Institute in the year 1993. I was put in the hostel of that Institute for a night. I could notice a strict security in the Institute and thought that the same shall prevail in hostel also. But I was very much wrong. It was a bit annoying to show your passport everytime you enter in the Institute's academic area. It was the era of President Yeltsin and economically Russia was really down. It wsa also reflected in the poor maintenance of the Institute. However, such a handicap did not deter their scientists from doing good reearch. There was an excellent team on plsma synthesis of nanomaterials.

While bidding good-bye to me on the first day, Dr. Andrievski did advise me not to open the door of my hostel room in night to unknown persons. I think his Institute had had some mishap in past. It did happen that at midnight I had the repeated loud bangs on my door. I followed the instructions given by him and luckily the episode was over within few minutes. I did not utter a single word during thr bangs. Next morning, I narrated this incident to my host. I was surprised that even the hostel care taker did not take my utterings seriously. I wish now the situation is Russia is better.

Professor Andrievski was keen to visit India. I feel guilty I could not do effectively in this. The officials at the Department of Science and Technology, Government of India in New Delhi were invariably rather indifferent., and a genuine request often gets missed. I am glad, at last, Professor Andrievski was deputed by the Russian Academy of Sciences to take part in the Bilateral Workshop on nanomaterials held in National Metallurgical Laboratory, Jamshedpur in the year 2008. He later narrated me his extremely tiring journey from Delhi to Jamshedpur.

After the death of Professor Samsonov (1975) my only source to get scientific Russian papers was Professsor Andrievski. We exchanged our publications and at times he even sent a book from his own personal library. Later with the advent of internet, the communication was much quicker.

I still vividly remember my meeting with Professor Andrievski in the year 1988 in Orlando (USA) during International Powder Metallurgy Conference, organized by MPIF. There, unlike other Russians, he was not shy in actively interacting with Russian expatriats. In a way he acted as a bridge. I am glad to hear that he is still continuing with his old Institute in capacity of an emeritus scientist

Late Dr. F. Benezowski (Austria)

Dr. Benezowski was a well known.materials scientist in Austria, who dedicatedly served Metalwerk Plansee as Director R & D till his death. I was extensively exposed to his research contributions while in Kiev. His major contribution has been in phase diagrams of muticomponent systems pertaining to refractory metals and compounds. I first met Dr. Benezowski in 1968 during the 6th International Plansee Seminar in Reutte, Austria, for which he was the convener. He was a tall, slim person with extremely pleasing personality. He continued to pilot the International Seminar at Plansee till his retirement. The seminar was initiated by the founder of the Plansee Firm Professor Paul Schwarzkopf in 1952.

At Metalwerk Plansee Dr, Benezowski worked along with Professor Richard Kieffer in the initial post World War II period. Both of them jointly authored many papers and books. The first research work on the effect of manganese on sintered steels was done by them. This historical event was the driving force for me to dedicate my Monograph 'Manganese in Sintered Alloys', published by Manganese Centre, Paris, to these two eminent materials scientists. In every Plansee Seminar, Dr. Benezowski used to oversee each and every event while sitting in the first row's corner seat His secretary used to be at reasonable distance. Whenever there was need, he just blink her. I vividly remember, how he solved my problem in few minutes. In Kiev (1968) we used to have an epidiascope for showing our illustrations. I had carried along with me the tracings of all the figures related to my paper, which I had to show duing the Plansee seminar. Dr. Benezowski immediately realised my dilema and instructed one of his staff to prepare the transparencies. Within ten minutes, the things were ready. He never reflected any irritation due to the lack of my preparation. In the next morning, before the start of the technical session, he handed over to me an envelop and just said 'It is for your drink'. I shot back and said' I don't drink.'He too responded immediately ;' Than it is for your milk'.We both laughed. In 1971 Plansee Seminar, there was a paper by a Russian metallurgist from Moscow on hot rolling of refractory metals under vacuum. Unfortunately there was no interpreter from their side. Dr. Benezovski requested me in public whether I can help. I responded in affirmative and did help in interpretation

The geographic location of Austria between West and East Europe balancing the opposite political camps rather constrained her to become a neutral nation. My own estimate is that the influence of East was on a higher side. Dr. Benezowski himself had migrated from Czekoslovakia. The Hungarian materials scientist Dr. Miller, whose pioneering work on doped tungsten filaments for lamp industry made him internationally famous, was another regular participant of the Plansee Seminars. In those cold war days, most of the East European scientists were looked upon by the hard core western Europe with an element of suspicion. Such an attitude was completely absent among the Austrian scientific community. In a way, they acted as a bridge between West and East. I think the Western world should be beholden to them.

My last meeting with Dr. Benezowski was in 1985 Plansee Seminar. He was a bit weak and frail. I could feel the heavy burden of coordinating the

Seminar on him. But, he was cheerful all the time. The real international gathering used to rejuvinate him. During a cultural program, he told me the recipe of his keeping in a reasonably good shape. Every evening he used to take a prolonged sauna. For many times, he edited the 'Plansee Seminar Proceedings', which were published by Springer Verlag, Berlin. But, later he started shedding off some of his responsibilities to his Juniors-mainly to Dr. Eck and Dr Ortner. Dr. Ortner took the responsibilty of conducting the Plnasee Seminar after the death of Dr. Benezowski. In early ninties, Dr. Ortner joined the University of Darmstadt as a Professor in materials characterization. He is now retired and leads a quiet life in Austria. He edits the International Journal of Refractory Metals and Hard Materials (Elsevier), of which I happen to be in the Editorial Board.

With the death of Dr. Benezowski passed the excellent cultural background of an Austrian scientist, whom I cherish even today

DR. GIAN F. BOCCHINI (ITALY)

If I search a real powder metallurgy personality from Italy, he is my friend Dr. Gian Bocchini, who is contemporary to me. I know him from the early seventies. Earlier he was attached with the Hoganas' Italy operation. As a matter of fact, he was one of the organisers of the International PM Conference held in 1982 in Florence. I could not attend that, but made up a point to attend the PM 2010 World Congress held in the same historical and beautiful city Florence Incidentally Dr. Bocchini's first name is just a Sanskrit word 'Gyan' meaning 'knowledge'. Really he is the most knowledgeable PM person in Italy

I met Dr. Bocchini in practically all the major PM conferences in the world. He is a person with full command on science and technology of powder metallurgy, particularly sintering aspects. His papers on sintering atmospheres and their control are lucid, original and at the same time written in style such that even a shop floor technician / engineer can understand. Dr. Bocchini became an intimate link between India and Italy. When the firm Andhra Sintered Products, in the South India State of Andhra Pradesh, started the venture with Merisinter of Italy. they preferred Italy as the economics was more favourable to have the tie up with Italy. Dr. Bocchini used to visit India, so as to give consultancy to Andhra Sintered Products. No doubt my good friend Mr. G.M. Krishnamurthy, formerly with Mahindra Sintered Producst, was the General Manager of the plant, he could not get the solid competent support from the local technical workers. Probably they could not realise how precisive technology is PM. Later Mr Krishnamurthy left the firm in frustration. Dr. Bocchini did not too much elaborate me his problems in India, but I could feel that he is not that happy, as he wished to be. In all he paid three visits to India in that connection. The promoters of the plant were also doing mere lip service. I heard they had received good help from the Banks in the form of loans, but alas in waste. I was sorry for Dr. Bocchini, but it was very difficult, at that late stage, to put life in the plant due to poor management.

Very recently I received an email from my friend Dr. Bocchini saying how happy he was in meeting with me in his own country Italy during PM 2010. He lives in Rappalo not far from Genova in Italy. He is active in helping the Italian Metallurgy Association. His good command in English has made him to reach to the PM World with greater ease.

MR. K. J. A. BROOKES (U.K.)

Mr Brookes can be undoubtedly called as Mr. 'Hard Material' of Europe. His background is in the area of cemented carbides. His extensive industrial experience and wide travel throughout the world have made him one of the most knowledgeable man in Hard Materials. He was the Technical Editor of the International Journal of Refractory Metals and Hard Materials' published by Elsevier. Earlier this Journal was edited and published by Mr Bernard Williams of Shrewsbury (UK). Mr Williams used to invite Mr Brookes to write on the status report of various cemented carbide industries all over the world. In those days when websites were not available, Mr Brookes' contributions were far from significance. One can find in him some sort of critic as well. He is a nice gentleman, but minces no words in pointing out any lacuna. I first met him in 1986 in Dusseldorf Conference of European Powder Metallurgy Association. Soon we became good friends. He is a person with whom you can talk for hours on a cup of coffee. His passion is cemented carbides and he compiled an International Handbook and Directory on Hard Materials, which he published himself. It was a profitable business for him, but one may not realise the pains which he took in compiling and updating this Handbook. Many editions of this Handbook and Directory have passed out.

One of the favourite research area of Mr Brookes was the role of chromium carbide in cemented carbides. As soon as there is a mention of this stuff, he uses to jump for contributing during the discussion. I too had worked on chromium carbide and during one poster presentation in 1997 International Plansee Seminar, he gave some useful tips to me. Sometimes his interpretations have been out of conventional track, but he boldly defends them. At times there use to be some elements of humour in his conversation. He is a regular contributor in summarising the relevant conference papers in the periodical Metal Powder Report. These summaries, many times, amount to critical reviews too. I always found Mr Brookes a cheerful and satisfied person. Although he earned good money through his publications, in a strict sense he is still a consultant,more with a bent of academia.

I would like to here recall one of the incidents during the Board of Editors meeting of the International Journal of Refractory Metals and Hard Materials in Austria during the summer of 1997. He was not happy with the treatment meted to this journal by the publisher (Elsevier). He told this very boldly and after him some passive members also became active including me. There was a dinner after this meeting. Mr Brookes had been very considerate in full length reviewing my book "Cemented Tungsten Carbides' published in USA. He did an excellent job, but in the end did mention that the book is more based on academia. As a matter of fact, this was the truth as I have not had any production experience in a plant on cemented carbides.

My latest meeting with my friend Ken was in Florence (Italy) during PM 2010, in the month of October. He instantly recognised me and welcomed with great warmth. He was still alert and did attend all papers related to hard materials. As in past, he asked numerous critical questions. In one case the paper presentor was confused. His abstract talked of WC-20 Co, while all his slides wrote Co-20 WC. Mr Brookes had not read his abstract, while I had. His question really made the situation in the lecture hall a bit comic. Athough Ken does not keep best of health now-a-days, he is still very active as a consultant in hard materials.

LATE PROFESSOR R.F. BUNSHAH (USA)

Professor Bunshah, a devoted Parsee, was an alumnus of Banaras Hindu University (1948). Late Dr. Kondal Rao (NFC, Hyderabad) was his class mate. After getting the B.Sc. degree in Metallurgical Engineering, he moved to USA and obtained the Ph.D. degree from the Carnegie Institute of Technology, in Pittsburgh, PA. As most of the people attached to Tata Steel have had education at Carnegie Tech, no wonder he intentionally selected this Institute. In the latter half of 1960 while doing research at BHU under Professor G.R. Bashforth, I purchased his edited book entitled 'Vacuum Metallurgy'. In those days it was a new technology, in which very few persons had the mastery. Professor Bunshah was one of them. Later he got engaged in coating research and invented 'activated physical vapor deposition method'. In all his researches, vacuum was an integral part of the experimental set up. He joined University of California, Los Angeles as a full professor, from where he trained a score of scientists including some from India eg. Dr A.C. Raghuram (formerly at NAl, Banglore), and Dr. A.C. Budhani (IIT Kanpur). In the year 1973, during Golden Jubilee Celebrations of our department at BHU, Dr. Bunshah visited his alma mater. I also happened to be in the award giving ceremony and here we got introduced. He was awarded the 'Distinguished Alumnus Award 'of the Departemnt on that occasion.

My next meeting with Professsor Bunshah was in the year 1977 during the famous Plansee Seminar at Reutte, Austria. He had just purchased his brand new diesel version Mercedes Benz in Stuttgart (Germany) and arranged the shipment of the car to USA. In the seminar, he spoke authoritatively on the physical vapour deposition. The audience was very much impressed by lucidity of his lecture. He, later, asked my full bio-data and as soon as he went through he suggested me to write a book on Refractory Carbides. He promised to arrange the publisher in USA (Nova Science Publishers, Inc, Commack, NY 1996). We were in touch with each other regularly through correspondance. My last meeting with Professsor Bunshah was in 1995 at Los Angeles. He was then an Emeritus Professoor in the University. His office was just adjacent to that of Professor John J. Gilman, who was also an Emeritus Professor. Dr. Bunshah was looking weak. I knew about her Iranian wife at Los Angeles. He fixed an appointment with me to show his famous laboratory and suggested to pick me from the hotel, not far from the University. As there was parking restriction, he advised me to stand out side the hotel's main door. We talked many things, including BHU and his old classmates, the rat race in USA for getting research funding etc. From our conversation, I could notice a sense of frustration in him, as if the university is not able to utilize him utmost. Or may be his health problem was an abstacle. He introduced me to Profesor Gilman, with whom I had an interesting discussion. Gilman was very skeptical of the computer modelling people and as a matter of fact he wrote a very thoughtful article in the periodical Materialstoday (Elsevier) about this. Professor Bunshah was knowing my limitation that I can not drive in USA. I had to pay a visit to the Pacific Metals Plant in Los Angeles and Dr. Bunshah very elaborately explained how to reach to my hotel, so that my host can pick me up conveniently. The next day I had to catch my coach for Palm Springs. It was Sunday and Dr. Bunshah volunteered to drop me to the coach terminal in the down town. During our parting off he shook hand very warmly, and I had no idea that it was our last handshake. After few years I received a mail about his sad death after a prolonged illness. An obituary was written by me and sent to the Indian Institute of Metals for publication. What a surprise? The Institute did not know that Prof Bunshah was a life member of theirs. The IIM Metal News published my write up in an abridged form..

LATE PROFESSOR R.W. CAHN (U.K.)

Professor Cahn, after completing his Ph.D. degree from Cambridge University (UK), joined the Physical Metallurgy department of the University of Birmingham as a lecturer. Professor Hanson, head of the department, was instrumental in bifurcating the existing metallurgy department into two Physical and Industrial.Metallurgy respectively. The theoretical emphasis in the former department attracted Dr. Cahn to join the same. During War time, young Cahn migrated from Austria to UK along with his parents, due to political reasons. In stead of calling him a metallurgists, I would prefer the term' Applied Physicist'-which later took the nomenclature of 'Materials Scientist'. Recrystallisation in metals had been an attractive area for Dr. Cahn, who for the first time propounded the concept of 'polygonisation'. Another area of Dr. Cahn was order-disorder transformation in crystalline systems.

My first meeting with Dr.Cahn was in the office of Professor McQuillan in January, 1961 on the very day I joined the University. He felt comfortable wearing tweed jacket. He had a well built body and was of middle height. There was a typical mannerism in him of closing the eyes while expressing something more intently, He had much fascination for Indian culture and philosophy. In those days the Trilogy of Satyajit Ray were being screened in UK. Personally, I did not like the deliberate direction in the film of utmost poverty. However,the Western world had a fancy to see those episodes, with a sense of doubting whether India was ripe enough to get independence. I used to dispute with other British research workers, justifyng that the British Rule was the sole cause of our poverty. Anyway, Dr. Cahn was a very polished person, with some degree of diplomacy. He was a great lover of art and liked my inclination to that. After visiting the Birmingham Art Museum, I had purchased one picture by Joshua entitled 'The Dreamers', which I mounted on a frame and positioned in my book rack. While passing through my working laboratory, Dr Cahn once suddenly stopped to have a look on that picture frame. Another love of his was classical Western music. He and his wife were regular audience in the Philharmonic Orchestra of the city. Incidentally, his wife was the daughter of late Professor Hanson, the head of the department of Physical Metallurgy at the University of Birmingham.

The Cahn's affection towards materials science began through crystallographyHe appeared to have immense appreciation for that subject and offered himself to teach X-ray metallography to the final year metallurgy undergraduate students.He was extempore while lecturing. I did attend some of his lectures. When I joined the University, there were no Ph.D. students under him. I was told that he is in look out for a professorial position in other UK universities and that is why he preferred to have no research student at that moment of time. After a year or so, Dr. Nutting of Cambridge University became professor at Leeds University and Dr. Cahn at the University of Wales (Bangor) as the first professor in Materials Science in UK. Later on, slowly, many universities in UK one after the other started including the term 'Materials'along with metallurgy, while renaming their departments. I could see the decline of extractive metallurgy in UK and consequently they wanted to give more impetus to materials on the whole.

Dr. Cahn trained some Indian students first at the University of Wales and later in the University of Sussex. Noteworthy among them are Dr. V.S. Arunachalam and Dr. M.L. Bhatia. The latter one was my student at BHU during his M.Tech. Program. After getting the Ph.D. degree, he joined NAL and later DMRL, from where he is now retired. His research topic at the Sussex University was on recrystallisation of copper. With the lapse of time I noticed that the attention of Professor Cahn got more involved in editing journals and compiling Encyclopedia.The latest being 'Materials Science and Technology: A comprehensive Treatment', coedited by (late) Peter Haasen and E.J. Kramer (John Wiley & Sons). Another publication is 'Concise Encyclopedia of Materials Characterisation 'solely edited by Professor Cahn, which is out in its second edition (2005). Another historical publication of Professor Cahn is' Coming of Materials Science' (Elsevier), which covers the exhaustive historical account of the developments in materials education and research. Its reading is a must for any person interested in materials science. It is worth mentioning here that the beginning of the book edting by Professor Cahn began with the monumental book 'Physical Metallurgy' in the year 1961, which got published in 1965.This went through four editions, the last one edited in collaboration with Peter Haasen of Gottinegen

Professor Cahn became editor of the new Journal of Nuclear Materials in 1959, while I was still a student at BHU. He was offered the editorship of the first jounal in the field, the Journal of Materials Science in 1964, literally en route between Bangor and Sussex Universities.This was the start of a spectacular burgeoning of the scientific editing work that was to be the trademark of his later years. He says in his memoirs that he regarded the years he devoted to creating this journal as the most important single editorial role he played. He later also acted as an editor of the Journal of Materials Research from 1985 and established a new journal, Intermetallics.

Professor Cahn had great fascination for India, which brought him here a number of times. He was invited by Indian Institute of Metals in many conferences, which he accepted readily. When in early seventies, I got interested to get enrolled as a Fellow of the then Institution of Metalurgists, London, Professor Cahn nominated me for the same. I was awarded the Fellowhip on the very first nomination. It was a great moment for all of his well wishers, when Dr.Cahn was elected the Fellow of the Royal Society. As the time of his retirement approached, Dr. Cahn preferred to be connected with the University of Cambridge. He took its Fellowship. The word 'retirement' was not in the dictionary of Professor Cahn. Of late in 2004, I was in correspondance with him regarding the balanced apolitical structuring of materials science and engineering. He replied my email promptly indicating that many view in their own style and each definition has its own complexion. I must add that Dr. Cahn preferred the terminology' Materials Science and Technology', unlike Professor Ashby of Cambridge, who gave emphsasis on 'Materials Enngineering'. As an engineer, I do agree with Professor Ashby, without decrying the noble contribution of Professor Cahn. 'Technology' is a precursor of 'Engineering' and thus, a medium to translate materials science into engineering.

Dr. Cahn died of myelodysplasia induced leukemia on April 9th, 2007 in Cambridge (UK).

PROFESSOR A. C.D. CHAKLADER (CANADA)

Professor Chaklader is a graduate of the college of Ceramic Technolgy in Calcutta and a Ph.D. holder from Leeds University, U.K. My first contact with his scientific work was from his paper on hot pressing, which he had authored with another Indian student Mr Kakar. Dr, Chaklader had been utmost loyal to his employer University of Bristish Columbia, Vancouver, which he joined as Assistant Pofessor, later rising to the position of full professor. His research has been prolific ranging from clay products to advanced ceramics. He trained a large number of students from many countries, including India. My personal contacts with him were through our association with IISS. He has been a global traveller, attending all major conferences in ceramics.

Professor Chaklader was a passionate speaker in many conferences. His questions also used to be very piercing ones. I remember his supplementary question to Dr. Kothari in the Delhi International Conference on Sintering, which was initiated by Professor Petzow. Later Professor Petzow jokingly told me that that he touched Dr. Kothari, but Dr. Chaklader nailed him. Such an attitude of Dr. Chaklader should not be interpreted as if he was a harsh man. As a matter of fact, he was a kind and religious person. He and his wife were diciples of an Indian Guru.

I met Professor Chaklader a number of times in various countries. In 1987 meeting of the IISS Committee held in Tokyo, it was decided that the next international meet shall be held in Vancouver, Canada in the year 1991. Professor Chaklader was unanimously declared as the Convener of the 1991 Conference. I may here mention the rivary between USA and Canada for the future choice of the conference venue. American representatives were numerous, while Professor Chaklader was alone. I and Professor Somiya of Japan strongly defended the case of Canada. My comment that big brother should show some favour to his young brother, did tick the American.delegates and the matter was resolved amicably.

Professor Chaklader is now retired. However,of late, I could not succeed in being in contact with him.

LATE PROFESSOR R.L. COBLE (USA)

Professor R.L. Coble of MIT could be graded as one of the top academicians in ceramic science and technology. I had read his papers on sintering mechanism and few Indian students did their Ph.D. research under his guidance. One of them was Dr. T.K. Gupta. I first met Dr. Coble in Poland in the year 1979, during the International Summer School on Sintering.He came from Italy, where he did some consultancy to the famous Fiat company in Torino. He was a tall person and I presumed he had some military training in past. In the conference, he presented an invited paper. Professor George Kuczynski was also in the audience.There was an interesting, discussion in which myself and a russian scientist took part. Of course, the dogged nature of Professor Kuczynski was quite vivid. The discussion centred around what is the ideal material to be taken for basic sintering studies. Dr. Coble justified his argument with the help of the diffusion data available till then. I questioned the reliability of those data and suggested that the best way is to take recourse of electronic structures. Dr. Coble did not reply to my suggestion, but during tea break he told Professor Kuczynski 'there is some merit what this Indian scientist said.' In that way, he was quite open. He had the habit of drinking coffee just after waking up in the morning.He used to keep a mini electric kettle for that. Unfortunely he could not use that in Poland because of voltage specifications.The hotel had a strict timing for beaakfast.

Although after 1979 I never met Professor Coble, we were in constant touch through correspondence (postal).In scientific meetings, I heard people talking about the politics in MIT. Professor Petzow once reminded me that too many heavy weights should not be in a single department.

On the academic side Dr. Coble did his Sc.D. degree in Ceramics from MIT. Before joining the MIT faculty in 1960, he spent five years at the General Electric Research Laboratory, where his work led to the development of LUCALOX, a dense aluminium oxide ceramic. At MIT, he concentrated on physical ceramics and the kinetics of ceramic processes until his premature retirement in 1988. He was the Honorary Member of IISS and the Emeritus Professor of ceramics at MIT. Professor Coble was the receipient of Frenkel Award of IISS and Ross Coffin Purdy Award of the Ameriacn Ceramic Society.

Unfortunately, Professor Coble met his end in a very tragic situation. He drowned at the age of 64 in the coast of the island of Mout in Hawaii, where he lived.

LATE PROFESSOR MORRIS COHEN (USA)

Professor Morris Cohen had been an illustrious example of a person, who was extremely loyal to his employer. He started his professional career from his alma mater MIT, first as the Assistant Professor rising to the post of Professor. He was the Ph.D. thesis supervisor of some Indians including Drs. Dara Antia and V.G. Paranjpe. Dr.Cohen earned his Ph.D. in 1936 and became a full professor in 1946. He was named Ford Professor of Metallurgy in 1962, and was recognised across MIT by promotion to Institute Professor in 1975. Morris Cohen's contributions to the physical metallurgy were broad and deep-from fundamental investigations on the properties of iron and steel, especially the martensitic transformation in steel, and how microsructure improves the mechanical properties of steel, to seminal contributions to the mechanism and kinetics of the martensitic transformation, tempering phenomena, strengthening mechanism, age hardening of alloys, strain-induced transformations and rapid solidification of alloys. His work resulted in a much more basic understanding of how to make steel strong and made practical the ultrahigh strength steels used today

My first meeting with Professor Cohen was in IIT Kanpur in 1966, when he came to participate in the National Conference on Materials Science Education, organized by Professor E.C. Subba Rao. He was a good advocate of materials science, but in the core of his heart, he still was a physical metallurgist. Other participants in the conference were Professor Azroff and Professor Dorn from USA. I could notice that Professoe Azroff was more a materials scientist as compared to Professor Cohen. My next meeting with him was in 1970 at Asilomar (California) during the 2nd International Conference on the Strength of Metals and Alloys organised by ASM. There Professor Cohen delivered a very lucid and inspiring lecture on MSE. Professor Walter Owen, the then head of the Department at MIT was also there along with his American wife. He was a Britisher and was earlier a professor in the University of Liverpool UK. I could notice a trait in Americans. Some how, they preferred to offer an administrative job to a Britisher. This is a trend in Canada too.

My third meeting with Professor Cohen was in 1971 during the Silver Jubilee Celebrations of IIM. Dr Antia, his past student, had made a special attempt, so that Professor Cohen could attend the celebrations. In his lecture, he appeared to get more shifted towards materials science. During the tea break, I had a brief conversation with him. There I found him differing with Professor Tangri of University of Winnipeg, Manitoba (Canada), who had spoken on the role of acoustic emission in predicting the mechanical behaviour of metals.

Professor Cohen's contribution in science in the United States included work on Committees of the National Academy of Sciences, the National Science Foundation, NASA and the National Academy of Engineering. Durng the World war II, he succeeded as Associate Director of the Manhattan Project at MIT and also contributed to the programmes at Los Alamos National Laboratory, the Oak Ridge facilities in Tennessee, and Hanford site in Washington. In 1970, the National Academy of Science (USA) chose him to cochair the COSMAT study (Committee on the Survey of Materials Science and Engineering). Materials and Men's Needs turned out to have a very large influence on U.S. national Policy on materials education and research.

The sad end of Professor Morris Cohen came on 27th May, 2005 at the age of 93 years MIT raised an Endowed MSE Graduate Fellowship in his honour. Professor Cohen was one of the Honorary members of the Indian Institute of Metals. My friend Dr Raghavan worked for few years as a visiting scientist in his laboratory on martensitic transformation.

PROFESSOE H. DANNINGER (AUSTRIA)

Dr. Danninger did his technological education in Vienna. I met him first in the International Plansee Seminar in the late seventies, when he was a doctorate student. His area of research was tungsten heavy alloys and through discussion with him I could notice a good blend of basic and applied authority of sintering science in him. He was a smart young scientist with full of vigour. Later, I met him in other International Conferences. Of late, his interest grew in sintered steels and he has many collaborations with MIBA, the biggest powder metallurgy plant in Austria. His approach has been to go deep into the phenomenon. Even a socondary topic like lubricants did attract him to go into deeper studies. Many PM people just do not bother much and assume all lubricants with generalised character.

Apart from his research interest, Dr. Danninger is an excellent teacher too. In International Sintering 2000 Meet in New Delhi, he attended and presented two papers.He was interested in liquid phase sintering in steels and attended the International workshop on cemented carbides, which was jointly organised with Sintering 2000. He told me that he always searches solutions from other material groups as well. In that respect he has been utmost innovative. His painstaking R & D contribution also paid him soon by getting promoted in quick successions. At presnt he is a full professor and Head of the Institute of the Inorganic Materials Chemical Technology in the Technical University of Vienna. I consider him one of the top powder metallurgist of the present generation.There are many more expectations from him. He has been a Skupy lecturer at the Hagen symposium in 2006. Very recently in 2010 he was honoured as the Fellow of American Powder Metallurgy Institute International.Dr.Danninger has worked as an effective bridge between Eastern and Western Europe.

Mr Edul M. Daver (USA)

During the 1970 International Powder Metallurgy Conference held in New York, I met a very energetic youth, who had just finished his M. Tech. under Dr. J.S. Hirschhorn and was on the staff of Alcan Metal Powders in New Jersy, USA. He approached me first and introduced himself as the past student of Professor Tendolkar at IIT Bombay. He was so eager to treat me that he invited me to his company's suite in the conference hotel venue Waldorf Astoria. With the passage of time he got regular promotions in his organisation, with which he was utmost loyal. Presently he is in top position of the Company as President. Alcan wound up the aluminium powder business and they did not mind to sell the major share of the company to Mr Daver.The present name of the company is A Cu powder LLC.

Mr Daver has been very helpful to me in giving per gratis different grades of Al-powder prenixes including Tribaloy intermetallics for my research at IIT Kanpur.This has been gratefully acknowledged in our various publications. I met Mr Daver in a number of times in various locations in the world during International PM Conferences. He is a sobre person, and has been a keen watcher of India's technological progress in all stages of economies; both command and liberalised ones.

Daver belongs to Parsee community of India, who are always peace loving. but are also shrewd businesmen. I was in 2010 World PM Congress in Florence and here too I met Mr Daver He had been the President of the prestigious Metal Powder Industries Federation of USA in the year 2006 and delivered the North American PM Status Report in the World PM Congress held in Busan (S, Korea) in September, 2006.

DR. J. DUSCZYCK (THE NETHERLANDS)

During my visit of Poland in the year 1979, Dr. Dusczyck and myself met briefly in the International PM Conference organised in the city of Poznan. He had a distinction of being both a scientist and an engineer. I was in touch with his publications in PM journals. Later he moved to The Netherlands in search of a suitable job. In those days there was a lot of political unrest and turmoil in Poland and the Government was not seriously looking after the interest of its scientists.This led to a major migration of scientists from Poland.

In 1981, during the International Plansee Seminar, Dr Dusczyck along with his family was in Austria and there I had a chance to interact with him in a greater detail. I found him a smart individual with a sense of humour. He was an effective speaker and one can make out the glimps of confidence in him. At the Delft Technical University, Dr.Dusczyck was entirely engrossed with PM of aluminium alloys including the extrusion aspects. His competent engineering education in Poland was handy for him in solving powder extrusion problems. In the year 1989, on my invitation, he attended the Sintering Conference in New Delhi organised by me. There I noticed his keen interest in Indian history and culture.

In the year 1991, during my European trip, while going to Canada to attend the International Sintering Conference organised by Professor Chakalader, I passed through Amsterdam by train. There at the railway platform in the broad day light I was robbed of my briefcase, which contained all important documents including the passport and money. I was in a real mess and approached the Indian Embassy at The Hague for the duplicate passport. Luckily my Eurail pass was in my pocket, so I could make the rail travel to The Hague.At Indian Embassy, I met Mr Shastri, who gave me the fresh passport. I engaged him in some conversation and he told me he is from coastal Andhra Pradesh. I was rather amused to find a government servant in foreign service with such a narrow mind as to tell the subarea of his province. Seeing my plight Mr Shastri was kind enough to contact the Delft University and eventually to Dr.Dusczyck. He fixed a time in the afternoon to meet me at the Delft railway station. There he gave me some Dutch money and also a very timely dinner in the restaurant of the railway station. No doubt I was hungry at that time. I did not forget the timely help from him all along. During 2010 World PM Congress held in Italy I knew Dr. Duszcyck shall be there.and I paid back the sum of money which he gave to me in Delft. It was so nice to meet my friend after the gap of nearly twenty years. Here I must tell another incidence too. I must confess my sin to travel from The Hague railway station to the Indian Embassy by bus without ticket.The bus was withot any conductor. I know it was an offence, but was determined to face the eventuality. May be my description of this Amsterdam episode may be useful to some of the readers of this passage. In order to compensate my sin, later I did give some money to a needy begger in Amstardam. Late Dr.L.R. Vaidyanath of Indian Copper Development Centre did tell me his story. That was still amazing. It was robbing right from the Amsterdam airport, which is not at all crowded like the railway station

DR. SUNIL DUTTA (USA)

In Cleveland's (USA) Indian community, practically every one knows Dr. Sunil Dutta. He is an extremely sociable person with much charm and wits. Dr. Dutta is an expert in advanced ceramics and works in NASA Centre for research in Clevelend. I met him first in 1987 in Tokyo's Sintering Conference. He was of similar age to me. There he presented a paper and had some tiff with the Technical Session Charman Dr. W.A. Kaysser. Kaysser like a typical German was very strict with timings. This annoyed Dutta. In Tykyo we went together to visit shopping malls along with another Indian scientist Dr. K. Ramesh, who was doing post doctoral research at the Tokyo Institute of Technology. I noticed Dutta being surrounded by many overseas delegates. Later, Dr. Ramesh told me that they were seekers of research fund, in which NASA was very rich. Dr. Dutta was a key man in such agreements. He is an expert in structural ceramics.The research training of Dutta was in Sheffield University, where he was awarded the Ph.D. degree. Professor Paul of IIT Kharagpur was his contemporary at Sheffield.

Dr. Dutta is a frequent visitor of India and particularly Kolkata, He is a Bhadralok Bengalee with a charming wife. In 1988 during my USA visit, I made a point to visit the Dutta family. I was staying in the Cleveland Clinic Hotel, where once the Shah of Iran used to stay. Dr Dutta treated me exceptionally well and showed his area of social activities among the Indian community. I felt such activities kept him pretty young. Although he never lived in North India, he had a good knowledge of Hindi. Luckily Professor Paul was also in Cleveland in those days. The Dutta family invited both of us on dinner and also Dr. Ranjit (Ron) Dutta who was working in General Electric's plant in Cleveland. As a matter of fact Ranjit came to pick me up from the hotel. He was still a bachelor and had no plans for marriage. On our arrival at his house,Dutta family greeted us warmly and we had a sumptuous Bengalee dinner. Paul was always talking in Bengalee, which Sunil could feel. I could understand Bengalee to some extent. I could guess that Dr. Paul was some sort of a political type person. Later I came to know that he was a member of Indian National Congress Party of India. Somehow he was not pulling on well with the then Director of his Institute,Professor K.L. Chopra. Paul was a proud person with an element of arrogance too. Incidentally Paul was with IIT Kanpur too for few years after his Ph.D. completion from Sheffield University in the area of glass technology. As it was late in night, I was badly feeling sleepy. Paul had no problem, because he was staying with Dr. Dutta. I did not like to disturb them in their animated talk. Dr. Ranjit Dutta was very rational; he could understand the whole thing. Any way we took leave from Dutta family and Ranjit dropped me to my hotel and said' You are my Guru.'I got surprised by this statement.He then elaborated that he had read our book on Metallurgical Thermodynamics and Kinetics, which was very educative. I was really flattered.

In the year 1989, I had invited Dr. Sunil Dutta to attend the New Delhi Conference on Sintering and present an invited paper. He accepted it readily and participated along with his wife. They did a lot of shopping in Delhi. I still remember his fine banquet speech in the conference dinner.

Last I heard from Sunil was after 9/ 11. He was very much agitated like all of us and was circulating messages on the emails. In one of the emails I replied saying that Bin Laden was originally pampered by USA and now he is a problem for all of us. I also mentioned that USA had double standard as far as terrorism is concerned. This is much before 26/ 11 incident in Mumbai of the year 2008. Of late, I have no news from my friend, but trust he is doing excellent in serving the Indian community in Cleveland and USA at large.

LATE PROFESSOR H.E. EXNER (GERMANY)

In the year 1970, the International Conference on Powder Metallurgy organised by the Metal Powder Industries Federation, USA was held in Warldorf Astoria Hotel in New York. There I saw a thin tall German among the delegates. I came to know he is from the Powder Metallurgy Laboratory of Max Planck Institute for Metals Research, Stuttgart. We were not introduced to each other in that big crowd., but I could gauge his sharp intelligence through his questions on various papers. It was in 1979 that I came to closer contact during the Powder Metallurgy Conference held at Penta hotel in London organised by the Institute of Metals, London. Exner was the student of Professor Fischmeister. Other past students who attended the meeting were Dr. Kehl and Dr. Arzt. The Stuttgart PM team was internationally known and every one in the audience listened to those papers with due attention. There I met Dr. Kaysser, who had just finished his D.Ing. degree. Dr. Exner can be regarded as one of the top physical metallurgists in Germany. An Austrian by birth, he did his education including the doctorate on cemented carbides from Leoben Technical University. He also collaborated with Professor Petzow and both wrote many seminal papers on sintering theory. In the year 1986, during my Stuttgart visit, Dr. Exner had moved to the laboratory of Professor Fischmeister in the down town campus. I took an appointment to meet him in his laboratory. He warmly received me and talked on various topics right from Indian Philosophy to sintering.

Dr. Exner was the editor of a very effective journal 'Practical Metallography', where each paper is in two languages : English and German. His wife used to do translation work in English. During my visit of Stuttgart in 1989, as a gesture, he presented me all the old issues of the journal 'Powder Metallurgy International', of which he was the editor. He did not attend the Dusseldorf European Powder Metallurgy Conference organised few weeks before my actual visit to him. On my becoming inquisitive, his answer was very simple.; He devotes his time more in science rather than technology'. My book on cemented carbides was full length reviewed by him in his journal' Practical Metallography'. He was so meticulous that he pointed out my inconsistency in the spellings of few proper nouns.

My interaction with Professor Exner made me convinced that he is plain talker and expresses his feelings with due robustness. I invited him to visit India and particularly to IIT Kanpur. He had in past visited India a number of times, but limited himself to only IIT Madras. He was much influenced by the ancient temples and architecture of South India.

After listening his many papers, I was convinced by the incisive approach of Professor Exner in research. He invariably started with first principles and reached the conclusion with much lucidity. A parrallelism I found in late Professor Easterling of UK. In the International Plansee Seminar of the year 1997, I met him again. This time Professor German (USA) was also a participant. Dr. Exner was not very happy with the costly experiments the Americans did in cooperation with NASA only to conclude the established trends in sintering.

Among Indians Professor Vinod K. Sarin of Boston University was a good friend of Professor Exner. Professor Exner had a soft corner for hard materials, an area which he commenced during his doctorate period in Stockholm. No wonder he never missed the chance to attend all the sequential international conferences on hard materials originally started by Late Professor Gurland of the Brown University at Rhodes Island in USA.

In the year 1998, Professor K.A. Padmanabhan, the Director of IIT Kanpur requested Professor Exner to extend his journay to Kanpur from Bangalore, where he was to attend the IIM Annual Technical Meeting. Professor Exner very kindly accepted the invitation and in the packed hall presented his overview on sintering mechanism. He visited my powder metallurgy research laboratory and was quite impressed. After his seminar, he took Dr. Padmanabhan in a corner along with me and enquired what he is thinking about the future of my laboratory at IIT Kanpur. He knew that I am retiring within two to three years. While talking to me, he emphasised how Germans plan well ahead to keep the continuity of their academic programmes.

Professor Exner received numerous awards from different countries. One of the Awards he particularly cherished is the award that is named after his academic teacher, the Roland-Mitsche which he received in 1998 together with his wife, in appreciation of his contributions in the field of metallographic materials' analysis.

Professor Exner expired on 14ᵗʰ October, 2009. His school fostered concise analytical thinking, stimulated to always substantiate experimental results theoretically, and, last but not least, required to present the results convincingly and with precise formulations. Myself, Professor Petzow and Dr Markus Rettenmayr wrote the obituary, which got published in the International Journal of Refractory Metals and Hard materials (Vol. 28, No 4, July 2010, p.558). His more than 100 Ph.D. students are with us to propagate the rigour of research in physical metallurgy, which my friend Eckart always cherished.

LATE PROFESSOR ERIC FITZER (GERMANY)

I met Professor Fitzer, first, in the International Plansee Seminar He was a native of Austria and was a professor in the chemical technology faculty of the Karlsruhe University. He was tall and robust in built. His lectures on carbon and carbon-carbon composites were very original and he developed techniques for drawing carbon fibres. In those days, the aerospace industries were in rise and so, Professor Fitzer was a much sought after scientist throughout the world. So much so, that he was not easily available in his University and most of the time was abroad. This did not mean that he neglected the University work. His very able faculty member was Dr. Schligting, whom I happened to know very closely. When I visited his department in the year 1979, Dr. Schligting took care of my comfort. Professor Fitzer and his wife visited India a number of times under the United Nations Development Scheme on carbon fibres. He loved visiting Kerala State and was fond of its beaches.

At Karlsruhe, I presented a seminar in the department of Professor Fitzer. Dr. Schlgting accompanied me and my wife to show near about places including Baden-Baden. He was an emotional person and from his conversations I could feel a pain in him of the divided Germany. On one occasion there was practically tears in his eyes. We still remember his sumptuous lunch in a lake side restaurant at Baden-Baden. He had a bad liver and was not in excellent state. We had to catch the train for Frankfurt and suddenly he heard the news of traffic jam in the highway. Somwhow through a different route he made us to reach the railway station in time. Unfortunately the life-span of this bright scientist was cut short and he died after major liver complications. I badly miss a sincere friend in him.

Professor Fitzer became a loner after the death of his loyal colleague Dr. Schligting. However, he never, missed the occasion to attend the International Plansee seminars in Austria. On one accasion (1985) he and his wife were with an Indian student, who was the son of an Indian Diplomat in Bonn. He rushed to introduce me that boy. The boy was a decent one with pleasing personality. Dr. Fitzer's contribution in training the scientists at National Physical Laboratory. New Delhi and Indian Space Research Organisation in the area of carbon fibre shall ever be remembered.

Unfortunately Professor Fitzer is no more with us. His widow lives in Germany.

PROFESSOR R. M. GERMAN (USA)

When the world renowned powder metallurgist Profesor F.V. Lenel of Rensselaer Polytechnic Institute (RPI), Troy (USA) was on the verge of retirement in early 1980s, his Institute was on the look out for his successor. They found a young scientist Dr. R.M. German for that. Dr German was then on R&D staff of Mott Corporation, of Connecticut State. He joined RPI as assistant professor and worked very hard to retain the stature of the laboratory. He received very liberal fundings and his laboratory got a number of novel equipments, which were not available earlier. In 1981 during the Sintering Conference in Yugoslavia, I met Dr. German for the first time. He had known my research work and as a matter of fact had referred my work in his papers too. In the year 1984 during the International PM Conference in Toronto, I visited Troy along with my wife and held discussions with him. My past student Mr Deepak Madan was doing his Ph.D. research under him. In addition, I saw a score of Chinese/ South Korean students too. What struck me most was the ambition of this young powder metallurgist. He always wanted to be on the top, but at the same time he toiled too. I found some sort of killer instinct in him. With the passage of time our cooperation increased more and more. In the beginning of 1990s, Dr. German decided to move to Pennsylvania State University as a full professor. He was worthy of that post and he made all his RPI students to move in the new location. Another student of mine at IIT Kanpur Mr. Rajiv Tondon joined his team at Penn State to work on PM stainless steels.

The scientific and technological contributions of Professor German are enormous. In addition, he is a much sought after consultant for PM industries. He often engages his students in cousulting projects. It is a good training to them for acquainting with the real industrial problems

Profesor German's publication list exceeds 750 papers, 20 edited books. He is co-inventor of numerous patents. His 12 books include Liquid Phase Sintering, Particle Packing Characteristics, Sintering Theory and Practice, Powder Metallurgy of Iron and Steel, Injection Moulding of Metals and Ceramics (with A, Bose) and User's Guide to Powder Injection Moulding-Design and Applications. In addition he a receipient of numerous awards from IISS and MPIF.

In November of the year 1995, Professor German along with Professor Messing organised the International Sintering Conference in Penn State University. I went to attend that. The added attraction was more so, since my son Anish was doing his Ph.D. research under him. The conference was a big success. There I met Professor Johnson of North-Western University after a gap of 25 years. Professor Palmour II of the University of North Carolina was also there. I was impressed after seeing the experimental facilities of German's laboratory. It was many times bigger than what I saw at RPI. It appeared that the industries in Pennsylvania State were very forthcoming to assist Professor German.

I and Professor German used to exchange our publications. We also reviewed each other's books and published the same in the PM journals here and in USA. There were critics of German too. Late Professor Courtney of Michigan Tech University and late professor H.E. Exner were notable. I recall in one of the Plansee Seminars held in 1997, Professor Exner was very critical of the costly research on sintering under microgravity in the space shuttles, which were quite predictive even otherwise

Profesor German is an untring person. He wanted to be away from any sort of bureaucracy. This led him to start a new 'Centre for Innovative Sintered Products' at Penn State University. It was a sort of research consortium in which many PM industries came forward to cooperate. I am pleased that this Centre is running presently in the able hands of Dr. Donald F. Heaney, Associate Professor. The profound zeal in Professor German did not rest in Penn State Univrsity only. Few years back, he decided to switch over to University in Mississipi, where he was the Director of the Centre for Advanced Vehicular Systems in its Department of Mechanical Engineering. I had an impression that now he will be settled in Mississipi State University, but I was wrong. Professor German moved again, and this time to the San Diego State University in the California State (USA). He has also, recently, started a new organisation named 'German Materials Technology'.

Professor German possesses the quality of a shrewd evaluator. After receiving the copy of our book 'Materials Science and Engineering' presented to him, he complimented it as a significant task (letter dated 22nd September, 2006 to the coaouthor).But at the same time added :' In the USA such text books need to be rewritten and issued as new volumes every year or so since answers to questions get out and the used books or illegal copies will kill sales.' It appears this symptom prevailing in USA is coming to be true in India as well.

LATE PROFESSOR N.J. GRANT (USA)

After graduating from MIT in the year 1944 in Metallurgical Engineering, Dr. Grant became an instructor there. He became a full Peofessor in 1956 and then served as the Director of the Centre for Materials Science and Engineering from 1968 to 1977. Dr. Grant did considerable research in dispersion strengthened alloy systems and I was very keen to meet him. In the year 1970 this got materialised, when in the summer I was the Visiting Associate Professor at RPI. I called him and fixed an appointment. I took the morning coach from Troy and reached Boston. From there I reached MIT, which is in Cambridge, just crossing the river. Uptil then I was not knowing that Professor Grant is of a Russian origin. He came to USA along with his parents, while he was just a child. I talked about our research on Al-based PM composites and he commented that I have selected a difficult system.The laboratory of Professor Grant was shown to me in detail by Mr Vinod Sarin, an Indian research student, who is now a professor in the Manufacturing Engineering Department of Boston University. I met in his laboratory my old friend at BHU Mr Mahohar Singh Grewal, a sikh,,who was one year senior to me. He was then a Ph.D. student under professor Grant.The laboratory of Professor Grant was very active in those days. He had just started work on rapidly solidified alloy systems. I could gather that he is a consultant of many giant metallurgical and manufacturing companies.That was one of the reasons why his students did not find any problrm in getting lucrative jobs. I could notice that his laboratory was full of experimentalists and the simulation studies had not yet infected them.

My second meeting with Professor Grant was in Kiev in 1977 during the International PM Conference organised by Academician Fedorchenko. There Professor Grant was specially treated by the hosts. The last visit of mine at MIT was in the year 1995. By that time he was retired and was an Emeritus Professor. He was then a relatively free man with no research students. I was interested in seeing his atomizing unit for preparing rapidly solidified alloy powders. He took me in the basement and showed me the facilities. They were all unattended and I felt a bit sorry. But, strangely he was not sorry at all. He smiled and said every good thing has an end. What a typical Indian philosophical approach. During my discussion in his office, the telephone receiver rang. It appeared he was not amused. The more he wanted to cut short the conversation, the more the other party was involving him. This made him annoyed and he just spoke loudly : 'Look I have a visitor with me, Plaese do not disturb me any more'. He kept the receiver a bit stoutly. He told me that the gentleman on the other side was a broker, pestering him to buy more and more shares. He, then, directed his conversation in a different direction and said the US economy is in plight. Every where there is deficit. I did not add anythings to his comment. I was curious to know the modern emphasis, which his department was putting in Materials Science and Engineering education. He introduced me to another gentleman (I don't recollect his name.), who explained me their new approach. I noticed how well they were integrating materials science with engineering, in contrast to us in India, who are fighting among each other being in two distinct camps. I took my lunch in the cafeteria of MIT, where I noticed practically every student wearing a serious look. The giggle and laughter of students seen in other universities were missing. This made me convinced, why MIT is with a difference and preoccupies an eminent position in international science and technology. Incidentally, some of the famous powder metallurgists of Europe were trained by Professor Grant. Professor Paul Schwarzkopf, the owner of the Plansee AG, Ausria sent his son Walter to do his Masters' thesis under Professor Grant. Walter, later, became the Chairman of Plansee AG. Unfortunatelt, he is no more with us and his son looks after this famous company.

Among the famous Indian students of Professor Grant were Dr. V.K.Sarin, Dr. M.S. Grewal, Dr. G Rai, and Dr. Dalal. The last two persons were products of IIT, Bombay, while Sarin did his undergraduate studies in USA. Dr. Rai was for a while at SAIL R & D Centre, Ranchi, but later migrated to USA. He got a good job at GE in USA. I have in my personal library the Proceedings of the conference, which the past research students of Professor Grant organised to commemorate his retirement from MIT.

Professor Grant published over 500 papers and held over 130 patents. In addition he worked with many Government Committees and Agencies, including NASA, NATO, the Atomic Energy Commission and the Department of Defence. Professor Grant had a unique ability to foster leadership. So many of his graduates went to very high positions of leadership in industry.

Professor Grant died on May 1, 2004 at the age of 88, after a battle with Alzheimer's desease.

LATE PROFESSOR H. H. HAUSNER (USA / AUSTRIA)

Professor Henry H. Hausner was born in Vienna, earned a degree of Doctor of Engineering from the Univesity of Vienna in 1938. His interest in PM began then when he joined the Incandescent Lamp Company and began working with tungsten PM products. He immigrated to the United States in 1940 and worked for American Electro Metal Corporation, General Ceramics Corporation and Sylvania Electric Company,where he developed PM nuclear fuel elements made from uranium, beryllium and zirconium. He was an adjunct professor at New York University and the Polytechnic Institute of Brooklyn, New York. He established a successful PM consulting business in 1956 when he left Sylvania, one of his clients including General Electric, Westinghouse, Battelle, Los Alamos National Laboratory and the U.S. Atomic Energy Commission.

Professr Hausner was a registered professional engineer and authored or edited more than 48 technical books and technical meeting proceedings. He wrote more than 180 technical papers.He had 9 patents and organised many symposia, conferences and courses around the world. He was the founding editor of International Journal of Powder Metallurgy and served as editor-in-chief for 20 years. When he was 84 he relinquished the reins of the Journal to Professor Alan Lawley in 1985.

My first acquaintance with Professor Hausner was in 1968 in the Plansee Seminar. I had gone there from Kiev. During the tea break I shook hand with him. He treated me warmly as if we knew each other for quite some time. I was not aware that only recently he had visited India. Professor Oleg Roman of USSR was a visiting professor at IIT, Kharagpur and had been in past in USA at RPI. At Kharagpur Professor Roman had organised an International Conference in which Professor Hausner was an invitee. I was not aware of Professor Roman by that time. When Professor Hausner mentioned his name, I thought he was some Indian scientist with the surname 'Raman'. At Brooklyn Polytechnic Institute, where Dr. Hausner was an Adjunct professor, he had many Indian students as his course takers. He always had praise for them.

Professor Hausner was the founder editor-in-Chief of the International Journal of Powder Metallurgy publishd by APMI International, Princeton, NJ. He used to review my manuscripts and offered valuable comments and suggestions. His old age was not an impediment with his editorial and consultancy work. His consulting office was right in Manhattan in New York city. He had been the Ph.D. external examiner of some of my students. In the examiner's report, he was very particular that all the powders used for the subsequent PM processing were fully characterised. Sometimes we did not take full cognizance of his advice. Now we appreciate how correct and wise his suggestions used to be.

The love and attraction of Austria, the motherland of Professor Hausner, brought him at the fag end of his life to settle in Salzburg. He was a keen musician and was a keen attendee of Salzburg Philharmonic group.

After the death of his first wife Professor Hausner remarried and lived together very harmoniously. I met her in 1971 Plansee Seminar, and presented her the famous silk scarf made in my native place Varanasi. She was having a poor health and, therefore, could not attend the 1984 award ceremony in Toronto, where Professor Hausner was awarded the' Powder Metallurgy Poineer Award'. After few months I heard the news of her death in New York. After donating his personal library to APMI International's Headquarters, Professor Hausner decided to shift to Salzburg permanently. We were in regular correspondence. My 1994 G.D. Birla Memorial Lecture of the Indian Institute of Metals was dedicated to him. He was extremely pleased to receive the printed copy of my lecture. His eyes gradually stopped functioning properly and he became practically blind. His assistant read my paper to him and he dictated his final thanks giving reply to me. The letter was signed by him in an imperfect style.

This event struck deep into my heart. It is practically difficult to get such a noble soul in modern times.

Dr. Hausner died on 4th July, 1995 at his home in Salzburg (Austria) at an age of 94 years.

PROFESSOR LAI HO-YI (PEOPLE REPUBLIC OF CHINA)

I first met Professor Lai Ho-Yi in the International PM Conference in the year 1984 at Toronto. The conference was organised by MPIF, USA. He was the Group Leader of the Chinese delegation, who were about 15 in number. In that conference, I was struck to see all the Chinese in the same make of suit, except that of Professor Lai Ho Yi. Seeing the respect he was getting not only from his Chinese fellows, I was convinced that he is undoubtedly an important personality. I introduced myself and developed some sort of friendship with him in a very formal manner. I knew that he had spent a number of years in Sweden in the Chalmers University under Professor Fischmeister. In that respect he was the first generation of Chinese scientist, who were sent by their Government to get research experience in Europe. Professor Ho-Yi was of my age. I would like here to praise the wisdom of Chinese authorities for their priorities so as to depute right type of persons at right places for advanced training abroad. The secret of the same type and make of suit was still baffling me and I was told that loose size suits were kept ready in the department stiores in China, so that they may be wearable by different sized persons. Because of language problem, the Chinese delegation always used to be together, even attending the same technical session.

Professor Lai Ho Yi was the Head of the Powder Metallurgy Departmet in the Beijing University of Science and Technology, one of the best Government funded Universities in China. His research contribution was prolific. He was an influential person in China. I recall one of our papers on PM aluminium alloy was publishd by a Chinese Publishing House in one of the Proceedings. Even after my repeted request, they rather ignored to reply me. At last I approached Professor Ho-Yi. He was instrumental in instructing them to act promptly. What a surprise? Within a week I received the proceedings by air mail from the publishers. I, thus, concluded that big persons do matter in China. Something like this is also here in India,

LATE PROFESSOR BERNARD ILSCHNER
(GERMANY / SWITZERLAND)

In the year 1973, the Metallurgical Engineering Department of the Banaras Hindu University had organised an International conference on the occasion of its Golden Jubilee Celebrations. It was there I first met Professor Ilschner. He was a good friend of Professor T.R. Anantharaman. Another interest of Professor Ilschner was the Indian culture. He had long association with the University of Erlangen, where he invited many BHU faculty members including Dr. K.A. Padmanabhan and Dr. R.P. Wahi. My acquaintance with him was rather brief Later I came to know his work on functionally graded materials. I invited him in the 1989 Delhi International Conference on Sintering. He was, then, a visiting professor at Stanford University, USA and deputed his coauthor to attend and present their paper. Dr. Ilschner can be regarded as one of the top materials scientists in Germany specialising in mechanical behavior of engineering materials. Later he moved to Federal Institute of Technology, Luissane (Switzerland) as a full professor and head of the mechanical metallurgy division. During one of my European visits in the year 1991, I visited his beautiful city and famous Institute. I was his guest and still remember vividly his utmost sense of hospitality. As soon as I alighted from the train in Lussane, he took hold of my suitcase and carried till the car parking station. I resisted him, but he did not agree. It was a real Indian hospitality. A much older person than me, his action really touched me. In the evening we took dinner in an open-air restaurant near the lake. He was an enthusiastic person, bubbling wth ideas.We talked on varied things right from national politics to professional subjects. He told me about his second marriage and the kids from his wife. He wanted to get them settled suitably and that was the main reason, why he and his family had moved to Switzerland. The economy of Switzerland was much more better than that of Germany. Professor Ilschner was an editor of the Series on 'Materials Technology' published by Springer, Berlin.

Next morning, I visited Professor Ilschner's research laboratory, which was rich in experimental facilities. The modern trend of simulation studies did not overshadowed his research team. Fatigue of metallic and ceramic systems had been one of the favoirite topics.

Professor Ilschner had been a frequent visitor of India and each time he never forgot to visit South India. The splendid high rising temples had been his greatest attractions.In addition, he used to interact with IIT, Madras as well, since the latter was basically funded by the German Government.

In the later part of his career, like other West European metallurgists, Professor Ilschner too got converted into the guild of materials scientists. In the 1996, he was in Delhi to attend the Golden Jubilee Celebrations of IIM. Some of the office bearers of IIM were too much fascinated with the term 'Materials Science', although there is another organisation in India 'Materials Research Society of India'.Their intention was to change the name of IIM. As a Council Member of IIM, I had differed with other Council Members. Some of them had probably briefed Prorfessor Ilschner in advance and requested him to speak few introductory words about it. Although his paper's topic was entirely different he devoted few minutes to sing the praise of the new trend. I could smell the matter and in the discussion time at the end of his paper lucidly presented the case of furthering extractive metallurgy in the developing countries like China and India. I could sense that Professor Ilschner felt a bit awkward. There was a big applause after my comments. Later some past Presidents including one current Vice-President of IIM thanked me for my timely intervention. I during the tea break, apologized to Professor Ilschner in case I was a bit abrasive. By that time he had understood the whole matter and reassured me by saying that I was right. He told me that he was saying that as a West European and your IIM people should priorotise the national needs. I wished he told this publicly.

My last meeting with Professor Ilschner was at IIT Kanpur in the year 1999 or so. Our Director Professor K.A. Padmanabhan had specially invited him to visit the campus. This was the first visit of Professor Ilschner to IIT Kanpur. He told me about his hugh preoccupation in edting the Encyclopedia of Materials Science and Technology, published by Elsevier. Few years after that I heard the news of the sad demise of this great materials scientist.

PROFESSOR SHINHOO KANG (S. KOREA)

I was not knowing about this bright South Korean materials scientist Dr. Kang till the year 2000, when I organised the International Sintering Conference in New Delhi. After seeing the scientific events columns in relevant journal, Dr. Kang wrote me his desire to attend the conference and present a paper. I was delighted and placed his paper in the invited category. Since my research work has been in the area of cemented carbides, I was particular to meet this scientist. He came to Delhi along with his wife. Both appeared to be very compatible couple. He presented his paper in the conference and made friendship with many. My next meeting with Dr. Kang was in his own country South Korea in the city Busan in the year 2006 during the World Powder Metallurgy Congress. He is always a man in low profile and never tries to oversell his ideas. But at the same time, he possesses a holistic scientific view in materials science ie. structure-properties-processing-performance relationship. This training he definitely got from his engineering education in USA first at RPI (1974-78, BS Degree) and later at MIT, from where he was awarded MS degree in 1980 and Ph.D in 1983. For both the latter two degrees his supervisor was the famous late Professor N.J. Grant. His interest in hard materials arose after getting appointment with GTE Laboratories at Waltham in Massachusetts State, where he worked for full 9 years (1983-92).His another MIT alumnus Dr. Vinod Sarin was also working in that laboratory. The GTE management wanted to avail the services of Dr Kang for solving many engineering problems in cutting tools and, therefoe, transferred him to their plant GTE Valenite Inc. at Troy in Michigan State. There Dr. Kang stayed for a short period of only one year and eventually took the decision to serve his motherland. In 1993 he joined Seoul National University as a full professor, which he is continuing with due vigour. In the area of hard materials he picked up Ti(CN) based cermets, which have nishe applications. With the dwindling resources of tungsten, it is very opportune to lay emphasis on titanium refractory compounds, which are much lighter in density than tungsten based compounds. Although South Korea is not poor in tungsten resources, but still they are having a correct future planning.

Last time when I met Dr. Kang and his wife, it was 2010 in Florence in Italy during World PM Congress. Here too he presented an invited paper, which was attentively listened by the delegates. Dr. Kang has 96 publications and 25 patents in his credit.The relatively large number of patents speak loud of his contribution to hard material industry. He has guided so far 49 MS and 23 Ph.D. theses at Seoul. He is a member of the Editorial Advisory Commttee of the International Journal Refractory Metals and Hard Materials (Elsevier). The hard materials community is watching closely the progress of this bright scientist, who is bound to receive many more laurels.

DR.A. Q. KHAN (PAKISTAN)

During the period of late Mrs. Benazir Bhutto's premiership of Pakistan, there was a thaw in Indo-Pak relations.The Ist circular of the Interntional Conference on Advanced Materials to be held in September, 1989 in Islamabad was duly received by me. I sent the abstracts of my two papers, which the organisers accepted in the Invited Category. My Institute, IITK, permitted me to attend the conference and I found not much difficulty to get the visa. I booked my air ticket with the Pakistan Airlines, the route was Delh-Lahore-Islamabad. At the New Delhi air port, I met two of my old colleagues of the University of Roorkee Dr.D.B. Goel and Dr. V.K. Tiwari, who were also going to attend the conference. On arrival in Pakistan,we were warmly received at the Islamabad airport and put up in the 'Hotel Islamabad',the conference venue. Next morning during registration period, we met Dr. A.Q. Khan, a tall, wheatish coloured gentleman. I had heard about his work in Belgium and the Netherlands and read his edited book entitled 'Advances in Physical Metallurgy' published by Butterworths, UK in end of fiftees I could visualise the great significance attached to Dr. Khan in Pakistan. Every one wanted to come closer to him and wish him. When the late President Zia-ul Haq visited his Institute, he announced the renaming of the Institute as A. Q. Khan Laboratory. This Laboratory is situated in Kohuta, not far from Islamabad. Most of their materials related scientists were attending the conference. They had their advanced education mostly in USA and Europe. I met Dr. Ortner of Plansee AG Austria He was a bit surprised to see me there. Probably, he thought that due to adverse relations the Indian nationals shall not be attending the conference. I also guessed there must be some business of A.Q. Khan Laboratory with Plansee AG. I attended a number of Plansee Seminars in Austria, but did never encounter any Pakistani delegate. Of late I found Dr. Ortner a bit over generous towards Pakstan in inviting a young Ph.D degree holder from a Chinese University to join the Editorial Board of the International Journal of Refractory Metals and Hard Materials. I got the impression that Pakistanis were intentionally not willing to have visibility and doing their job more secretly. The fundings for nuclear activities were first made by Lybia and then by Saudi Arabia.

A very strange thing happened during that period. The BCCI Bank in UK became broke. There was a rumour that the whole money was channelised to the secret nuclear programme in Pakistan. Some of the overseas delegates from Europe were of dubious affiliations. Some of the famous participants were Professor Bunge of Clauthal, Germany, and Professor Braber from Belgium. Professor Bunge was with his wife, who was always well covered, so as not to hurt any Muslim sentiment.

My conversation with Dr. Khan, during the conference, was twice: first during the registration time and second during the dinner. Among the Pakistanis was one old retired Professor in Physics. He originally belonged to Hyderabad in South India prior to partition of India. Though the Pakistanis of the Uttar Pradesh origin were very keen to talk with me, this old professor always avoided me. Dr. Khan warmly informed me that he had read our text book 'Metallurgical Thermodynamics and Kinetics'. He also narrated about his late father, who got settled in Bhopal and then in Nagpur. His father was a teacher and was not in an excellent relation with Dr. Khan's grandfather. His grandfather, a Pathan, was doing the business of horse trading and they used to pass through the G T road regularly. Kanpur too was a stop for them. During partition, the mother of Dr. Khan along with her young son movd to Karachi in Pakistan. This city is populated by Mohazirs (the muslim migrants from India). During our conversation, he spoke how our reputed Journalist Mr Kuldip Nayar interviewed him at his residence in the mid-eighties. The interview was facilitated by a Pakistani journalist, who was known to Dr. Khan. Dr. Khan was a proud person and wanted to show to others that they were in no way inferior to any one in the world.

I was not much acquainted with all the works directed by Dr. Khan. However, maraging steel was the favourite topic of his, including it's tube forming. He was naturally very much involved in the uranium enrichment. After 9 / 11, the whole world knew about the clandestine activities of Dr. Khan. My impression was that Pakistanis, unlike Indians, were more mission oriented. They did not believe much in paper publications. May be their masters were predominantly targeting the production of nuclear devices.

I could also see the apparent nexus between the Pakistani army and the A.Q Khan Laboratory. The conference was fully videographed and at the end of each day the army elites usd to view the same, particularly the question / answer periods. They were very keen to read between the lines.

This information was gauged by me while talking with an army man in a civilian dress. One thing is clear-a better Indian strategy shall be to give more power to some of her top scientists/ technologists and at the same time to remain focussed in few areas. Spreading thin for any country is not at all advantageous. Whatever negative aspects we mark on Dr.A.Q. Khan, he made his country to be noticed with utmost attention. Sometimes an element of deception becomes a boon.

Very recently I read in the newspapers that this disgraced scientist has been allowed by Pakistani authorities to attend public functions after being kept in 'protective custody' for the past six years following his acknowledgement that he ran a clandestine nuclear proliferation network.

LATE PROFESSOR RICHARD KIEFFER (AUSTRIA)

Professor Kieffer's contribution in the area of refractory metals and their compounds is phenomenal.He was the scientist who switched over to academia from industry. He was the right hand man of Professor Paul Schwarzkopf, the famous Austrian professor and industrialist, who founded the Metalwerk Plansee in Reutte, Tirol, Austria. For few decades they were very congenial partners, but later their relations got strained. Professor Kieffer decided to move to Vienna as Professor and Head of the department of Inorganic Materials Technology, the post presently occupied by Professor Danninger (see Danninger). There he trained a score of students, including his son late Bernard Kieffer, who did his doctorate dissertation at Vienna. Bernard decided to immigrate to USA, where in Albany he organised the famous Wah Chang Co.This firm has been pioneer in refractory metal production in the world.

My very first meeting with Professor Kieffer was in the 6th International Plansee Seminar in the year 1968. The meeting was a formal and a very short one. He had a medium height with well groomed hair. There was a twinkle in his eyes. He was in the conference along with his wife, who appeared to be much younger to him. My next meeting with Professor Kieffer was in the summer of 1970 in New York during the PM International Conference organised by MPIF. He presented a very lucid lecture on sintered tool steels. I heard him for the first time speaking in English, but his command was good and flawless. In mannerism, Professor Kieffer was akin to a German professor, full of authority and aura. I too had my presentation in the conference on alloy refractory carbides. Since he was a specialist in that area, he appreciated my paper and enquired about Professor Samsonov. He was knowing him personally since Professor Samsonov served as an officer in the USSR Ministry of Defence, when Austria was under occupation during the World War II. It was here that he got interested in high temperature materials for varied applications.

My third meeting with professor Kieffer was in the year 1977 in his office at Vienna at his famous Technical University.He showed me his laboratory in great length. I could see an air of authority and a deep sense of discipline in him. He used to give instructions to his research students while walking. Some of his colleagues were Professor Jangg and Professor Ettmayer. Dr Jangg was a bit shy person, but the latter was very amicable and warm. After spending the whole forenoon in his department, Professor Kieffer took me to a restaurant for lunch. During conversation, I could gauge his conservatism. He was very unhappy with the hippy cult of USA, which was then spreading in Europe too. He admired USA for business adventures, but from the cultural contents viewpoint, he was very proud of Europe. From Vienna I had planned my flight to Munich and from there to Innsbruck. My reservation of the Munich-Innsbruck was in some very small airline operating in that difficult mountain terrains. Professor Kieffer advised me to take train journey from Munich to Reutte, changing the train at Garmisch. This routé was more convenient and less hazardous. I followed his advice and since then I always take that route to reach Plansee.

After 1977 Plansee Seminar, I did participate in other future seminars too. Each time I found in Professor Kieffer an increased degree of warmth. In conferences, he was an attentive listener, and did not raise questions to paper presenters. He was a shrewd person and always inching to innovations in new ventures. Undoubtedly he was. a much sought after international consultant in the area of hard materials.

After retirement from the Vienna Technical University, Professor Kieffer's position was taken over by Professor Lux, who had much exposure to USA and world at large. Austria should be proud of two doyens-one Professor Nowotny in the field of Materials Science and the other Professor Kieffer in the area of Materials Technology. It is pity Professor Nowotny immigrated to USA to join the University of Connecticut.

DR. N.C. KOTHARI (AUSTRALIA)

I first saw Dr. Kothari in the year 1964 in Bombay during the IIM Annual Technical Meeting. He was then working in the Atomic Energy Establishment of Denmark in Riso. He presented a technical paper on which Dr. K. Tangri of Indian Atomic Energy Establishment asked a number of questions. Soon after, Dr. Kothari moved to Australia at Queensland University, where he trained a large number of Australian students in powder metallurgy. Apart from teaching, he did significant research on sintering, for which IISS admitted him as a full member. In 1983, I actually interacted with him in the Sintering Conference organised by me in New Delhi. He was a frequent visitor of India, but he mostly touched only Bombay. In Delhi he spoke on dispersion strengthened PM systems, which evoked good length of discussion. He again participated in the next International Sintering Conference in 1989 (New Delhi), where he reviewed on the sintering aspects of oxide superconductors, a burning topic of that time. Dr. Kothari was a forceful speaker. In between these two conferences, he visited our Institute IIT,Kanpur in 1985, when an International Conference on the Metallurgical Processes was held. The time was the celebration of the Silver Jubilee of our institute. On this occasion I came to know that he was an excellent expert on failure analysis. As a mater of fact he fought many cases in the court as a pleader and forensic expert. He earned quite a lot of money through such avenues. Dr, Kothari also cooperated with a number of PM industries in Australia. One can easily claim him as a leading star in Australian Powder Metallurgy. He was a frequent traveler across the globe and never missed any PM conference. I heard that he now leads a retired life in Australlia. Currently, I have lost link with him.

LATE PROFESSOR GEORGE KUCZYNSKI (USA)

Professor Kuczynski can be regarded as one of the founders of the solid state sintering theory. No scientific library anywhere in the world is without his name in the catalogue. He initiated the sequential seminars in 'Sintering and related Phenomena' in the University of Notre Dame, which was later moved to other universities in USA. They formed a consortium for this series of seminars. I have been an ardent reader of the Seminar Proceedings. It was his broad vision which made him to add 'Related

Phenomena'in the seminar title. He was in search for a generalised theory of sintering. As a matter of fact he did propound the statistical theory for sintering, which is very close to the generalised theory. Professor Kuczynski never divided materials into metallic and nonmetallic. All along he had in view only one term 'Crystalline Materials'. At Notre Dame University, he guided few Indian students too. But according to him they were more interested in getting lucrative jobs just after completing their M.Tech. studies.

Professor Kuczynski was a Pole and had studied physics in Poland. He moved to USA as an immigrant and studied at MIT. He and his wife were extremely devoted catholics. I met the couple in Warsaw during the Sintering conference (1979). He was very fond of speaking in Polish, but in an American accent. In Warsaw the Polish hosts were extremely proud that he could visit his motherland. As soon as we met in the dinner on the eve of the conference, he said he had read the abstract of my paper and would like to talk with me tomorrow morning. I became a bit nervous to face this giant in sintering theory. Next morning there was a trip to historical places by coach. He suggested me to sit beside him. My wife and his wife were on the other side of the coach. He began discounting my approach, but I argued back since he was an advocate for the generalised theory of Sintering. At times he was some what vehement. I could sense that he wanted to convert me. My wife could sense that this professor was grilling me. After some time our discussion ended and we started talking other things. Unfortunately, Profesor Kuczynski was never in India. This never materialised.

In the year 1981, I was again lucky to meet Professor Kuczynski in Yugoslavia in Portorozh (now in Slovenia) during the sintering conference organized by IISS. He was in good shape. He, myself and Dr. Stuijts (the famous materials scientist from Philips Co, The Netherlands) were on the dinner table. Professor Stuijts talked about his wife and complimented how she is so helpful to him in this old age, when he is not putting up a good health. Professor Kuczynski looked at him intently. During the technical session, Professor Kuczynski came heavily on the paper by Dr. W.A. Kaysser of Max Planck Institute, Stuttgart. The topic was 'Ostwald Ripening during Liquid Phase Sintering.'

After 1981, the next conference under the auspices of IISS was in New Delhi in December, 1983. I was the convener of the conference. Professor Kuczynski could not come to the conference. His wife informed me that he has some heart problem. After great persuation by the famous Japanese materials scientist Professsor S. Somiya, he could participate in the 1987 International Sintering Conference held in Tokyo. Incidentally, Professor Somiya was the organiser of this conference. In the conference, I could see the frailness of Pofessor Kuczynski.However, while talking science he exhibited his usual vigour. During his paper he showed only few transparencies and talked in relatively few chosen sentences. He was hoping that his audience might have already read his past relevant papers, and so, needed only few tips. This was my last meeting with this great scientist of sintering.

Professor Kuczynski died on 16th May, 1990.

PROFESSOR ALAN LAWLEY (USA)

Dr.Lawley prior to joining the University of Drexel in the year 1967 as a faculty member, was with Franklin Rsearch Institute in Philadelphia. He completed his Ph.D. degree from the University of Birmingham, UK in the year 1958 from where I, too, received the M.Sc. degree in Physical Metallurgy (1962). I met him first in the Educators' luncheon in the year 1970 duirng International PM Conference held at New York.On that occasion the PM text book by J.S. Hirschhorn, published by APMI,was released. My paper submitted for the International Journal of Powder Metallurgy and Powder Technology on 'The Challege of PM Education' (Vol. 13, No3, 1977., 227) was edited by him at the instance of its Chief Editor Professor H.H. Hausner. After the retirement of Professor Hausner from the editorship, Dr. Lawley took over this responsibility in the year 1985. I always appreciate his 'Editor's Note' in each issue of the Journal, particularly the last paragraph in which he always writes something spicy. As an example I would like to quote him from the recent issue of the Journal (Vol. 46, No 3, May/ June,2010). He derived the idea from the writing of Benn Schott in New York Times (2/26/2010) titled 'On the Timing and Duration of Sleep'. Dr. Lawley wrote, 'As a morning person, I am up and about before dawn but fade early and have been frequently been accused of resting the eyelids during cocktail before dinner.' As a Britisher, Dr Lawley has a characteristic sense of humour, which is reflected in these notes.

At Drexel, Dr. Lawley turned out a large numer of Ph.D. The students were from various countries including India. Most of his overseas students preferred to stay back in USA. One of my past M.Tech student Mr. Shiva Nand Majagi did his Ph.D. under him. Dr. Lawley had been one of the external examiners of one of our Ph.D. students, Mr Kadam, who had worked on Particulate Lead based alloy compoites. He read his thesis rather too well, so much so that when our Institute received back the thesis it was full of read markings, mainly pertaining to English language. However, he had the praise for the thesis too.

In one of the issues of his journal. International Journal of Powder Metallurgy' (October 2001) published soon after my retirement from IIT Kanpur, Dr. Lawley published a very touching article about me written by Mr Peter K. Johnson in the 'Newsmaker' columns. I continue to be a member of APMI International, more than 35 years, with which Dr. Lawley is so sincerely and devotedly associated.

The biggest service of Dr Lawley has been to the International Journal of Powder Metallurgy, pubished by APMI International. It is an extremely challenging job. How right is Mr Pirre Tabenblat, Chairman of the Editorial Review Committee, when he writes on the occasion of the 25 years of completion by Dr. Lawley as editor of the journal :' Alan has a unique style in approaching authors and is always responsive to their needs and gives constructive feedbacks. By combining theory and practice, he has made the journal into a seamless entity and a much respected publication.' (Int. J. PM, Vol.46,No4, 2010 p.8).

Professor Lawley retired from Drexel in the year 2006 as the Grosvenor Professor in Metallurgy. Presently he is an Emeritus Professor at the University.

LATE PROFESSOR F.V. LENEL (USA)

Professor Lenel is well known for his dislocation model for the mechanism of the early stage of sintering. One of his most favourite student was Professor George Ansell, who soon after his Ph.D. program from Rensellaer Polytechnic Institute joined the same Institute as a faculty member. Professor Lenel immigrated to USA in the thirties after a doctorate in physics from Germany. After reaching New York he contacted the noble metal producers 'Herman and Hardy', where he took the job. Soon he moved to Ford Motors R&D Centre, Michigan, where he did pioneering development work on sintered materials and engineering components. His academic bent of mind made him to resign from there and to join RPI as a professor. Here he founded the world famous school in powder metallurgy.He was so modest that he did not like to expand his empire and was always at low key. However, the flow of researchers at his laboratory never diminished and he produced a score of powder metallurgists, who are presently scattered throughout the world.

In the summer of 1970 while attending the International PM Conference in New York, I wished to prolong my stay in USA, so as to gain more experience. Keeping this in mind I wrote to Professor Lenel. He immediately responded and offered me the Visiting Associate Professorship in his department. Dr. Ansell was then the head of the department. In developing the theory of liquid phase sintering, we can identify two doyens : Professor Kingery of MIT and Professor Lenel of RPI. Profesor Lenel worked mainly on metallic systems, while Professor Kingery was interested in ceramic systems. In this way both complemented each other.

At RPI, I did an additional job too. The famous book by Ukrainian scientist Professor Geguzin entitled 'Physics of Sintering' was published in Russian. Professor Lenel wanted to read its English translation, which I did gladly. He also used to invite me at his residence on week ends for lunch and also for swimming. I found him a fast car driver. His wife Peggy was extremely faithful to him. They were inseparable. Wherever he went, she was with him.I met Professor Lenel and his wife in practically all the major international PM conferences.When I joined IIT Kanpur in February, 1976 as a full professor, Professor Lenel was just departing from South Korea after completing a short term visiting appointment in the Korea Institute of Technology. He wrote me and expressed his desire to visit India including my Institute too. I welcomed the couple. He and his wife did some railway journeys too to visit some historical places including Varanasi. The brother of Dr. Harb Nayar, who lived in Delhi, took care of them there. Professor Lenel ended his Indian visit at Bomaby and met Professor Tendolkar. Here at IIT Kanpur Profesor Lenel presented a technical seminsr. I had just joined the Institute and there was nothing to show him on PM. But, the couple gave me blessing, which made me to achieve so much at IIT Kanpur. Professor K.P. Singh, our the then head of the department took him and me to meet the Director of our Institute for a courtesy call. There Professor Lenel praised my erstwhile work to the Director Dr. J.B. Lal. From Bombay the Lenel couple went to Saudi Arabia, which turned out to be very costly proposition. After a day or so, they decided to cut short the visit and return to USA. Myself and my wife visited him in RPI in the year 1984. By that time he was retired. He proposed us to accompany them in their car for going to Toronto to attend the International Conference. We accepted their offer, although the confirmed ticket for the coach service was with us. We passed through Kingston. Professor Lenel had some eye problem, but as usual he was driving very fast. On one occasion we missed a major accident. His wife Peggy, then, took command of the car. She was an excellent driver, and possessed good health too. At Toronto conference Professor Lenel and Professor Hausner were awarded the 'Poineers in Powder Metallurgy' Award.

Professor Lenel was not very fond of editing or writing technical books. But, after his retirement, his past students persuaded him to write a book on powder metallurgy. He did not disappoint them. His famous book 'Powder Metallurgy: Principles and Applications' was published by MPIF, NJ in the year 1984. He very graciously dedicated the book to his past students, spread throughout the world.

During my next visit to USA in the year 1995, I wanted to meet Professor Lenel in Troy, but I was told that he is suffering from acute Alzeimer. One can realise the hardship which his faithful wife Peggy faced during the final stage of her husband's life. Certainly with the death of Professor Lenel, the era of contemporary powder metallurgy ended.

MR PER LINDSKOG (SWEDEN)

To my first Ph.D. student (1977) at IIT Kanpur Mr M. Hamiuddin, I gave him the research topic 'Sintered Ferrous Alloys cantaining Phosphorus'. In that connection we needed well characterised Fe-P premixes. I had known the pioneering work of Mr Per Lindskog at RPI for his M.S. degree on Fe-P sintered alloys under the guidance of Professor Lenel. As he was the Managing Director of Hoganas AB, Sweden, I considered prudent to ask for the powders. He brought the idea of Fe-P powders back to his plant in Sweden and developed a number of master alloys like PNC 45, PNC 60 etc. He helped me in sending good amount of powder for our research free of charge. As a matter of fact Mr Lindskog was the external examiner of the Ph.D. thesis of Mr Hamiudddin. In the year 1996 I could personally meet him in New Delhi in the PM conference organised by PMAI under the Presidentship of Mr. B.M. Kataria of Mahindra Sintered Products. We welcomed each other as if we had long standing friendship. At that time he had retired from Hoganas and was an International Consultant based in Germany.

Mr Lindkog has profound PM industial and management experience. This made him very much sought after by major industrialists both in developed and developing countries. He always has profitability in mind. A Swede by birth and educated in USA, these two factors brought in him the competences in precision engineering and technoeconomics. I was much impressed by his plant in Sweden, which was completely computer controlled. There were only a few technicians in the shop floor. The plant was so clean and tidy, as if it was just inaugurated. There I met Mr. Tengzelius, the R & D Manager. The R&D Centre did many pioneering research including PM warm pressing. In order to enhance the use of their powders, Hoganas were never behind in developing prototype products and demonstrating them to the prospective automotive and machine makers.The company has recently published a six volume Handbook on iron powder for the first time.

In the later period of his retirement, Mr Lindskog took over the Presidentship of a famous steel plant in Rumania 'Ductil Iron' and transformed the same into the biggest manufacturer of iron powder. Presently Mr Lindskog is no more with the above company and is a freelance consultant.

LATE DR. SYLVANA LUCKYX (SOUTH AFRICA)

I met Dr.Luckyx in one of the Plansee Seminars, probably it was in the year 1981. Prior to that I had read her important papers on cemented carbides. She received her scientific and technical education in Italy and then moved to South Africa. There,she did further research work under the world renowned physical metallurgist Professor Nabarro. There are few individuals, who are devoted solely to specialise on one and one type of material. Dr.Luckyx was one of them. She had been a serious researcher and did not like to publish too many papers, for the sake of publishing. I find that this scientist did not receive adequate recognition, which she deserved. I was instrumental in nominating her for the membership of IISS. I am glad she accepted my suggestion for getting her nominated. Throughout her life she was a teacher. She retired as Professor from the School of Chemical and Metallurgical Engineering, University of Witwatersrand, Johannesburg, South Asrica.

Structure-properties relationships in cemented carbides have been the major attractions for Dr. Luckyx. In this respect she followed the footsteps of the famous expert in cemented carbides late Professor Gurland of USA. As South Africa has plenty of mineral resources for refractory metals extraction, Dr. Luckyx was much sought after by their materials processing industries. She participated in Sintering 2000, an International Conference held in Delhi in the month of February, where she presented two papers. She had a plan to visit Montego Bay, Jamaica to attend the Ninth International Conference on the Science of Hard Materials (10-14 March, 2008) and present a paper. Unfortunately this could not materialise. I through others knew that she was not keeping a good health. Sylvana died on 5th November, 2007. I am sure her unselfish soul rests in peace. The Issue no. 2, 2009 of the Interational Journal of Refractory Metals and Hard Materials, which constituted the Proceedings of the above conference was rightly dedicated to her memory.

DR. HAR BHAJAN (HARB) SINGH NAYAR (USA)

Dr H.S.Nayar in USA is popularly known as 'Harb' Nayar.He holds a Ph.D. degree from RPI, Troy under the guidance of Professor Lenel. He is a devoted Sikh. His first wife was a Canadian and the present one an Indian. His parents were in Delhi during partition. His father was running an engineering concern near Delhi. Soon after completing his higher secondary certificate, Harb left for USA to study engineering. I met him first in the summer of 1970 durng the International PM Conference organized by MPIF in the New York city. However this meeting was a very brief one. Soon, I came to know that he joined the British Oxygen Co. in New Jersey State on its R&D staff. The biggest contribution of Dr. Nayar had been in designing the sintering atmosphere in different zones of a continuous furnace. The idea was quite original and the whole international PM community welcomed his innovation. He carried a numbr of patents. In the year 1975 or so he published a status report on PM in India published in the Internatiol Journal of Powder Metallurgy. There he did warmly mention about me. In those days I was attached with the University of Roorkee. Although most of his prime life was spent in USA, there is a nostolgia for the motherland India in him.

It was in June, 1984, I was supposed to attend the International PM Conference in Toronto. This was again organised by MPIF. Before the

Canadian visit, I along with my wife wished to visit USA and Dr. Harb Nayar's meeting was on the itinerary. While in Delhi we knew about the tragic news of the Blue Star Operation by our Army, which was ordered by our the then Prime Minister Mrs Indira Gandhi. It was a very very sad event, in the root of which the then Indian National Congress Party was very much involved. Our hotel room was reserved by Harb in the Holiday Inn in New Jersy. Next morning Mr Philip, another R&D man in British Oxygen, came to take us to Dr. Nayar. Mr Philip, a young man and graduate from IIT Madras, originally belonged to Kerala State of India, and is a catholic christian. He knew very well Mr N.T. George, the Honorary Secretary of PMAI. On the way he expressed his anger and anguish about the 'Blue Star' tragedy. He also felt as if the minority was not safe in India. I consoled him and briefely narrated the religo-political unholy alliance in India. I suppose he was partially satisfied by my answer. After about an half an hour drive, we reached the R&D Centre, where PM Division was headed by Dr. Nayar. Harb greeted us warmly, but he was too sad and pained. I also could see the hidden anger towards our Government. I did not interrupt him and listened very attentively. Some of his ststements were highly emotional. At the end of our technical meeting he told Mr Philip to show me the facilities at the R&D Centre, which he did very dutifully. After the visit, Harb and myself had technical discussion, although I could make out that on that sad day his heart was not really for the discussion. After taking a quick lunch at the Centre we returned to our hotel.

Few days after our visit to Harb at his work place in New Jersy,we again met him in the Toronto PM Conference. There he was much composed. In International Confereences, it is an usual convention that big companies do organise dinners for selected gathering. Dr. Harb Nayar on behalf of British Oxygen also organised one in which myself and my wife were invited. There I could feel Harb's real influence and popularity in the PM community of USA. Every one appreciated his amicable nature. Harb, in his welcome speech, also mentioned about me as a valuable friend from India.

In the year 1988 the International PM Conference was held in Orlando. Here I again met Harb. There he was with his Indian wife and a baby daughter. Dr. Sachdeva, my excellent PM friend from Bombay was also there. Here too like the previous occasion, his Company invited many delegates for a dinner. Mr Kemp Roll, the past Executive Dierector of MPIF was also there along with his wife. I knew Mr Roll right from 1970. In Harb I find a sound scientist and a shrewd PR man. I could sense his gradual disenchantment with British Oxygen. At present he is running a consulting company under the banner 'TAT Technology Inc' in New Jersy. He used to visit India practically every year and I did make a point to see him in Delhi. Of late, his travel frequency has decreased drastically. He mentioned me about the long tiring journey to USA from India, particularly at an old age. Our friendship is stable and growing with time. He pities that the environment in India is not that easy for consulting as it is, in general, in USA.

PROFESSOR R. PAMPUCH (POLAND)

I first met this internationally famous ceramic scientist in the year 1981 in the International Conference on Sintering organized by IISS in Yugoslavia. He was there along with his beautiful and petit wife. Our interaction was rather brief. No doubt we were in correspondence on academic matters. It was in 1989, he accepted my invitation to attend the International Sintering Conference organised by me in New Delhi. He was accompanied by one of his assistant professors. As soon as we met, he presented his famous text book on ceramics in Polish. I requested his collegue to translate its table of contents in English, which he did readily. His research work on combustion synthesis of ceramis had become internationally known by that time. Profeesor Pampuch in the next morning's technical session. presented his paper in chaste English, unusual for other Poles. Sooner, I came to know that he was a well travelled person, including Western Europe and USA. Professor Pampuch had an attractive personality with some pomp, but full of humility. He had a good knowledge of Russian language and had read my papers on refractory carbides in Russian. During my visit of Poland, I could notice a sense of frustration and suspicion in Polish people towards Russians. No wonder the fall of Berlin wall and reunification of Germany brought Poland closer to Western Europe.

Professor Pampuch had a good knowledge of our epics like Ramayana and Mahabharata. I was astonished,when he talked about those in the toast offerings during the conference banquet. Currently his Polish book on ceramics has been translated into English and is published by Elsevier. He is undoubtedly instrumental in presenting ceramic science to the world,in general, and to Poland in particular. He is presently an Emeritus Professor in Poland.

DR. HENRI H. PASTOR (FRANCE)

I met Dr. Pastor first in the year 1971 in the International Plansee Seminar in Austria. He was then the R & D Manager in Eurotungstene (Grenoble, France), the refractory metal powder producer. He was with his Chief Mr.Rene Meyer. Dr.Pastor approached me in one of the tea breaks and said he has read many papers of Samsonov, my teacher. He was a soft spoken person with mild smile at his face. Sooner I realised the depth of physical metallurgy knowledge in him. He had researched on practically all the refractory compounds, notably carbides and carbonitrides. As I did not have the schedule of the visit to France on that occasion, I promised him to visit Grenoble next time. This became possible in the year 1979. I was invited by Mr Meyer to attend the Annual Technical Meeting of the French Metallurgical Society in Paris. I presented a paper on the status of metallurgical research in India, as they had shown interest on this topic. In my lecture the world famous Professor P. Lacombe was in the chair, for whom I had heard quite a lot. Another famous scientist was Professor Accary, who had in past worked in the French Atomic Energy, and currently was a professor in Paris. After the lecture, there was a dinner in a restaurant. During the informal conversation, I found a respect for India and Indians, their political and social systems, but they were not so conversant with our educational system. It is worth mentioning that one of the first Directors of our National Metallurgical Laboratory was the eminent French metallurgist Dr. Crussard, whom I had met in Asilomar Conference of ASM on 'Strength of Metals and Alloys' in the year 1970.

After two days stay in Paris, myself and my wife reached Grenoble by train in the afternoon. It was very windy and chilly, as Grenoble is at a height. Next morning,I visited the R& D Centre and plant of Eurotunstene.What struck me most was that all processing units in the R&D Centre, were planned so as to have a miniaturisation of the big scale production. It was desirable as PM processing of cemented carbides in the plant had to be carried out under full knowledge and reproducibility control. Dr Pastor took us for the lunch in the restaurant of the famous French School of Catering, while their teachers had their vigilant eyes over their students, who served the courses. Since then whenever I visited

Grenoble, I never missed that restauarnt. Grenoble in those days was full of hotels of all categories.

I found that the PM industries in France were prone to use their own make equipments. However, LECO carbon analyzer (USA make) was an exception. During our drive Dr. Pastor told me that he was born in Algeria, from where his French parents migrated to France. He is still a bachelor and does not have desire to get married. Recently her ailing mother died, whom he cared very devotedly. I use to correspond at his home address, which remained unchanged for last many decades.

Dr. Pastor visited New Delhi in the year 1989 for attending the International Sintering Conference organised by me. Prior to this on other occasion he had visited Pune, so as to interact with Sandvik Asia R & D Centre. There Dr.Sanjay Basu, the Vice-President of the firm, was his host. In Delhi Conference, he spoke on the recycling of cemented carbides. The techno-economics was the first and foremost priority of his company which by that time was taken over by Sandvik Coromant of Sweden. The Swedish style of management was quite different and I wonder whether the French industry could adopt that so cheerfully. I did not raise this sensitive question in our conversation. The Sandvik management, later, decided to transform the R&D Centre at Grenoble, France under a new name CERMep, of which Dr. Pastor was made the first Managing Director I do not hear much about CERMep now-a-days. May be the the management has wound up this company ? Dr. Pastor retired from CERMep few years back, but still is active in independent consultancy. It appears he is not putting up a good health, as he could not attend the World Congress on Powder Metallurgy PM 2010 held in Florence in October, 2010, which is not far from France

PROFESSOR GUENTER PETZOW (GERMANY)

I had heard about Professor Petzow while I was in Kiev doing my Ph.D. research. He was the founder editor of the journal 'Powder Metallurgy International', published in Germany. He used to invite papers from powder metallurgists of Kiev. Some of my friends there wrote papers in Russian, and I did translate some of them in English. My first meeting with Professor Petzow was in the summer of 1968 during the Sixth International Plansee Seminar in Reutte (Austria). It was rather a brief meeting, as he was much sought after by other delegates. From

Roorkee in early seventies, I began my correspondence with him, which he invariably replied very promptly. Unlike most Germans, Professor Petzow was well verse in written and spoken English. In 1979 during my European visit, I visited his famous laboratory at Max Planck Institute for Metals Research, Stuttgart. There I presented a seminar too. On that very day he was supposed to go to Berlin for a radio interview, but still could make out to stay for my seminar. I always found him an animated person with full of enthusiasm and ideas.

Professosr Petzow's first visit to India for scientific participation was in 1983, when I, in capacity of the convener, invied him to deliver the keynote lecture in the International School on Sintering.He gave a very lucid lecture on liquid phase sintering. I invited him for dinner on two consecutive evenings along with some selected dignitories. Dr, Somiya of Japan was one of the guests in the dinner. Professor Petzow always enjoyed the company of Dr. Somiya.

With passage of time, the comradeship between Professor Petzow and myself became more deeper. In 1984 I met him in Toronto, Canada, where he gave me an open invitation to come and work in his laboratory. I selected the time as 1986, when there was an European Powder Metallurgy Conference in Dusseldorf in the month of July. It was coincident that his 60th Birthday was celebrated during the conference. Professor Petzow was very busy in those days and his biggest challenge was to build a world class laboratory for advanced ceramics. Many industrialists of Germany used to visit his laboratory and were looking for his cooperation with their R & D projects. Professor Petzow was in look out for a reputed scientist for his laboratory who could be his successor too after his retirement. I may mention here that in Germany the process of searching a prospective professor is very tedious and meticulous. I recall the visit of Professor De Jonghe of University of California, Berkeley, who gave a seminsr. Probably he was a prospective candidate. Profeessor Brookes of UK was offered the post, which he joined. Later I heard that he was not too comfortable in the European continent.

Professor Petzow revisited India in 1989 to participate in the International Sintering Conference convened by me in New Delhi. This time he was accompanied by two more scientists of his laboratory. Unfortunately, his visit was short. Each time, he never missed to visit our Bhabha Atomic Research Centre (BARC). Professor Petzow's laboratory did poineering research on beryllium and naturally BARC people did interact with them. As a keen observer, he noticed the bureaucratic attitude of some of their people. He confided me this impression of his. To us it is not that strange, as we treat BARC as a Government Organisation with built-in hierarchy. At BARC he was received by Mr. H.C. Katiyar (an old BHU graduate), the then Director of the Materials Group.

During my frequest visits of Europe, I never forgot to include Germany in my itinerary. Some how, I have great regards for the solid German scientific traditions. The introduction of Indian philosophy including the Sanskrit language in Europe was done by the German indologists. My late father used to narrate those features. Sanskrit was accepted as an Indo-European language. I wonder whether the present German youth counts this or not. The other reason for my affinity with Germany was the fact that she never had any sort of colonial ambition towards India. When I was in Birmingham University, some of the Indian metallurgists of Sheffield University left UK just after their Master's program for doing Ph.D. research in Stuttgart. One of them Dr. Upendra Roy did substantive research on the effect of interstitials in refractory metals under Professor Gebhard. They were somewhat annoyed with the racial attitude of Britishers over them.

I also attended the Diamond Jubilee Celebrations of Max Planck Institute for Metals Research in Stuugart during one of my visits. The visit was only for few hours, as I had to catch my flight to other European destination. There I met most of my old friends including the Indian friends like Dr. K.A. Padmanabhan, Dr Wahi, and Dr. Kutumba Rao.

The biggest scientific contribution of Professor Petzow has been in advanced ceramics. particularly on silicon nitride. While in USA in Michigan University as a visiting professor, Petzow did original rsearch on phase equilibria in multi-component Sialon sytems. There he also translated the then very popular text book in materials science written by the American Professor A.G. Guy. Professor Petzow was, no doubt, much influenced by the US advances, but at the same time he influenced many USA materials scientists by the sound impact of German research. There has been consistent mutual trust and respect among these two Groups. He invited Professor Coble, Professor Kuczynski, Professor Hausner, Professor German in his laboratory as visiting scientists. The outlook of Professor Petzow was an international one, but from the core of his heart he was nearest to Japanese. He admired the hard work of Japanese in a situation, when they do not possess all the basic raw materials, needed for any modern industry. Japanese Government and organisations did honour Professor Petzow on many occasions. The contribution of German scientists in development of Tokyo Institute of Technology, one ot the oldest and biggest school of engineering, is well known, for which the Japanese are ever grateful to Germany.

In scientific meetings, Professor Petzow used to ask very few questions, but very lucid ones. His aim was never to embarrass the speaker, but to ask the question in such a way, that speaker himself would get aware of his failings. Only recently I sent a copy of our book entitled 'Powder Metallurgy' published by CRC Press, USA to Professor Petzow, to whom we had dedicated the book. Immediately after getting the book, he wrote:'Thank you for the book, which you have dedicated to me.It is very generous of you and a great honour to me'.

After retirement from the Max Planck Instiute, Professor Petzow is an Emeritus Professor and visits his past working place periodically. I regret missing the great occasion, when his past students and colleagues marked his retirement by holding an International gathering at Stuttgart. Although he has crossed the age of 80, he still is active and quite alert. I, particularly, feel grateful to him for writing the Preface of our text book on' Materials Sceince and Engineering' (Anshan, UK). Although his international travel has been curtailed drastically, we still fondly look forward his next visit to India.

Another seminal contribution of Professor Petzow has been in the editing of the old and internationally famous journal 'Zeitschrift fur Metallkunde', which for the last few years is renamed as 'International Journal of Materials Research'. In the international competition Germans are unusually smart and, unlike French,. do not shy in recognising English as an International language. The publisher is Carl Hanser Verlag Gmbh of Munich and they have admirably maintained the international standard of the journal. They issue periodically IJMR—Alert on internet for the convenience of the scientists at large.

ACADEMICIAN PROFESSOR M.M. RISTIC (YUGOSLAVIA/ SERBIA)

In the year 1969 while in Kiev, I heard about Professor M.M. Ristic of Belgrade, Yugoslavia. He had just initiated the Series of the World Round Table Meetings on Sintering in Yugoslavia, and edited the journal

Physics of Sintering, which was later renamed 'Science of Sintering' in the year 1975. The idea was a novel one. Professor Samsonov was one of the full members of the team, and he mentioned about Professor Ristic to me. That period was the era of Cold War and it was only Yugoslavia, a nonaligned country, which could accomplish this difficult task in bringing scientists from both the sides in single platform. Each part was keen to know about the scientific activities of the other and both used to participate in good strength. The number of the members was limited and thus, the discussions used to be informal and in depth. One can see the old Proceedings of the Round Table Meetings to verify this fact.

In the year 1975, the name of the International Team of Sintering was changed to 'International Institute for the Science of Sintering'(IISS). In doing this Professor Samsonov played maximum role. In the same year, I was elected as the Corresponding Member of this Institute. In those days I was attached to the University of Roorkee. In 1977 a year after joining the IIT Kanpur, I attended the International Conference on Powder Metallurgy in Kiev (Ukraine). Academician Fedorchenko of the Institute of Materials Science Problems, Academy of Sciences Ukraine, had organised the conference. It was there I met Professor Ristic. He was a man of enormous energy and vigour. He invited me to participate in the IISS activities more intensely, which I do till today.

Academician Ristic has a very close relation with scientific Institutes of East Europe, mainly Ukraine, where many scientists from both the sides undertook exchange visits. Academicians Ristic and Skorokhod, present Director of the Institute of Materials Science, Kiev, have many in-depth collaborations and they are very good friends too. The second man in command in Acdemician Ristic's Institute is Dr. Drago Uskokovich, who, I gather is now on the verge of retirement.

PROFESSOR P.K. ROHATGI (USA)

I was one year senior to Pradip at BHU. He topped the list of graduating students of Metallurgical Engineering program in the year 1961. Just after graduation, he joined MIT as a graduate student under Professor Flemings. After getting his Sc.D. degree from MIT, Pradip joined International Nickel Co's R&D Centre at Suffern, N.Y. as a research metallurgist. He was also a metallurgist at Bethleham Steel Co. in Pennsylvnia State. Around 1972 or so, he joined Indian Institute of Science as a Joint Professor in metallurgical, mechanical and industrial management departments. It was in Bangalore that he consolidated his research on cast metal matrix composites, which actually he had initiated at IIT, Kanpur where he was a Visiting Assistant Proessor. He wrote a number of monographs on cast metal matrix composites. While he was at Bangalore, I was at the Universty of Roorkee. I noticed that quite a few metallurgists, even big ones, in India were not taking metal matrix composites with due attention. My reminder to them was to watch the progress done in Japan. We missed the bus due to such laggardness. Another topic of interest to Profeesor Rohatgi was "Technology Forecasting'. He worked on cast composites in contrast to my work on powder metallurgy composites. He always supported me and treated my contribution as complementary.

Council of Scientific and Industrial Research of India soon realised the contribution of Professor Rohatgi and appointed him the first Director of Regional Research Laboratory, Trivandrum in Kerala State and subsequently of Regional Research Laboratory, Bhopal. At Trivandrum, he had good associates like Dr. K.G. Satyanarayana, Dr. Prasad, Dr. Mazumdar and Dr. Surappa. As a matter of fact Dr. Surappa did his Ph.D. under his guidance at the Indian Institute of Science, Bangalore and is now the Director of a new Indian Institute of Technology, at Ropar. Many of our M.Tech. students after getting their degrees joined RRL, Bhopal, where they are doing very well. Dr. Rohatgi was an experimentalist par excellence and was a believer in hard results. Since he was the very first Director of these two laboratories of CSIR, he had the satisfaction to build them as per his mission. This is always an advantage for the beginners. I also felt so in my career at the University of Roorkee and IIT Kanpur.

While Dr. Rohatgi was in Bhopal, there was an acute shortage of funding. Moreover there was some selective treatment to different CSIR laboratories. This did not make Professor Rohatgi happy. Dr. Varad Rajan was then the Director-General of CSIR. All of a sudden I heard the news of Dr. Rohatgi's departure to USA after resigning his post. I was not amused as I was confident that this person had in the very beginning retured to India from USA with utmost seriousness. Dr. Rohatgi moved to the Unversity of Wisconsin-Milwaukee as a full professor in its department of Materials Engineering. Here he was busy and still busy in research on metal matrix composies. I know one of his able Indian students Dr. Asthana, who after his Ph.D. degree worked in NASA. A side reason for Dr. Rohatgi's departure was to inpart good education to his son and daughter. Both of his deserving wards did not disappoint him.

Professor Rohatgi was a towering personality and this was a point of envy for some of our scientists. Politics prevails in practically every society, but its story in Indian Science is very complex. You have to satify many criteria to get recognized. Some of them are your region, your caste, your language, your godfathers in Indian science, if any, and above all your luck. It is irony that Dr. Rohatgi did not become the Fellow of INSA (Indian National Science Academy) or receive Bhatnagar Prize. He got recognition mainly from overseas. It is good that he became the Fellow of Third World Academy Sciences.

Professor Rohatgi is a regular visitor of India and whenever he comes, he never forgets to visit IIT Kanpur campus. Kanpur city is his native place and he has a soft corner for the Institute, where he taught metallurgy to young bright students during his visiting assignment. Professor Rohatgi ia full of hope and vision, which I wish do not wither away with time.

LATE PROFESSOR RUSTOM ROY (USA)

During my university days in BHU,I was a student member of AIME. In their monthly periodical' Journal of Metals', news columns, the name of Professor Roy was very common. In the shaping of the Materials Science discipline in USA, Professor Roy shall ever be remembered. Dr. Rustom Roy was born in 1924 in Ranchi (India). The family was the Christian arm of a family of Kulin Brahmin Hindus-the priests to the priests going back to 33 generations. His father Narendra Kumar Roy was a Senior Civil Servant and a christian social radical, who had been trained in village cooperatives in Denmark. Dr. Roy after graduating in chemistry (1942), volunteered for the Air Force Officers School. He was selected but then turned down for being too young. After studying M.Sc. in Geochemistry at Patna University (Bihar State), young Roy moved to Penn State University. He left India by ship with 8000 US troops arriving in New York on 28th December, 1945. The desire of Dr. Roy to go to USA in stead of U.K., which was prevalent in those days, may be due to the curiosity for a less known country. In a matter of tradition the Americans are in a fortunate position because they have no ancestors and no classical soil. Goethe, the famous German poet in a poem Amerika, fu hast es baser, wrote 'your fate is happier than that of your old continent.

You have no ruined chateux. You are not troubled by vain memories and useless quarrels'.

Soon after completing his Ph.D. degree under Professor Osborn, Dr. Roy joined the faculty in Minerology as Assiatant Professor. He married with Della a coscientist. Dr. Roy and his wife returned to India. They were in contact with Tata Steel, not far away from his native city Ranchi, where they met the then Prime Minister Mr Nehru. Mr Nehru introduced him to CSIR authorities and Dr. Roy joined the Central Glass and Ceramic Research Institute in Calcutta. Six month later his stay, it became evident to him that he could not effectively do scientific research in India. The pace was far too slow and bureaucratic. In September, 1950 Dr. Roy and his wife returned to USA as permanent immigrants and settled in Penn State University.

At Penn State Professor Roy got quick promotions rising to the post of full professor at the age of 33. After the USSR program on Sputnik, the department of U.S. Defence realised the significance of materials research and in early sixties founded eight major Centres for Materials Rsearch in different US Universities. The Penn State University was one of the first to start the interdisciplinary approach and the first Director of MRL (Materials Research Laboratory) was Professor Roy. I think the University was very correct in not naming it as 'Materials Science Centre'. The term materials is much global and encompasses both fundamental and applied aspects of materials research. Professor Roy was fully conscious of the fact that such centre needed a brand new types of young scientists, who were nurtured in the congenial atmosphere of interdisciplinarity. To meet such a requirement, a number of materials science and engineering departments emerged in different U.S. universities including the Penn State. Professor Roy continued on the Director's post for 23 years.

My first meeting with Professor Roy was in the year 1983, when he visited IIT Kanpur to deliver a scientific lecture. His past Ph.D. student, Professor Dipankar Chakravorty, Head of our Materials Science Programme was his host. The lecture was related to sol-gel processing of advanced ceramics. I was much influenced by his manner in explaining difficult concepts in simple words. Some times, he expressed the concepts with some French mannerism. He was very different from the straight-jacketed English speaker. While delivering the lecture, for a while he sat on the table, which remided me of the great ancient Indian scholars.

Professor Roy contributed utmost in founding the Materials Research Society in USA in the seventies. Other countries, including India copied this pattern and we have our own 'Materials Research Society of India' (MRSI), which was founded by Professor C.N.R. Rao of the Indian Institute of Science. It is strange that Americans write MRSI as MRS-I, as if, we are a branch of MRS. I raised this issue before our stalwards in Materials Science, but each time they looked on the other side. They lacked courage to protest with MRS. My own letter to MRS was conveniently ignored and replied in a round about manner. It is worth mentioning that I am a member of MRS for many many years.

My second meeting with Professor Roy was in 1995 at the Penn State University. We had a lengthy discussion in his office. The office of Professor Roy was like a mini museum; a stand was full of conference badges. Professor Roy had just returned from Russia, after attending the meeting called by Mr Gorbachev, the erstwhile President and the father of USSR Perestroika. He had much admiration for the selfless contribution by the Russian scientists. Professor Roy had been an undisputed link between West and East and his contribution in cooling down the cold war era misunderstandings in U S scientists can not be minimised. He has been a consistent fighter, full of conviction. I had a chance to meet his learned and faithful wife Della, who is also a professor in the same department.

Professor Roy has always been proud of his Indian inheritance and at the same time of the scientific progress made in USA. No wonder that he named one of his grandsons 'Naren', which was the first name of his father. Like in any society, I did find some adversaries of Professor Roy too in USA. They were jealous of his self esteem. It is not that Professor Roy erred in identifying those adversaries, but he just ignored them and marched alone (Ekla Chalo) on the line of our great poet Ravindra Nath Tagore. When I expressed my own reservations, he advised me to write those in scientific magazines' columns. I feel sorry, I could have done much in that direction. Recently, I read Professor Roy' column in the periodical Materialstoday, published by Elsevier, UK. He very candidly advocated the socialisation of basic scientific researches. It is wrong to say that innovative spirit is present only in engineers. Scientists are equally prone to that.

Any one who has closely worked with Professor Roy is aware of the courage and outspokenness in articulating his concerns. His colleague

Gerhard Barsch at Penn State recalls how in the late sixties at a buffet-style dinner at a Gordon Conference for scientists, Professor Roy got up at the dinner table and expressed embarrassment at the blatant disparity between the extravagance of the lavish feast the well fed participants were enjoying and the glaring poverty and hunger world wide. It is good that Professor Roy had not attended any gala dinner of the Indian scientific conferences in the five star hotels. Had he been there,he would have certainly remarked 'save the wasteful expenditure and save for the cause of education '.

Apart from science, Professor Roy had many more interests. He was involved in women, minorities, art, religion and society. He was also much concerned with human sexuality and his book 'Honest Sex' written along with his wife is a good testimony of the time. Although he was a christian, his ideas were universal in appeal and more close to theosophy. This universality is more like our 'Sanatan Dharma'. His ancestral Brahmanical origin was, perhaps, something genetic in nature.

Professor Roy had an international outlook, He was the one, who initiated the US-Japan cooperation in ceramics. Professor Somiya of Japan has elaborated this aspect in his article titled' Friend of many Japanese Scientists'. There he mentions how Professor Roy mediated in the Ryonaji Shrine in Kyoto, very different from other Americans.The Indian root in Professor Roy still remained intact. Another former student and later colleague of Professor Roy, Robert Newnham in his reminiscences wrote about the first scientific meeting of MRS, organised by Professor Roy on 'Application of Phase Transformations in Materials Science' (Refer Phase Transitions 1973, MRS). Professor Roy's contribution to the Proceedings was a thought provoking article called 'A Syncrotist Classification of Phase Transitions' in which he compared the kinetics, thermodynamics, thermochemical and structural aspects of phase transitions in ceramics and minerals. Syncretism means an attempt to combine or reconcile differing beliefs.He was really marvellous in using new and unique terminology. Newnham so vividly concludes his article as follows: 'Rustom has shown us how participating fully in the phase change is how we become loving, caring human beings and this is how he and we, should prepare for the letting go'.

An outstanding aspect of Professor Roy's life was his capacity and dedication to breaking artificial boundaries in order to integrate science, religion, health, art and social action for human benefit. His insight into the world's main religions led him to work to break down the boundaries between Christianity, Hinduism, Islam Buddhism and other religions.At the fag end of his life, Professor Roy became a champion of integrative medicine.He was also a long time promoter of art and the field of art and science and was responsible for bringing the works of artists to the Penn State University. He served as Science Advisor to the number of successive Pennylvania Governors and chaired for many years the Science and Society section of President Mikhail Gorbachev's State of the World Forum.

Near the end of his life, Professor Roy became somewhat pessimistic, but he never stopped the crusade in bring together science / technology with society. His latest publication in India was in Current Science (Vol 98,No 2,Jan. 2010, p. 131). He wrote: 'In the seventies half a dozen high level scientists and engineers at Cornell, Penn State, Stony Brook, Stanford, MIT etc launched the science, technology and society movement. For a couple of decades it flourished and spread throughout academia in the US and UK. It slowly decayed due to lack of energetic participation by international scientists or engineers. Today I weep as I see the old silos of learning rebuilt, as tall as ever'.

On the occasion of his 80th Birthday Celebration,held on 27th November 2004 in Boston, Mr John B. Balance, the then Executive Dirctor of Materials Research Society, described him as the "most creative original thinker-may be outrageous".The motto of Professor Roy was :" Why don't we try something different".

While concluding it would be appropriate if I quote from the article of Rob Fischer about Professor Roy: 'Rusty is an ear when few will listen, a mind where vision is hard to find; a voice of clarity among muddled thoughts. (Passionate Realist: Rustom Roy, Crickle Wood Press., State College, Penn., 1994, p.20). Professor Roy died on 26th August, 2010 in Foxdale Village in Pennsylvania State, USA. He is survived by his wife, three sons and their wives and two grandchildren.

PROFESSOR VINOD K. SARIN (USA)

Vinod is a proud Indian-Ameriacn metallurgist, who is currently a professor in Manufacturing Engineering Department of the University of Boston. In the year 1970, when I visited the laboratory of Professor N.J. Grant at MIT, it was Vinod,who gave me the conducted tour of the facilities.He has a fairly white complexion and many of the white Americans mistake him as one of them. My association with him at MIT for an hour or so was very formal. I was taking track of the academic activities of this metallurgist. His Ph.D. work was on rapidly solidified copper alloys on which he had publications as well. Later he moved to Sweden to join Sandvik R & D Centre. It was here that he got involved with hard materials, with which he is till presently associated, It was in Stockholm, he came in contact with late Professor Dr. Exner of Max Planck Institute for Metals Research, Stuttgart, another authority on cemented carbides. Dr. Exner was in Sweden on a sabbathical. They both collaborated in research on hard materials. After some time I came to know that Dr. Sarin has joined GTE's Research Laboratory at Waltham, in Massachusetts State. For my 1983 International Conference on 'Sintered Metal-Ceramic Composites' held in New Delhi, I sent an invitation to him, which he readily accepted. Not only he presented a paper in the conference, he made up a point to visit us at IIT Kanpur, where he presented a seminar. He visited our house in IIT campus and since then we are personal friends too.

Dr. Sarin's father was a big shot in the CSIR's head office in New Delhi. He desired his son to get trained in engineering. Vinod did not disappoint him. He proceeded to USA and completed his B.S., M.S. Programs from Michigan and Wisconsin Universities respectively. After the M.S. program, he did return to India and was posted at National Physical Laboratoty in New Delhi. As he was not very happy with the Indian bureaucracy, he decided to move back to USA. This time he preferred to join MIT under the guidance of Professor Grant, about whom I have described elsewhere in this chapter. After that there was no looking back for this young man.

My next meeting with Dr. Sarin was in 1984 at Toronto during the International Powder Metallurgy Conference. He was with his other colleague Dr. Buljan of GTE. There Dr. Harb Nayar had also invited Dr. Sarin in the Company's dinner.

Late Professor Gurland of Brown University was the originator of the International Conference on the Science of Hard Materials. Dr. Sarin and Professor Gurland were good colleagues. Their work place locations were also not far from each other, and so they used to meet frequently. Professor Gurland suggested Dr. Sarin to take command of running the 1987 International Conference, which was held in Nassau (Bahamas). I was in their International Committee and was extended an official invitation with some financial grant. I made up the plan to travel to Bahamas, which turned out to be a costly one. Unfortunately this time IIT Kanpur did not help me financially. I very much enjoyed the fresh breeze of the Nassau's shores. Here I met important persons like Professor Nabarro FRS from South Africa, (late) Dr. Almond from NPL, UK, Professor Fischmeister from Germany, Dr. Subra Suresh of Brown University, Professor Gurland of Brown University, my friend Dr. Henri Pastor from France and many others. Any meeting organised in a resort has many distinctive advantages. Here Dr. Sarin had come along with his wife 'Rani', who was introduced to me. Rani is the daughter of a well known Hindi literateur and was studying in Boston when Vinod was at MIT. Soon Vinod and Rani fell in love and got married. Vinod's family was very selective about the geographic and cultural background of its settlement. The excellent academic atmosphere of Boston always attracted them. Boston is the city of American Brahmins and one can feel this only after visiting the city and interacting with the people.

At Boston University Professor Sarin got interested in Diamond like coatings on cemented carbides. He earned a number of patents based on his research. He had been instrumental in training some Indian scientists in his laboratory—notably being Dr. Arya. It is pity I could not visit Sarin's laboratory during my Boston visit though only for a day in the year 1995. The confusion in communication was responsible for this. Any way I am glad that I could then meet his old teacher (late) Professor N.J.Grant at MIT.

Of late, I have had no occasion to meet Dr.Sarin personally, but at the same time I know that he is too busy with his research on coatings and also in raising research grants,an arduous task, which any U.S. professor has to do.

LATE PROFESSOR W. SCHATT (GERMAY)

I had heard about Professor Schatt from Professor Samsonov, while I was in Kiev as his Ph.D. student. Professor Schatt was supposed to attend the International Sintering Conference convened by me in New Delhi in the year 1983. He was to be decorated as the full member of IISS. Unfortunately he could not do so. In 1985, I met him first in the Plansee Seminar. In was only in 1986 that I had a chance to interact with him in Stuttgart in Professor Petzow's laboratory. He had specially come to attend the European Powder Metallury Conference held in Dusseldorf. It was the time when the communism in East Germany had started to crumble.

Professor Schatt's theory on dislocation activated sintering did catch the attention of International researchers quite favourably. I could notice in the conference that practically all the scientists from West Germany used to look him with great admiration. They also pitied him. But, as matter of fact, he was a satisfied man and bore a similarity with classical Indian Gurus: simple living and high thinking. His height was short, but his speech was loud and clear. He liked his son to become academic. Unfortunately he was not that happy with the success of his son, which he did not hide to me. Professor Schatt knew Russian language too well. As a German soldier he was a prisner of War in a Russian camp during the Second World War. However, he did not have any ill feelng towards the Russian people. He had a fond memory of his late wife.

The merger of two Germany East and West, brought Professor Schatt still much closer to the West. The European Powder Metallurgy Association (EPMA) invited him to write a text book on powder metallurgy. He completed the project and the book is a highly acclaimed one (W.Schatt and K.P. Wieters, Powder Metallurgy : Processing and Materials, EPMA, Shrewsbury, UK, 1997).

Professor Schatt possessed a child like curiosity, always eager to know other's view point. He believed in accurate experimentation. The whole scientific career of his was passed in Dresden. Professor Lenel of RPI, USA had a good friendship with him, both being of more or less of same age. In addition, their approaches on sintering mechanism were based on dislocation model.

For the last one decade I was not in contact with him. Of late, I enquired about his health from Professor Petzow. He informed me about his death on 24th July, 2009. The last semblence of a classical German academician, with a spirit of selflessness, is no more to be seen.

PROFESSOR S. SOMIYA (JAPAN)

I had known about Professor Somiya of the Tokyo Institute of Technology through ceramic literature for quite some time, but it was only in 1981 during the IISS International Sintering Conference held in Slovenia (then Yugoslavia), that I first met him.I found him to be very reserved and his replies used to be in few words and not sentences.There, he was very attentive in going through all the poster papers. With his vast international experience, he appears to be the best evaluator of the ceramic

R&D of any country. Professor Somiya was admitted as full member of IISS in 1983 on the occasion of the Delhi Sintering Conference convened by me. I was, therefore, very hopeful that he shall attend and he did. I was at the New Delhi Palam airport to receive him in the evening and led him to Ashok Hotel the venue of the conference. His first act,while reaching his room in the hotel, was to open the bag and present me his edited book in English and a Sony pocket calculator. I accepted those with due humility. I requested him to come along with me to the restaurant for dinner. The long air travel had tired him and he really enjoyed my conversation with a glass of beer. Now I realised he is a different person, since I saw him in Yugoslavia. He appeared to be a very meticulous person. He, prior to his departure from Japan, had enquired all the details of taxi charges, tips etc., in case due to some reason I could not be present in person at the airport. Next day we all met at the registration desk. During the conference I and Professor Petzow used to go in different restaurants of Ashok Hotel and Professor Somiya was always a welcome addition.

It will be interesting to the readers to know about an incident, which happened with Professor Somiya at Ashok Hotel. His return flight from Delhi to Tokyo by Alitalia was in night, and so he checked out the hotel in noon and deposited his suitcase in the hotel's cloak room. In the evening, when we wanted to hire a taxi, he noticed his baggage missing from the cloak room. He was upset, while I was very angry on the hotel administration. I threated to report this to the Minister of Tourism, as this Governemnt hotel was directly in their control.The hotel administration assured us to locate the suitcase and despatch the same by earliest air flight to Tokyo. It appeared that his baggage was transferred to the Austrian Embassy in Delhi, as one of their guests had checked in the hotel the previous day. Dr.Somiya was on the verge of missing the flight. We, therefore, decided to trust the hotel administration. At Delhi airport my self and Dr. Somiya took dinner and I bid him good bye with due apologies.While going to the security check, I heard him telling to the security staff about his agony in a child like manner. Later he wrote me the receipt of the suitcase, but the custom people at Narita Airport had to break open the lock for examination.This mishap made me so cautious that in future I invariably told my conference delegates to be careful. I wish now the situation in India is not that bad.

Professor Somiya is an international authority on hydrothermal synthesis of advanced ceramics. He had Ph.D. from Penn State University in USA and was a big facilitator for the intimate cooperation between American and Japanese materials scientists. Japanese in general are rather reserved in making new friends, but when they develop friendship, it becomes a life long one.

During the Delhi Conference (1983), a decision was taken to hold the next conference in Japan in the year 1987. Professor Somiya was unanimously elected as the convenor. He accepted our offer, but there was a rider; no USSR scientist would be invited. I could not understand his limitations, which made him to suggest so. May be it was hang over of cold war syndrome. Anyway, the 1987 conference in Tokyo held in Sunshine City was a big success in which scientists like Professor Kuczynski, Professor Kingery, Professor Lenel were specially invited. It was a good opportunity for us to interact with Japanese scientists. I still remember Professor Somiya with his deliberately well stuffed conference bag, always hanging in his shoulder. In capacity of the past organiser of the conference in New Delhi (1983), I was specially requested to participate in the official banquet ceremony rituals. It was really an honour. The conference Proceedings was published in two volumes under the title' Sintering 1987' (Elsevier).

Dr. Somiya could be recognized as an International ambassador for scientific cooperation. Few years back he donated funds for instituting 'Somiya Prize' of Materials Research Society (MRS) of USA. It is an award to scientist / scientists, who have made active research collaboration in more than two continents. Professor C.N.R. Rao of India has been a recipient of this covetted prize. Of late, Professor Somiya has become very active in networking various materials related scientific organisations and institutes. For the last few years, I have had no contacts with him, but I hope he is hale and hearty

PROFESSOR KEN-ICHI TAKAGI (JAPAN)

Dr. Takagi has done seminal research on complex refractory borides and poineered in developing tool materials based on them. He was the Head of the Technical Research Laboratory of Toyo Kohan Co. Ltd in Kudamatsu in Japan. This ceramic system for R&D attracted me since the binder iron was much cheaper and the sintering temperatures not too high. I corresponded with him for giving me few kilograms of the starting raw material ie. complex borides for research of one of my Ph.D. students,

Mr P.K. Bagdi. He very promptly agreed to my request and sent me the material by air mail. I was already aware of his publications in English and very much appreciated his holistic approach in developing new materials for varied applications. We were in constant communication with our results. Incidentaly this student happened to be my last Ph.D. student at IIT Kanpur.

It was in the year 1995 that I first met Dr. Takagi at Penn State University in USA. He had a good working relation with Professor German, who had organised the Sintering Conference in his University. There we had lengthy technical discussion. Dr. Takagi was a soft spoken person with a very pleasant smile. In that conference I had an invited presentation on this group of novel materials. Dr. Takagi very attentively listened to my paper and I was expecting questions from him during the discussion period. To my surprise there was none from his side. But during the tea break, he quietly approached me, took to a corner and gave few tips for a still better sintering results. Later I came to know that in Japanese culture, as a gesture, one does not dispute in public with elders. I was very glad to hear his suggestions. We had many fruitful exchanges of ideas on R & D. After a gap of five years, Dr Takagi came to attend my conference on Sintering organised in New Delhi in the year 2000. There he delivered an invited paper on the complex ternary boride based cermets. I was extremely pleased to see him in my own country.

After my retirement fom IIT Kanpur in the year 2001, my research activities practically stopped and I turned more towards consultancy and book writing. This was the main reason why our correspondences became few. I got shifted to Varanasi, my native city. Among the text book s published by me with my son Anish, a professor in powder metallurgy at IIT Kanpur, was the text book entitled 'Powder Metallurgy: Science,Technology and Materials', which got published in India in the end of 2010 and copublished in USA by internationally famous publisher CRC Press, Florida. I was in search for a preface writer, who is a specialist in both PM theory and practice. It was a publication under the Series in Metallurgy and Materials Science under the auspices of the Indian Institute of Metals. I found none better person than Professor Takagi, Now he was the professor and Head of the Mechanical Engineering Department at the Tokyo City University. I emailed my request to him, which he agreed readily with a rider for one month at his disposal. He wrote the Preface with great care and thought. I very much appreciated the last sentence of the Preface: 'This book will be one of the desk-books not only for undergraduate and postgraduate students, but also researchers and engineers who are engaged in powder metallurgy." I very much hope to meet Professor Takagi in the next World Congress in Powder Metallurgy to he held in Yokohama, Japan. in the year 2012.

PROFESSOR A. THOLEN (DENMARK/SWEDEN)

I knew Professor Tholen as fellow member of IISS. He was, earlier, a student of Gottenberg School of Materials Science, His biggest contribution is in the role of adhesion in cold sintering of powder mass, which he established very intelligently through electron microscopy. During one of the European visits in early eighties, I made a point to visit his research laboratory in the Technical University at Lubek in Denmark. My train from Germany was scheduled to reach Kobenhavn in the morning around 6.00 AM or so and he was punctually at the railway platform to personally receive me. It was still some what dark on that morning. He drove me straight to the University and initiated scientific discussion. I was somewhat perplexed to do that without a morning cup of coffee. I was also amazed seeing his stamina. My research seminar was scheduled in the afternoon and I was supposed to check in the hotel after that. In his department I met another colleague of his Dr. Hanson. Till then, I was not aware that he had married to a British lady metallurgist. Professor Tholen took pains to show me other materials related departments in the University. I liked the calm atmosphere of the University and the utmost dedication of the students. Professor Tholen was a man of few words with a look of a thinker and philosopher. The dinner arranged in his house was a memorable one. His wife had made a number of delicacies. I was picked up from my hotel by Dr. Hanson. His wife Carol and one young son were also in the car. Carol was educated in London in physical metallurgy and had moved to Canada's Queens University in Ontario State as a faculty member. During an International Conference she and Dr. Hanson met each other and fell in love. Subsequently, they got married. Carol did a big sacrifice in resigning from her job in Canada and came over to Denmark. She was a scientist in some laboratory in Kobenhavn. They had adopted an African boy, who was a smart child. The parents were really very loving and caring ones. Carol was still knowing only English and so I could make out the gist of their conversations during the dinner. She was naturally concerned as a mother in the upbringing of the child and was not much aware of the Danish's society record on race. Tholen did comfort her. I told them about Dr. David Woodford, who was my contemporary as a research student in the University of Birmingham. Later he joined General Electric R&D Centre at Schenectady, NY. He and his British wife had also adopted an African child. Carol was aware of this. Durng our conversation Professor Tholen narrated his yatching experience. At the end of the wonderful dinner, Dr. Hanson and Carol dropped me to my hotel. Tholen family was surprised by my pronunciation of the word' Kobenhavn' as most of the nonscandinavians utter it incorrectly as Kopenhagen. This correct version I leraned from the Danish wife of late Dr. Pradeep Chowdhury of IBM Research Center, while being treated on a dinner in their home along with my BHU acquaintance Dr. M.L. Koul., who was contemporary of Dr. Chowdhury at MIT.

It is pity I am no more in contact with Dr. Tholen. However I have been told that he left Denmark and joined some Swedish University as a Professor.

PROFESSOR F. THUMMLER (GERMANY)

When I came in contact with Professor Thummler, he was occupying the chair at the University of Karlsruhe. Before that he was a professor in Stuttgart University. There is an interesting story how this learned scientist from East Germany (Dresden) entered into West Germany. When I met him for the first time in Plansee Seminar in 1968, I found him a modest person, with full of humility. Some Indian students had already done their Diploma Projects and Ph.D. theses under him. One of them was Mr. Kirit Dalal, who after graduation settled in Germany and married a German girl. Another was Dr. Leo Prakash, an IIT Madras Mechnical Engineering graduate, who researched on cemented carbides with modified binders. Dalal was in PM plant at Krebsoge as research metallurgist and later on moved to Goetze, and currently at Bleistahl Gmbh & Co.,the premier automobile parts manufacturing companies in Germany.There was another gentleman from Goa Dr. Nazare, working at Karlsruhe. In Plansee Seminar, I took part in the discussion of the paper by Professor Fischmeister. I was not aware that he was a big shot. Later in the tea break Professor Thummler complimented me saying I am a good speaker. I don't know what he was trying to convey. Next morning during the breakfast at the hotel, I took a seat just beside him. He discussed some scientific ideas and told me that his work on sintering of Fe-Mo alloys very well fits with the Samsonov's model, which I had reviewed in the previous days's technical session. I suggested him to get it published in the Proceedings and he fulfilled his promise. In the fourth volume of the Proceedings of the 1971 International Seminar, there is a written communication from him. In the year 1979, I visited his department in the Nuclear Research Centre in Karlsruhe, where Dr. Holleck was working. I knew Dr. Holleck right from the Plansee meeting in the past. In those days the European Atomic Centres were lucratively financed. Dr. Leo Prakash was my escort. Professor Thummler's department in the University was not so richly equipped as in the Nuclear Centre.

Professor Thummler's strength has been the equal emphasis to powder metallurgy of metallic and ceramic systems. He never rushed for quick publications unless he had elaborately completed the project. Most of his researches were on the border of theory and applications. One can read his lucid treatment on this in the International Journal 'Science of Sintering'. One of the proud student of Professor Thummler was Dr. Albano Muller, who became the Technical Director of the biggest powder metallurgy plant of Europe at Krebsoge (Germany).

My next meeting with Professor Thummler was in the year 1984 in Toronto in the International Powder Metallurgy Conference organised by MPIF. He was there along with his wife. After one of the papers of Dr. German, presented by his Indian student Mr Deepak Madan Professor Thummler asked a question. The student fumbled a bit. I also took another question, but a bit stoutly. The authors knew our views very well. In one of the free evenings, I and my wife met Professor and his wife in the mall of the hotel. We offered coffee to the couple, which they gracefully accepted. He commented to me that he initiated during the discussion the question and you finally nailed him. He was meaning the question/answer session after German's paper.

In the year 1986, I met Professor Thummler again, but this time in Dusseldorf in connection with the International PM Conference. He was chairing the technical session in which our paper on master alloy modified steels were presented. He spoke high about our work.

My last meeting with Professor Thummler was in Austria during the International Plansee Seminar in the year 2001. He was appearing weak, because of his age. His text book on Powder Metallurgy published by the

Institute of Materials, London is still an excellent book, where for the first time metal and ceramic processings were described symbiotically. His contribution in powder metallurgy nuclear materials has been profound, particularly during the cold war period. With the passage of time, Professor Thummler devoted all his energy on non-nuclear materials with an eye on innovation and technoeconomics.

PROFESSOR JOSE M. TORRALBA (SPAIN)

In 1987 during the International Sintering Conference held in Tokyo, I met a young scientist/ teacher from Spain. He was Dr. Torralba, who was very attentively going through most of the poster papers on the stand. He was very inquisitive and appeared to be ambitious. He interacted with me occasionally during the conference. In those days, Spain was not a major player in powder metallurgy and one can undoubtedly say that as far as academia is concerned Dr.Torralba brought it in the fore front. His research activities range quite widely from sintered steels to powder injection moulding. He has been an excellent organiser too. The European Powder Metallurgy Conference held in Spain is much acredited to his hard work. EPMA also owes quite a lot to him. He was the first to organise in Spain the short term course on powder metallurgy recently under the auspices of EPMA.

My second meeting with Professor Torralba had been in the year 2000 in sintering conference held in New Delhi. He presented two invited papers and took active part in the discussion. The third meeting with him was in 2006 in Busan in connection the World PM Congress. Here he appeared to be very busy, since many delegates used to surround him.On every occasion he met me with cheer and with some element of respect. My last meeting with him was in Florence in 2010 October in the World PM Congress. Here he was in full form and Chaired a technical session on Powder Injection Moulding along with Dr. Animesh Bose. I presented him my latest new publication 'Powder Metallurgy' copublished by CRC Press of USA, which he gratefully accepted. I have still to hear his critical comments on the book. Another attribute to Professor Torralba is his cosmopolitan views. He mixes with scientist of any country with ease and poise. Spain and the PM world, in general,are looking ahead much from this scientist.

Professor O. Van der Biest (Belgium)

Professor Van der Biest is a renowned Professor in advanced ceramics at Katholike University, Lueven. I wished to meet him during my Belgium visit in the year 1991, which he readily accepted with hospitality. I was supposed to deliver a seminar on our recent results on cemented carbides. I was well aware to the educational background of Professor Van der Biest. His University car picked me from Mol, where I was visiting the Atomic Research Centre to deliver a seminar on PM dispersion strengthened ferritic stainless steel, an area of much interest to them working on fast reactors. Dr. Van der Biest warmly welcomed me and introduced his other colleague Dr. Ludo Froyen. He was then an Associate Professor with specialisation in metal matrix composites. His department of materials engineering was in a building of a typical old European architecture, but with all modern scientific research facilities. I was in good know how of the department, which, in past, did excellent research on shape memory alloys and corrosion. Our ex-colleague; late Dr. Raj Narayan was a visiting scientist in their corrosion group for a year.

In my seminar, I met a young gentleman (I forget his name) from the famous cemented carbide plant of Luxembourg, presently known as Ceratizit Luxembourg S.A., who was well verse with my research work carried out at IIT Kanpur. After the seminar, he asked many questions to me in private with which his company was facing problems. I explained him without hiding any fact, as I was much impressed by his tenacity. I could realise the very quick transport facilities in Europe, which is yet not so easy in India. I remember the patchy road of Kanpur which discourages one to drive.

After visiting the facilities of the department, we went for the lunch in the restaurant of the University. In the University I saw many students from Middle East including from Algeria. On the table we were six persons in total. Unfortunately Dr. Van der Biest forgot to introduce all of them to me. This created an embarrassment. Only few days back I was in Rome to attend the International Conference on Recrystallisation and Grain Growth, where I had a paper presentation too. There on a conference tour trip an Algerian lecturer in Physics, also a conference delegate, was sitting beside me. We got involved in conversation. After some time I found him to be a fanatic person with always Jehad in mind. On the lunch table I was just going to describe this episode and as soon as Dr. Van der Biest heard me he said tactfully 'Let me introduce you my research fellow from Algeria'. I understood his hint and changed the topic immediately. The dinner invitation from Professor Van der Biest, on the same day, in the city restaurant was a very quiet affair. We were only two. We talked about many things, including the topic of nuclear India. The small atomic test by our late Prime Minister Mrs Indira Gandhi was an irritant. I assured him that we are a responsible nation and his focus must be more towards Pakistan. He did not say anything further. In this connection I have some doubt about the fair deals in business as far as Middle East countries and Belgium is concerned. The sad death of Dr. Huet the eminent metallurgist of Belgium Atomic Energy, while repairing his car on a holiday all alone in his private garage seems to be intriguing. I tried to ask many investigative questions, but nobody replied to my satiafaction. They said that the hugh car just fell down over his body, while he was in a lying position. No body was a witness. It was just a conjecture.

Dr Van der Biest had and is probably having a great fascination for USA. This is reflected in his frequent reference of USA during conversation. Incidentally he is a Ph.D. degree holder of the University of California, Berkeley. He is a very sought after thesis external examiner in Europe. One of his ex-Indian student Dr. Bikramjit Basu is an Associate Professor in Materials Science and Engineering department of IIT Kanpur.

PROFESSOR RICHARD WARREN (SWEDEN)

My research on refractory carbides brought me near to Professor Warren. From his biodata, I knew that he is an alumnus of the University of Birmingham. He was an undergraduate student (1961), when I was doing my postgraduate research in Birmingham. Unfortunately, we were not introduced at Birmingham. During one of my European visits in the year 1981, I made up a point to visit the famous Chalmers University at Gothenberg in Sweden.I was then aware that famous powder metallurgy scientists like Professor Fischmeister, late Easterling and late Exner were engaged there one time or the other. Dr. Warren was then a Reader (Dotsent) in the Department of Materials. He was kind enough to receive me at the railway station and dropped me at the hotel by his car. I knew from him that his wife is a Swede. That may be one of the reasons for his settlement in Sweden. His initial research interest in particulate composites, later grew into continuous fibre composites. His results on dihedral angle relationships in cemented carbides are invariably referred in any paper related to metal matrix particulate composites. While in Gothenberg, I told him about the ensuing International Conference on Sintered Metal-Ceramic Composites.to be held in New Delhi in December, 1983. He was very much excited and promised his participation in the conference. Incidentally he was in the International Advisory Committee of the conference.

During the Delhi visit, Dr. Warren was very much impressed by the conference. He never left the venue even for a minute during the paper presentations. In those days there was no fax facilities, but still our contacts were quite frequent and timely. During the valedictory session of the conference, he warmly spoke about his impressions and gave the impression as if for the last few months we were located just in adjacent rooms.

Dr. Warren and Dr. Almond at NPL, Teddington (UK) were very good friends.Unfortunately Dr. Almond, whose research on cemented carbides was seminal, could not attend the New Delhi Conference. Later, I met these two famous scientists at Nassau,Bahamas in the Conference on the Science of Hard Materials (1987). It is pity, soon Dr. Almond expired. Later, Dr. Warren moved to another University at Lulea in Sweden as full professor. Of late I have had no communications from him. I have a great admiration for this unassuming quiet, but nevertheless alert friend of mine.

EPILOGUE

In the first four chapters I have desctibed about my past teachers, my peers and colleagues both in India and abroad, who have been my men of metals and materials. In this epilogue, I would like to present some of my own thoughts based on my academic journey of the last five decades full of ups and downs and and sometimes adventures. My stay at IIT Kanpur has been a very productive one. The combination of teaching and research, which is abundant in IIT system is doubly rewarding.

NEED FOR GOOD TEACHING AND GUIDANCE

A good teaching makes one to efficiently convey difficult aspects to the students of all standards. The development of right type of human resource is the primary responsibility of any academic institute. A good teacher can assess the absorption of his lecture by the student by sheer body language of the latter in the class room. But here comes the limitation of student / teacher ratio. The repeated suggestion by the Central Ministry to increase the ratio at IITs is a detriment to the over-all quality upgradation. As the Governemnt gives grant, it has a tendency to dictate terms. I remember how in past we fought vigourously in the Academic Senate various dictats of the Governemnt, for example shortening of the duration of 4 semesters M.Tech program to 3 semesters and the increased intake of students with one pretence or the other. I am glad that the Government now realised its mistake and corrective measure for the duration of the M.Tech programs has been made. I can proudly say that IIT Kanpur, in many respects, has been a pace setter among all other IITs. On the flip side we ought to be really global. We should not shy in opening IITs offshore, particularly in developing countries.

Students need guidance whether in class room or in research laboratory. This should not be misunderstood as spoon feeding. There are some guides,who treat students merely as work force.This is highly deplorable. The relationship must be of a comrade. A good guide should watch his students from a distance. The students' genuine problems must be addressed sympathetically.In a way carrot and stick policy is not bad. When researchers work together, there is all possibility of some differences among themselves. The guide must be fair and fearless.He should brush aside those, whose habit is to unnecessarily complain. Only a fair guide can command respect.

A question arises, what should we expect from a good researcher. Firstly, he must have the zeal and tenacity. He must be uptodate, but at the same time should not hang around on internet all the time. Many informations there are biased, without peer reviews. A good researcher must weigh any statement with criticality. Because the guide is more experienced,this should not prevent his juniors to raise doubts. Periodical seminars in the laboratory should be an integral part of the schedules.The interaction with the guide and his students must be in person-to-person basis. To entertain discussion on the primary results in a group is not a correct practice. The concerned research student in a group does not open himself with ease. During the group seminar, the matter is different. Here the research student comes prepared and coveres in all the pros and cons of his findings.

It is not out of place if I write how our Metallurgical Engineering Departments are gradually switching over to new name 'Materials Science and Engineering'.I am a protagonist of MSE and have coauthored a good selling text book in India, which has got copublished in UK. Nevertheless, from the Indian point of view, it is geat folly that extractive metallurgy is getting gradually wiped off from the syllabus.This is dangerous symptom. In a big country like India full of mineral resources, the country should lead the world in extractive metallurgy education. Unfortunately, there I find no serious attempt by the Institute/ Universities or the concerned Ministry to see how to attract good teachers in this area.The existing faculty in this area is getting retired at a fast pace and sooner the situation shall be bleak. In case we can not train teachers locally in the area of extractive metallurgy, better to send the budding young scientists abroad to get adequate training / education. For this a strategy has to be worked out by our metal producing captains in industry, who can play a significant role.My colleague at IIT Kanpur Professor Ahindra Ghosh has lamented how the teaching in the area of iron making and steel making in our metallurgical engineering departments is weak and inadequate.(IIM Metal News.Issue No 1, 2008, p.29).The picture in nonferrous is not different from that.

NEED FOR R & D

The division of any research into tight compartments of basic and applied is meaningless.As a matter of fact, both are enshrined in the spectrum. The question only arises in which portion of the spetrum the researcher feels most at home. The significance of any project cannot be gauged on the basis of whether the project is of basic or applied nature. Its productivity in a short or long range must be the basis. My personal opinion for any continuing project is that the real success is primarily based on its contribution to the techno-economics.The utmost success of Japanese researchers is mainly based on this philosophy.

The controversy between science and technology is an unreal one. It is worth to quote here the Nobel Laureate Professor Gross: "The entire range of sciences might be compared to a tree. If basic science is its roots, fruits of this tree are the technological advancements.". Another quote is also interesting: 'Scientists seek to understand what is, whereas engineers seek to create what never was.' A rivalry between basic science and applied sciences is uncalled for. otherwise the things get politicised. The new frontiers in basic science are always welcome, but no one should frown on those, who are busy in researches leading to cheaper materials or processing. This class conciousness is unfortunately more prevalent in India. I would like here to refer the autobiography of Dr. A. P. J. Abdul Kalam, our Ex-President, who wrote: "In India even today, the term technology for most people conjures up image of smoky steel mills or clanky machines.This is rather inadequate conception of what technology denotes.The invention of horse cable in the middle ages led to major changes in agricultural methods and was as much a technological advance as the invention of Bessemer furnace centuries later. Moreover, technology includes techniques as well as machines that may or may not be necessary to apply them. It includes ways to make chemical reactions occur, way to breed fishes, eradicate weeds, light theatres, treat patients, teach history, fight war or even prevent it."(Wings of Fire, APJ Abdul Kalam, Universities Press, Hyderabad, 1999, p.164)

Technical Manpower

It is worthwhile to consider here what, in India, makes some passing out engineering graduates to drift from the main stream profession presently. The reasons are manifold. The absence of any central monitoring for the supply and demand aspect of technical human manpower is the biggest hurdle. Another reason is the emoluments, which our M.Tech. / Ph.D. students get after placements. It is worthwhile to see, also, whether the employed young engineer has been productively utilised by the employer. I remember how a big Gevernment research organisation got impoverished of its bright young scientists, because they were more or less ordered to sit in the library in their entry stage for quite some time. May be they did not have the work plan for their employees? There is something wrong in the real appraisal of the technical manpower requirement. A student out of less competent Institute does stick with such Institutes. They later on get time bound promotions and eventually when they become boss, they attract mediocre staff. Thus mediocracy breeds another mediocracy of a still higher order.

We need not be unnecessarily jealous of the private rsearch organisations in India like G. E. Science Centre or General Motors Science Centre, but we must learn something positive from them. We must be clear in chalking out our strategy. We must have a real feel of what we in any organisation can do best. Any ambition is to be linked with pragmatism. Many times a big goal is accomplished more through collaboration than by a solo attempt. ISRO is a noticeable example, where good coordination among Institute/ industry has paid off.

There is a general tendency in India, to let the metallurgist's job in industry get done by other engineers, particularly mechanical engineers. This is the mistake which the plant management realises much later, when their products fail to reach the proper quality. The management wrongly believes that one person can do the job of two. Some of the real case studies have been highlighted by me elsewhere (Consulting Ahead, Vo.3, Issue No 1, 2009, p.43).

Another aspect which bothers me is the need for the emphasis on quality. There is a talk on the 'University of Excellence' in India. Such an experiment shall be of not much value. This will unnecessarily bring forth an inferiority complex among the existing Universities. The need of the hour is to have a in-depth monitoring of present universities rather ruthlessly.But for this the Ministry must have a clear vision and persistence. Any gain is achieved after great toiling. There is no short cut for that. Considering that India is one of the global emerging and knowledge dependent economies, it is a serious concern in terms of quality of advance education that is being offered by our national universities.

ROLE OF MATERIALS RELATED PROFESSIONAL SOCIETIES

The materials world is extremely rich. It's introduction to the school level students should be an integral aim of professional societies, in which we the teachers can contribute. An initiated student in the professional courses is far more productive than an uninitiated one. The Institute of Metals,Materials and Minerals in UK and TMS / ASM in USA are doing yeomen service in this direction. Our own Indian Institute of Metals does organise an All India Quiz, known as Dr. Brahm Prakash Memorial Quiz, centrally carried out by the Kalpakkam Chapter of IIM. We should not rest only with this, but even think of mobile road shows for metals and materials. Unfortunately, we, in general, are prone to cozy options. In technical meetings, we rarely come to business quickly, but waste quite some time in inaugural etc. Practically half a day is lost in inaugural session, which is superficial in nature. In the past three International Conferences on Sintering organised by me, I have been very careful to be free from this trait. We used to come to real technical aspects after a mere five minutes of introductory speech. Most of our professional societies are more busy in soliciting industries for sponsoring lunches and dinners, but not to that extent in framing good technical programs. If we always focus on revenue, the real reputation of the conference or seminar is lost.

Last item over which I wish to dwell upon is the theme of the conference. The titles of our technical conferences in the seventies used to begin with the term 'Advances'. This trend is still tody prevalent.The theme is, often, too general.May be in those days the aim was to attract relatively large audience? Too broad a topic with not much depth makes the purpose of the conference less productive. Another feature is that, we are very eager to name the conference as 'International', even with very limited presence of overseas delegates. Some of the lectures from overseas, particularly from industries, are more of public relation exercises.As we are in engineering profession the technical programs must include a session covering design aspects

The tremendous growth in the number of Institutes/ Societies in India has not brought forth commensurate progress. They appear to be more ritualistic and do not shy in asking fund from the Government Agencies. When the Agencies offer them help, they do expect the pound of flesh in return. One Indian Academy I know does have a separate undeclared quota for Geverment Bureaucracy for the Fellow category. The whole thing looks messy and out of tune in the modern egalitarian society. Our Institutes / Societies copy many things from West, then why not the selection process of office bearers too. I have been a member of MRS for last few decades and have closely watched how they publicise even the biodata of the Council Member aspirants in their periodical well before the election. There each aspirant does highlight his/ her vision for the Society's future.

When I look back from the slide rule age to modern computers, India's progress has been significant, but our goal must be to reach on the top in Asia at the least. This is not achievable by mere wishful thinking, but through hard work, where each stratum of the society contributes cheerfully with the sense of hope and pride. A good honest dedicated leadership is always a need of the day. I am sure we can achieve that.

APPENDIX I

Bio-Data

Full Name: Prof. Dr. Gopal Shankar Upadhyaya

Designation:

    Materials Consultant
    37B, Ravindrapuri
    Lane 17, New Colony, Varanasi 221005 India
    E-Mail: gsu@iitk.ac.in
    Phone: 9935202935

Date & Place of Birth:

    15 June, 1939 (Varanasi)

Educational Qualifications:

B.Sc., Banaras Hindu University 1956
B.Sc. (Met. Engg.), Banaras Hindu University 1960
M.Sc. (Phy. Met.), University of Birmingham (U.K.) 1962
Ph.D. Kiev Institute of Technology, Ukraine 1969

Professional Experience:

Employment Held:

Reader, University of Roorkee 1964-1969
Assoicate Professor, University of Roorkee 1970-1975
Professor, Indian Institute of Technology, Kanpur 1976-2001

AICTE Emeritus Fellow, Indian Institute of Technology, Kanpur 2002-2004
Materials Consultant 2005-Present

Visiting Assignments:

Visiting Associate Professor, Rennselaer Polytechnic Institute, U.S.A., Summer 1970.

Guest Scientist, Powder Metallurgy Laboratory, Max Planck Institute of Metals Research, Stuttgart, Germany, Summer, 1986.

International Conferences organized:

- International School on Sintered Metal-Ceramic Systems, December, 1983, Ashok Hotel, New Delhi.
- International Conference on Sintering of Multiphase Metallic and Ceramic Systems, January/ February, 1989, Ashok Hotel, New Delhi.
- International Sintering Conference SINTERING 2000, February, 2000, Hotel Le Meredien, New Delhi.

PUBLICATIONS

Books Published
Total: 15 (4 text books, 7 monographs, 4 edited books)

- Physical Materials Science of Carbides, Naukova Dumka, Kiev, 1974 (in Russian)
  (Co-author G.V. Samsonov, V.S. Neshpor).

- Metallurgical Thermodynamics and Kinetics, Pergamon Press, Oxford, 1977
  (Co-author R.K. Dube); Also Translated in Spanish by Editorial Geminis S.R.L., Buenos Aires, 1979.

- Materials for Advanced Energy Systems, (Ed.), Indian Institute of Technology, Kanpur, 1984.

- Sintered Metal-Ceramic Composites, (Ed.), Elsevier Science Publishers B.V., Amsterdam, 1984.

- Manganese in Powder Metallurgy Alloys, Manganese Centre, Paris, 1986.

- Sintering of Multiphase Metal and Ceramic Systems, (Ed.), Science Tech. Publication, Vaduz, 1990.

- Powder Processing of High Tc Oxide Superconductors and Their Properties
  (Co-author A.C. Vajpei), Trans. Tech. Publications Ltd., Switzerland, 1992.

- Nature and Properties of Refractory Carbides, Nova Science Publishers, Inc., 1996.

- Powder Metallurgy Technology, Cambridge International Science Publishing, Cambridge, U.K., 1997.

- Dhatuo Ka Itihas, (coauthor), U.P. Hindi Sansthan, Lucknow, 1997 (in Hindi).(co-author A.C. Vajpei)

- Cemented Tungsten Carbides: Production Properties and Testing, Noyes Publications, Fairfield, New Jersey, U.S.A., 1998.

- Sintered Metallic and Ceramic Materials: Preparation, Properties and Applications, John Wiley & Sons Ltd., U.K., 2000

- Materials Science and Engineering, Viva Publications, New Delhi, 2006. (C0-author Anish Upadhyaya)

- Sintering Fundamentals, (Ed.), Trans Tech Publications, Zurich, 2009

- Powder Metallurgy: Science, Technology and Materials, (coauthor), Universities Press (P) Ltd, Hyderabad, 2010, 2011, (Co-author Anish Upadhyaya)

List of Papers Published

1. Crystal structure of saturated mixed hydrides of Ti and Nb.
    G.S. Upadhyaya, A.D. McQuillan.
    Trans. AIME, Vol. 224, 1962, p. 1290

2. Lattice parameter study of Ti-Mo, Nb-Mo alloys.
    G.S. Upadhyaya. Trans. IIM, March 1967, p. 53.

3. Properties of alloys of Nb and Ti carbides in their homogeneity range.
    G.V. Samsonov, G.S. Upadhyaya.
    Poroshkovaya Met., No. 9, Vol. 70, 1968 (in Russian).
    Soviet Powder Met. And Metal Ceramics, Plenum Press, New
    York (EnglishTrans.).

4. Some physical properties of alloys of Nb-and Ti-carbides in homogeneity
    range.
    G.S. Upadhyaya.
    Proceedings of conference of research scholars, Institute of
    Materials Science,
    Kiev, 1968, p. 133 (in Russian).

5. Some relationships of constitutional diagrams of III-VI transition metals.
    G.S. Upadhyaya, G.V. Samsonov.
    J. Less Common Metals, Vol. 17, 1969, p. 161.

6. Some electrophysical properties of alloys of Nb and Ti carbides in
    homogeneity range.
    G.V. Samsonov, G.S. Upadhyaya.
    High Temperature Materials, 6th International Plansee Seminar,
    Austria, 1969, p. 652.

7. Physical properties of monocarbides of transition metals in homogeneity
    range.
    G.V. Samsonov, G.S. Upadhyaya.
    Porosh. Met., No. 5, Vol. 6, 1969 (in Russian, trans. in
    English).

8. Physical properties of alloy carbides of transition metals.
   G.V. Samsonov, G.S. Upadhyaya.
   Dop. AN Ukr. SSR, Ser. A, No. 3, 1969, p. 250 (in Ukr.).

9. Constitutional diagrams of transition metals.
   G.S. Upadhyaya, G.V. Samsonov.
   Izv. Vyz., Tsvet. Met., No. 3, 1969, p. 114.

10. Temperature dependence of electrical resistivity and thermo e.m.f. of alloy carbides of transition metals.
    G.V. Samsonov, G.S. Upadhyaya.
    Teplofizika Visoko Tem., Vol. 7, 1969, p. 449.

11. Microhardness of alloy carbides of Nb and Ti.
    G.S. Upadhyaya, G.V. Samsonov.
    Vestnic Kiev Tech. Institute, No. 6, 1969, p. 161.

12. Stacking faults in crystals and stable electronic configurations model.
    G.S. Upadhyaya.
    Izv. Vyz. Fizika., No. 8, 1969, p. 38.

13. Emissivity of Monocarbides of titanium, niobium and their alloys in homogeneity range.
    L.N. Okhremchuk, I.A. Podchernyaeva, G.S. Upadhyaya, V.S. Fomenko.
    Izv. Vuzov Fizika., No. 11, 19969, p. 126 (in Russian).

14. Work functions of Ti and Nb carbide in homogeneity range.
    G.V. Samsonov, L.N. Okhremchuk, G.S. Upadhyaya, V. Ya. Naumenko.
    Teplo-Fizika Visok. Temperature, No. 4, 1970, p. 921 (in Russian).

15. Temperature dependence of hardness of titanium carbide in homogeneity range.
    G.V. Samsonov, M.S. Kovalchenko, V.V. Dzamelinskii, G.S. Upadhyaya.
    Physica Status Solidi (I), Vol. 1, 1970, p. 327.

16. Wetting of carbides of Ti, Nb, and their alloys by liquid copper.
    G.V. Samsonov, G.S. Upadhyaya, G.K. Kozina.
    Fiziko-Mekh. Mater., No. 4, Vol. 6, 1970, p. 106 (in Russian).

17. Electro-erosion resistance of refractory carbides in homogeneity range.
    A.M. Lemeshko, V. Ya. Naumenko, G.S. Upadhyaya.
    Electro-Obrabotka Mater., No. 4, 1970, p. 6 (in Russian).

18. Stacking faults in crystals and stable electronic configuration model.
    G.V. Samsonov, G.S. Upadhyaya.
    Proceedings of the 2nd International Conference on the Strength of Metals and Alloys, Asilomar, ASM, Vol. I, 1970, p. 373.

19. Electronic nature and material cutting.
    G.S. Upadhyaya.
    Annual Number, The Institution of Engineers (India), Roorkee Sub-Centre, 1970, p. 23.

20. Equilibrium diagrams of rare earth metals.
    G.S. Upadhyaya.
    Rare Earth Metals and their Compounds, Naukova Dumka, Kiev, 1970, p. 57 (in Russian).

21. Self diffusion data and stable electronic configuration model.
    G.S. Upadhyaya.
    Metallurgical Transactions AIME, April, 1971, p. 912.

22. An electronic approach to sintering.
    G.S. Upadhyaya.
    Paper at the Symposium on 'Powders and Sintered Products', Department of Atomic Energy, Bombay, Feb. 1971.

23. Physical properties of monocarbides of Nb and their alloys in homogeneity range.
    Modern Developments in Powder Metallurgy, Vol. 5, Plenum Press, New York, 1971, p. 235.

24. Properties of alloys of ZrC and NbC.
    G.V. Samsonov, G.S. Upadhyaya.
    Poroshkovaya Met., No. 2, 1971, p. 85.

25. Properties of ZrC in its homogeneity range.
    G.V. Samsonov, G.S. Upadhyaya.
    Neorgani, Materiali, Vol. 7, 1971, p. 1351.

26. Heterogeneous diffusion in alloys and stable electronic configuration model.
    G.S. Upadhyaya.
    Scripta Metallurgica, Vol. 5, No. 12, 1971, p. 1125.

27. Stable electronic configuration model and its role in metallurgy.
    G.S. Upadhyaya.
    Trans. IIM, Vol. 24, No. 4, 1971, p. 48.

28. Electronic mechanism of basic technological processes in powder metallurgy of high temperature materials.
    G.V. Samsonov, G.S. Upadhyaya.
    Planseeber, fur Pulvevment, Vol. 20, 1972, p. 269; also in High Temperatures—High Pressures, Vol. 3, 1971, p. 635.

29. Steel plant for vacuum treatment.
    G.S. Upadhyaya.
    Indian Steel Age, Jan. 1972.

30. Mechanical behaviour of refractory carbides,
    G.S. Upadhyaya.
    Proceedings of the Symposium on 'High Temperature Materials', DAE, Bombay, Feb. 1972, p. 17.

31. Emissivity of zirconium and niobium carbides in the region of homogeneity.
    L.N. Okhremchuk, G.S. Upadhyaya.
    (Translated from Russian in 'Technology of Producing New Materials, Report JPRS—59873,
    Department of Commerce, U.S.A.).

32. Thermomechanical treatment of 18, 19, 25% Ni maraging steels.
    M. Lal, G.S. Upadhyaya.
    Trans. Indian Institute of Metals, Vol. 26, No. 4, 1973, p. 37.

33. Activated sintering of Al-bronze.
    G.S. Upadhyaya, P.S. Misra, S.S. Singh.
    Proceeding of 3rd International Round Table Meeting on
    Sintering, Herceg Novi, Yugoslavia, 3-8 Sept., 1973
    (Ed. M.M. Ristic), The Boris Kidric
    Institute of Nuclear Sciences, Beograd, p. 227.

34. Annealing behaviour of cold worked aluminium Dispersed with
    refractory carbides.
    P.S. Misra, G.S. Upadhyaya.
    Poroshkovaya Metallurgica, Sept., 1974.

35. Properties of P/M parts dispersed with refractory carbides.
    G.S. Upadhyaya, P.S. Misra.
    Proceedings of IV Internacional Conference on Powder
    Metallurgy, High
    Tatras, Czechoslovakia, Oct., 1974, Vol. II, p. 189.

36. Stable electronic configuration model and properties of rare earth
    metals and their compounds.
    G.S. Upadhyaya.
    Proceedings of 11th Rare Earth Research Conference, Traverse
    City, U.S.A., Oct., 1974.

37. Scope of powder metallurgy in cutting tool industry.
    G.S. Upadhyaya.
    Trans. Powder Metallurgy Association of India, Vol. 1, 1974, p. 31.

38. Nature of constitutional diagrams of some transition metal boride
    systems.
    G.S. Upadhyaya.
    Bor-poluchenic, Structura I Svoistva, Mitsniereba, Tbilisi,
    1974, p. 115.

39. Prospect of sponge titanium production in India—A technological study.
    G.S. Upadhyaya.
    J. of Mines, Metals and Fuels, August, 1975, p. 237.

40. Properties of sintered aluminium dispersed with TiC and WC.
    P.S. Misra, G.S. Upadhyaya.
    Int. Journ. Of Powder Metallurgy and Powder Technology, Vol. 11, No. 4, 1975, p. 120.

41. Preparation and properties of Al-carbide particulate composites.
    G.S. Upadhyaya, P.S. Misra.
    Proceedings of IV European Symposium for Powder Metallurgy, May, 1975, Grenoble.

42. Activated sintering of Al-Cu alloys with boron addition.
    G.S. Upadhyaya, P.V. Thareja.
    Proceedings of IV International Powder Metallurgy Conference, Zakopane, Poland, 7-9 Oct., 1975, Vol. II, p. 101 (also in Trans. PMAI, Vol. 2, 1975, p. 22).

43. Sintering of Ni-Cu-Mo-Cr low alloy steels.
    J.P. Tewari, G.S. Upadhyaya.
    Trans. Powder Met. Assoc. of India, Vol. 2, 1975, p. 32.

44. Powder metallurgy of RCo_5 permanent magnets—A review.
    G.S. Upadhyaya.
    News Letter, PMAI, Vol. I, No. 1, 1975.

45. Status of powder metallurgy in India.
    G.S. Upadhyaya.
    Powder Metallurgy International, No. 4, 1975, p. 197.

46. Refractory carbides in high temperature high strength alloys.
    G.S. Upadhyaya.
    Rev. on High Temperature Materials, Vol. III, No. 1, 1975, p. 25-50.

47. Sintering of low alloy steels.
   G.S. Upadhyaya, J.P. Tewari.
   Tool & Alloy Steels, Vol. 10, No. 2, 1976, p. 65.

48. Production of metal powders by gaseous reduction from solution.
   R.D. Agrawal, G.S. Upadhyaya.
   J. of Inst. Of Engrs. (India), Vol. 51, MM No. 2, Nov., 1976, p. 50.

49. Energy conservation in P/M industry.
   G.S. Upadhyaya.
   News Letter, Powder Metallurgy Association of India, Vol. 2, No. 3, June, 1976, p. 11.

50. Activated sintering of Al under thermal cycling.
   P.S. Misra, G.S. Upadhyaya.
   Powder Met. Int., Vol. 8, No. 4, 1976, p. 165.

51. Sintering of low alloy steels with varying Cu and Sn additions.
   J.P. Tewari, G.S. Upadhyaya.
   Trans. PMAI, Vol. 3, 1976, p. 26.

52. Potentiality of P/M forging of Al and Al-3 Cu alloy.
   P.N. Garg, G.S. Upadhyaya.
   Trans. PMAI, Vol. 3, 1976, p. 33.

53. Sintering behaviour of Ni-Cu-Mo low alloy steels.
   J.P. Tewari, G.S. Upadhyaya.
   Trans. IIM, Vol. 3, No. 6, Oct., 1977, 345.

54. The challenge of P/M education.
   G.S. Upadhyaya.
   Int. J. of P/M and Powder Technology, Vol. 13, No. 3, 1977, p. 227.

55. Critical evaluation of sintered products.
   G.S. Upadhyaya.
   ISI Bulletin, Vol. 29, No. 10, 1977, 354.

56. Samsonov's contribution in science of refractory carbides.
     G.S. Upadhyaya.
     Science of Sintering, Vol. 9, No. 1, 1977, p. 105-120.

57. Effect of Ni and Mn addition on sintering of tin bronze.
     A. Chandra, G.S. Upadhyaya.
     Trans. Of PMAI, Vol. 4, 1977, p. 46.

58. Sintering of aluminium refractory carbides dispersed systems.
     G.S. Upadhyaya, P.S. Misra.
     Science of Sintering, Special issue, Vol. 10, 1978, p. 157-174.

59. Powder from swarf and their applications.
     G.S. Upadhyaya.
     PMAI News Letter, Vol. 4, No. 4, Sept., 1978.

60. Effect of iron and cobalt addition on densification of Cu-7 Al premix.
     S.K. Singhal, G.S. Upadhyaya.
     Trans. PMAI, Vol. 5, 1978, p. 68-72.

61. Present status of coated carbides.
     G.S. Upadhyaya.
     In 'Tungsten and its Technology", (Ed. N.T. George), PMAI, Hyderabad, 1978, p. 47.

62. An electronic approach to wear mechanism.
     G.S. Upadhyaya.
     Proceedings of National Conference of Industrial Tribology, 7-9th March, 1979, Dehradun, p. 217-224.

63. Effect of repeated thermal cycling on densification of 4600 sintered steels.
     U. Gangopadhyay, G.S. Upadhyaya, M.L. Vaidya.
     Proceedings of the Symposium on Sintering and Sintered Products, BARC, Bombay, Oct., 1979, p. 489.

64. Effect of Ni on the sintering of phosphorus containing iron.
     Md. Hamiuddin, G.S. Upadhyaya. ibid, p. 537.

65. Strength differential effect in sintered lead based particulate composites.
    P.B. Kadam, G.S. Murty, G.S. Upadhyaya, M.L. Vaidya. ibid, p. 545.

66. Preparation and characteristics of lead base P/M composites.
    P.B. Kadam, G.S. Murty, G.S. Upadhyaya, M.L. Vaidya.
    Trans. PMAI, Vol. 6, 1979, p. 7.

67. Effect of copper on sintering of phosphorus containing iron.
    M. Hamiuddin, G.S. Upadhyaya.
    Trans. PMAI, Vol. 6, 1979, p. 57.

68. Investigations on sintered Al-carbide composites impregnated with lubricants.
    K. Gopinath, G.S. Upadhyaya.
    Proceedings of the National Conference on Aluminium Metallurgy, Bangalore, 5-7 Oct., 1979, p. 293-297.

69. Effect of transition metal carbides master alloy MCM on sintering of iron and Fe-P powder premix.
    M. Hamiuddin, G.S. Upadhyaya.
    Powder Metallurgy International, Vol. 12, No. 2, May, 1980, p. 65.

70. Effect of nickel on sintering of P containing iron.
    M. Hamiuddin, G.S. Upadhyaya.
    Int. J. of Powder Metallurgy and Powder Tech., No. 1, 1980, p. 57-67.

71. Managing quality in P/M industries.
    G.S. Upadhyaya.
    News Letter PMAI, Vol. 6, No. 1-2, 1980, p. 8.

72. Effect of Mo on sintering of iron and iron-P premixes.
    M. Hamiuddin, G.S. Upadhyaya.
    Powder Metallurgy, No. 3, 1980, p. 136.

73. Effect of Mo and Cu on sintering of Fe-0.45 P premix.

Md. Hamiuddin, G.S. Upadhyaya.
Trans. PMAI, Vol. 7, 1980, p. 12.

74. Effect of dispersoid volume fraction on strength differential in Pb-base P/M composites.
P.B. Kadam, G.S. Murty, G.S. Upadhyaya, M.L. Vaidya.
Trans. PMAI, Vol. 7, 1980, p. 91.

75. Effect of repeated thermal cycling on densification of 4640 sintered steel under load.
U. Gangopadhyay, G.S. Upadhyaya, M.L. Vaidya.
Trans. PMAI, Vol. 7, 1980, p. 96.

76. Powder forging—Problems and prospect.
G.S. Upadhyaya.
Proceedings of All India Seminar on 'Forging for Automobiles', Jan., 1981,
Chandigarh, IIM Chandigarh Chapter.

77. Effect of repeated phase transformation on sintering of 4640 steel.
U. Gangopadhyay, G.S. Upadhyaya, M.L. Vaidya.
Science of Sintering, Vol. 13, No. 2, 1981, p. 113-123.

78. Carburizing behaviour of sintered ferrous alloys.
Md. Hamiuddin, G.S. Upadhyaya.
Proceedings of VII International Powder Metallurgy Conference, Dresden,
Germany, Sept. 22-24, 1981, p. 191-312.

79. Electronic models and sintering of refractory carbides—An overview.
G.S. Upadhyaya.
Synthetic Materials for Electronics (Ed. B. Jakowlew et. Al),
Elsevier Scientific Publishing Company, Amsterdam, 1981, p. 133-152.

80. Consolidation of lead base P/M composites and their mechanical properties.
P.B. Kadam, G.S. Murth, G.S. Upadhyaya, M.L. Vaidya.

Proceedings of Int. Seminar on Pb, Zn and Cd—Retrospect and Prospect, 18-20 Nov., Indian Lead-Zinc Information Centre, New Delhi, 1981, p. M38-48.

81. Effect of silicon addition on densification of aluminium bronzes.
S. Chopra, G.S. Upadhyaya.
Trans. PMAI, Vol. 8, 1981, p. 33.

82. Effect of alloying elements on densification and mechanical properties of Fe-powder premixes.
M. Hamiuddin, G.S. Upadhyaya.
Trans. PMAI, Vol. 8, 1981, p. 56.

83. Wear behaviour of sintered ferrous alloys containing phosphorus.
M. Hamiuddin, K. Gopinath, G.S. Upadhyaya.
Trans. PMAI, Vol. 8, 1981, p. 63.

84. Abrasive wear of some heat treated P/M tool steels.
G.S. Upadhyaya, J.P. Misra, A.K. Patwardhan.
Proceedings of the 10th Plansee Seminar, June 1-5, 1981 (E. H.M. Ortnor), Vol. 3, p. 89-96, Metallwerk Plansee, Reutte, Austria.

85. Effect of copper on sinered properties of P containing ternary iron powder Premixes.
M. Hamiuddin, G.S. Upadhyaya.
Powder Met. Int., Vol. 14, No. 1, 1982, p. 20.

86. Carbide-binder phases in cemented carbides.
G.S. Upadhyaya.
In 'Powder Metallurgy Alloys' (Ed. P. Ramkrishnan), Oxford and IBH Publishing Co., New Delhi, 1982, p. 77-89.

87. An electron approach to the wear mechanism
G.S. Upadhyaya.
Wear, Vol. 80, 1982, p. 1-6.

88. Wetting of ceramics with metallic melts.

G.S. Upadhyaya.
Proceedings of Int. Symposium on Ceramics, 27-30th Nov.,
1982, BHEL, Bangalore.

89. Metallography of iron alloys containing P.
M.M. Amin, M. Hamiuddin, G.S. Upadhyaya.
Pract. Metallography, Vol. 19, 1982, p. 403-412.

90. Sintering of age hardenable 2041 Al-alloy based P/M composites.
A.K. Jha, G.S. Upadhyaya.
Trans. PMAI, Vol. 9, 1982, p. 11.

91. Preparation and properties of cast Al-composites containing P/M
inserts.
S. Lal. G.S. Upadhyaya. ibid, p. 28.

92. Sintering of 9% tin bronze with iron additions through premix and
prealloyed routes.
M.M. Collur, G.S. Upadhyaya. ibid, p. 36.

93. Effect of alloying additions in sintering of Fe-P premixes.
G.S. Upadhyaya, M. Hamiuddin.
In 'Sintering—Theoery & Practice' (Ed. D. Kolar, S. Pejovnik
and M.M.Ristic), Elssevier Science Publishing Co.,
Amsterdam, 1982, p. 291-298.

94. Preparation and properties of Al-10% Mn based cast composites
containing P/M inserts.
S. Lal, G.S. Upadhyaya.
Aluminium, Vol. 59, No. 4, 1983, p. 299.

95. Sintering of ferritic stainless steel-Al_2O_3 particulate composites.
S.K. Mukherjee, G.S. Upadhyaya.
J. of Powder and Bulk Solids Technology, Vol. 7, No. 1, 1983,
p. 27-31.

96. Sintered 434L ferritic stainless steel-Al_2O_3 particulate composites
containing P.

S.K. Mukherjee, G.S. Upadhyaya.
High Temperature Technology, Vol. 1, No. 4, May, 1983, p. 229-233.

97. Sintering of submicron tungsten based heavy alloys.
V. Srikanth, G.S. Upadhyaya.
Int. J. of Refractory and Hard Metals, Vol. 2, No. 3, Sept., 1983, p. R1.

98. Sintering of 434L ferritic stainless steel containing Al_2O_3 particles.
S.K. Mukherjee, G.S. Upadhyaya.
Int. J. of Powder Metallurgy and Powder Tech., Vol. 19, No. 4, 1983, p. 289-298.

99. Properties of sintered 2014 Al-alloy composites containing WC.
A.K. Jha, G.S. Upadhyaya.
J. Of Mat. Sc. Letters, Vol. 2, Dec., 1983, p. 801-804.

100. Transmission electron microscopy of Al-Cu based powder metallurgical composites.
A.K. Jha, T.R. Ramchandran, G.S. Upadhyaya.
Pract. Metallography, Vol. 20, No. 11, 1983, p. 562-569.

101. Effect of reactive transition metal addition on sintering of 434L ferritic stainless steel-Al_2O_3 particulate composites.
S.K. Mukherjee, G.S. Upadhyaya.
Trans. PMAI, Vol. 10, 1983, p. 27.

102. Sintering of some covalent-ionic bonded ceramics.
G.S. Upadhyaya.
Ceramurgia, Vol. 13, No. 5, Sept.-Oct., 1983, p. 195-199.

103. Effect of tungsten particle size on sintered properties of heavy alloys.
V. Srikanth, G.S. Upadhyaya.
Powder Technology, Vol. 39, 1984, p. 61-67.

104. Wetting of ceramics by metal melts—An electronic approach.
G.S. Upadhyaya.

In 'Sintered Metal-Ceramic Composites' (Ed. G.S. Upadhyaya), Elsevier, Amsterdam, 1984, p. 41.

105. Tensile strength and ductility of Pb-base P/M composites.
P.B. Kadam, G.S. Murty, G.S. Upadhyaya, M.L. Vaidya. ibid, p. 247.

106. Bonding in sintered aluminium-refractory carbides composites.
P.S. Misra, G.S. Upadhyaya. ibid, p. 255.

107. 2014 Al-alloy-metglass sintered composites.
A.K. Jha, G.S. Upadhyaya, P.K. Rohatgi. ibid, p. 259.

108. Al-Ti based cast composites containing P/M inserts.
S. Lal, G.S. Upadhyaya. ibid, p. 265.

109. Activated sintering of 434L ferritic stainless steel-Al_2O_3 particulate composites.
S.K. Mukherji, G.S. Upadhyaya. ibid, p. 253.

110. Sintering of W-Cu-Ni heavy alloys with phosphide addition.
V. Srikanth, G.S. Upadhyaya. ibid, p. 297.

111. Sintering of high speed steel bonded TiC particulate composites.
G. Suresh. G.S. Upadhyaya.
Trans. PMAI, Vol. 11, 1984, p. 9.

112. Sintering of T15 high speed steel-TiN particulate composites.
Y.K. Mathur, G.S. Upadhyaya.
Trans. PMAI, Vol. 11, 1984, p. 13.

113. Sintering of WC-Co hard metals conaining nickel.
D. Basu, G.S. Upadhyaya.
Trans. PMAI, Vol. 11, 1984, p. 1.

114. Corrosion behaviour of sintered 434L ferritic stainless steel-Al_2O_3 composites containing early transition metals.
S.K. Mukjerji, G.S. Upadhyaya.

Materials Chemistry and Physics, Vol. 12, 1985, p. 419-435.

115. Sintered ferritic stainless steels.
G.S. Upadhyaya, S.K. Mukherji.
Pre-print, UNEEC Conference on Powder Metallurgy, Minsk (Belorussia), March 25-29, 1985.

116. Anodic polarization study of sintered 434L ferritic stainless steel and its particulate composites.
S.K. Mukherji, A. Kumar, G.S. Upadhyaya.
Powder Metallurgy International, Vol. 17, No. 4, 1985, p. 172.

117. Effect of Fe_2P additions on corrosion behaviour of ferritic stainless steel composite compacts containing 6 Vol. % Al_2O_3.
S.K. Mukherji, A. Kumar, G.S. Upadhyaya.
British Corrosion J., Vol. 20, No. 1, 1985, p. 41.

118. Corrosion behaviour of sintered 434L ferritic stainless steel-Al_2O_3 composites containing phosphorus.
S.K. Mukherji, G.S. Upadhyaya.
Corrosion Science, Vol. 25, No. 7, 1985, p. 463-470.

119. Effect of Ni_2P addition on sintered W-Cu-Ni heavy alloys.
V. Srikanth, G.S. Upadhyaya.
Int. J. of Refractory and Hard Metals, Vol. 4, No. 3, Sept., 1985, p. 138.

120. Effect of different ball millings on size distribution of tungsten powder.
A. Asthana, G.S. Upadhyaya. ibid, p. 146.

121. Effect of binder composition and sintering period on the properties of W-Fe-Ni heavy metal alloys.
G.S. Upadhyaya, V. Srikanth.
Proceedings of 11th Int. Plansee Seminar, 20-24 May, 1985, Reutte (Austria), Vol. 2 (Ed. H. Bildstein and H.M. Ortner), Metallwerk Plansee, Reutte, 1985, p. 203.

122. Iron and nickel substituted WC-10 Co hard metals.
     G.S. Upadhyaya, D. Basu. ibid, p. 559.

123. Mechanical behaviour of sintered ferritic stainless steel-Al$_2$O$_3$ composites containing ternary additions.
     S.K. Mukherji, G.S. Upadhyaya.
     Mat. Sc. And Engineering, Vol. 75, 1985, p. 67-78.

124. Sintered 34L ferritic stainless steels.
     G.S. Upadhyaya, S.K. Mukherji.
     Materials and Design, Vol. 6, No. 6, 1985.

125. Oxidation behaviour of sintered 434L ferritic stainless steel-Al$_2$O$_3$ composites with ternary additions.
     S.K. Mukherji, G.S. Upadhyaya.
     Oxidation of Metals, Vol. 23, No. ¾, 1985, p. 177-189.

126. Effect of milling variables on powder character and sintering behaviour of 434L ferritic stainless steel-Al$_2$O$_3$ composites.
     S.K. Mukherji, G.S. Upadhyaya.
     Trans. JIM, Vol. 26, No. 10, Oct., 1985, p. 763-771.

127. Role of solidification in powder metallurgical processes.
     G.S. Upadhyaya.
     Metals, Vol. 1, No. 1, 1985, p. 29.

128. Effect of binder composition and sintering period on properties of W-Co-Ni heavy alloys.
     V. Srikanth, G.S. Upadhyaya.
     Trans. PMAI, Vol. 12, 1985, p. 16.

129. Effect of transition metal additions on the sintering of prealloyed α-Brass P/M compacts.
     V.C. Srinivastava, G.S. Upadhyaya.
     Trans. PMAI, Vol. 12, 1985, p. 22.

130. Effect of tungsten particle size and binder composition on sintered properties of heavy alloys.

V. Srikanth, G.S. Upadhyaya.
Modern Developments in Powder Metallurgy, Vol. 15-17, Ed.
E.N. Aqua and C.I. Whiteman, Metal Powder Ind. Federation,
Princeton, 1985, p. 51.

131. Sintered Al-based particulate composites.
G.S. Upadhyaya.
Proceedings of International Conf. On Aluminium, Nov.,
1985, New Delhi, Indian Institute of Metals, Delhi Chapter,
1986, p. 281.

132. Sintered heavy alloys: A review.\
V. Srikanth, G.S. Upadhyaya.
Int. J. of Refractory and Hard Metals, Vol. 5, No. 1, March,
1986, p. 49-54.

133. Properties of composites of 2014 Al-alloy with Ni-Mo based metallic
glass particles.
A.K. Jha, P.K. Rohatgi, G.S. Upadhyaya.
J. of Mat. Sc., Vol. 21, 1986, p. 1502-1508.

134. Effect of various dispersoids on the sintering of powder premixes
based on the age-hardenable Al-alloy 2014.
A.K. Jha, G.S. Upadhyaya.
Aluminium, Vol. 62, No. 6, 1986, p. 458-460.

135. Powder metallurgy in India.
G.S. Upadhyaya.
Powder Metallurgy Int., Vol. 18, No. 3, 1986, p. 223.

136. Decomposition sintering of Al-TiH$_2$ powder premixes.
A.K. Malhotra, A.K. Patwardhan, G.S. Upadhyaya.
Powder Metallurgy Int., Vol. 18, No. 4, 1986, p. 264.

137. Sintered properties of W-Cr-Ni heavy alloys.
V. Srikanth, G.S. Upadhyaya.
J. of the Less Common Metals, Vol. 120, 1986, p. 213-224.

138. Contiguity variation in tungsten spheroids of sintered heavy alloys.
     V. Srikanth, G.S. Upadhyaya.
     Metallography, Vol. 19, 1986, p. 437-445.

139. Sintered tungsten based heavy alloys containing Ni_2P.
     V. Srikanth, G.S. Upadhyaya.
     Trans. PMAI, Vol. 13, 1986, p. 56.

140. Sintering and heat treatment of low alloy steels made from partially
     prealloyed powder.
     S,V,V, Ramana, M.L. Vaidya, G.S. Upadhyaya.
     Trans. PMAI, Vol. 13, 1986, p. 126.

141. Sintering of stainless steel and their based composites.
     S. Lal, G.S. Upadhyaya.
     Review on Powder Metallurgy and Physical Ceramics, Vol. 3,
     No. 2, 1986, p. 165-203.

142. Role of early transition metals on sintering behaviour of ferritic
     stainless steel-Al_2O_3 composites.
     S.K. Mukherji, G.S. Upadhyaya.
     In 'Proceed. Of VI Powder Metallurgy Conference', Katowice
     (Poland), 19-21September, 1984, Central Section of Powder
     Metallurgy, Gliwice, 1986, Vol. II, p. 357-372.

143. Sintering of steel bonded titanium carbides.
     G. Suresh, G.S. Upadhyaya.
     In 'Horizons of Powder Metallurgy', Vol. 1 (Ed. W.A. Kaysser
     and W.J. Huppmann), Veriag Schmid, Freiburg, 1986, p. 275.

144. Effect of Y2O3 addition and sintering period on the properties of
     P/M 316 austenitic stainless steel.
     S. Lal, G.S. Upadhyaya.
     J. of Mat. Sc. Letters, Vol. 6, 1987, p. 761-764.

145. High performance engineering ceramics—An overview.
     G.S. Upadhyaya.
     In 'High Performance Ceramics' (Ed. B.V.S. Subba Rao),
     Oxford and IBH Publishing Com., New Delhi, 1987, p. 3.

146. Microstructure and properties of sintered low alloy Cr steels with molybdenum addition.
    S.V.V. Ramana, M.L. Vaidya, G.S. Upadhyaya.
    Pract. Metallography, Vol. 24, 1987, p. 105-118.

147. Densification and spheroid growth of liquid phase sintered tungsten heavy alloys.
    V. Srikanth, G.S. Upadhyaya.
    Trans. PMAI, Vol. 14, 1987, p. 56.

148. Effect of milling period and sintering temperature on the properties of 316L austenitic stainless steel and 4 vol. % Y_2O_3 containing particulate composites.
    S. Lal, G.S. Upadhyaya.
    J. of Powder and Bulk Solids Technology, Vol. 11, No. 3, 1987, p. 1-12.

149. Extending role of powder metallurgy in advanced ceramics.
    G.S. Upadhyaya.
    PMAI News Letter, Vol. 14, No. 1, 1987, p. 6.

150. Role of Samsonov's Stable Electron Configuration model in sintering of real systems.
    G.S. Upadhyaya.
    Science of Sintering, Vol. 20, No. 1, 1988, p. 23.

151. Effect of sintering atmosphere and alumina addidtion on properties of 6061 aluminium P/M alloy.
    A.K. Jha, S.V. Prasad, G.S. Upadhyaya.
    Powder Metallurgy International, Vol. 20, No. 5, 1988, p. 18.

152. Effect of copper and bronze additions on the sintered properties of 216L austenitic stainless steel and its composites containing 4 Vol. % Y_2O_3.
    S. Lal, G.S. Upadhyaya.
    Powder Metallurgy International, Vol. 20, No. 3, 1988, p. 35.

153. Ferritic stainless steel-Al$_2$O$_3$ particulate sintered composites: Interface interaction.
     G.S. Upadhyaya, S.K. Mukherji.
     In 'Interfaces in Polymer, Ceramic, and Metal Matrix Composites', Ed. H. Ishida, Elsevier Sc. Publishing Co., Inc., N.Y., 1988, p. 389-397.

154. Sintering of 70 Ni/30 Cu powder compacts through prealloy and premix routes.
     G.S. Upadhyaya, R. Hulyal.
     In 'Mod. Dev. In Powder Metallurgy', Vol. 21 (Ed. P.U. Gummeson and D.A. Gustafson), MPIF, Princeton, 1988, p. 139-154.

155. Effect of ternary additions on the sintered properties of 316L stainless steel and its yttria containing composites.
     S. Lal, G.S. Upadhyaya.
     In 'Modern Dev. In Powder Metallurgy', Vol. 18 (Ed. P.U. Gummeson and D.A. Gustafson), MPIF, Princeton, 1988, p. 581-594.

156. Kinetics of neck growth during loose stack sintering.
     A.M. Gokhale, N. Basavaiah, G.S. Upadhyaya.
     Metallurgical Trans. A, Vol. 19A, September, 1988, p. 2153-2161.

157. Powder metallurgy in India.
     G.S. Upadhyaya.
     Int. J. of Powder Metallurgy, Vol. 24, No. 3, 1988, p. 259.

158. Dry sliding wear of sintered 6061 aluminium alloy based particulate composites containing solid lubricants.
     A.K. Jha, S.V. Prasad, G.S. Upadhyaya.
     In 'Wear Resistance of Metals and Alloys' (Ed. G.R. Kingsbury), ASM International, Ohio, 1988, p. 73-80.

159. Cadmium in sintered electrical products.
     G.S. Upadhyaya.

In Proceedings of `ILZIC Silver Jubilee Conference 1988',
India Lead Zinc Informational Centre, New Delhi, 1988, p.
47.1.

160. Sintering of submicron WC-10 Co hard metals containing Ni and Fe.
G.S. Upadhyaya, S.K. Bhaumik.
Mat. Sc. & Engg. A105/106, 1988, p. 249-256, also reprinted
in Science of hard Materials-3, Ed. V.K. Sarin, Elsevier Applied
Sc., Barking, U.K., 1988.

161. Effect of cold work and annealing on the mechanical properties of
90 W-7 Ni-3 Fe heavy alloy.
V. Srikanth, G.S. Upadhyaya.
J. of Mat. Sc. Letters, Vol. 7, 1988, p. 195-197.

162. Effect of carbide powder type and refractory compound additions
on properties of sintered WC-10 Co hard metals.
D. Basu, S.K. Bhaumik, G.S. Upadhyaya.
Int. J. of Refractory and Hard Metals, Vol. 7, No. 3,
September, 1988, p. 145.

163. Some contributions of electron theory of sintering in real systems.
G.S. Upadhyaya.
In 'Sintering 87', Ed. S. Somiya et. al, Elsevier Applied
Science, Barking, U.K., 1988, p. 303-308.

164. Effect of binder composition on sintering of tungsten based heavy
alloys.
G.S. Upadhyaya, V. Srikanth.
In 'Sintering 87', Ed. S. Somiya et. al, Elsevier Applied
Science, Barking, U.K., 1988, p. 475-480.

165. Sintering of 434L ferric stainless steel-Al_2O_3 particulate composites.
G.S. Upadhyaya, S.K. Mukherji.
In 'Sintering 87', Ed. S. Somiya et. al, Elsevier Applied
Science, Barking, U.K., 1988, p. 719-724.

166. Sintered 6061 alloy-solid lubricant particle composite sliding wear and mechanisms of lubrication.
     A.K. Jha, S.V. Prasad, G.S. Upadhyaya.
     Wear of Materials, 1989, Vol. I (Ed. K.C. Ludema), American Soc. of Mech. Engineers, N.Y., 1989, p. 233-238 (also in Wear, Vol. 133, 1989, p. 163-172).

167. Sintering of WC-10 Co hard metal containing intermetallic compound.
     S.J. Majagi, G.S. Upadhyaya.
     Int. J. of Refractory and Hard Materials, Vol. 8, No. 2, June, 1989, p. 111.

168. Status of ceramic industry in India.
     G.S. Upadhyaya.
     Industrial Ceramics, Vol. 9, No. 2, 1989, p. 55.

169. Liquid phase sintering of P/M high speed steels.
     P.K. Kar, G.S. Upadhyaya.
     Tool and Alloy Steels, Vol. 23, No. 7, 1989, p. 249-255.

170. Effect of Y_2O_3 and Cu additions on the corrosion behaviour of sintered 316L austenitic stainless steel.
     S. Lal, M.N. Mungole, K.P. Singh, G.S. Upadhyaya.
     Materials Forum, Vol. 13, 1989, p. 134-138.

171. Surface roughness of sintered 6061 Al-alloy based particle composites.
     G.S. Upadhyaya, A.K. Jha, S.V. Prasad.
     Powder Metallurgy Int., Vol. 21, No. 4, 1989, p. 15-16.

172. Extending role of powder metallurgical products for automobiles.
     G.S. Upadhyaya.
     Proceedings of National Symposium on Automotive Materials and Manufacturing Technology, 28-29 August, 1989, The Automotive Research Association of India, Pune, 1989, p. 258.

173. Effect of phosphorus and Si addition on the sintered properties of 316L austenitic stainless steel and its composites containing 4 Vol. % yttria.
    S. Lal, G.S. Upadhyaya.
    Journal of Mat. Sci., Vol. 24, 1989, p. 3069-3075.

174. Dry sliding wear of sintered 6061 Al-alloy graphite particle composites.
    A.K. Jha, S.V. Prasad, G.S. Upadhyaya.
    Tribology International, Vol. 22, No. 5, Oct., 1989, p. 321-327.

175. Sintering of WC-10 Co hard metal containing superalloy.
    S.J. Majagi, G.S. Upadhyaya.
    Int. J. of Refractory and Hard Materials, Vol. 8, No. 4, 1989, p. 232-235.

176. Powder metallurgy metal matrix composites: An overview.
    G.S. Upadhyaya.
    Metals, Materials and Processes, Vol. 1, No. 3, 1989, p. 217-228.

177. Preparation and properties of 6061 Al alloy/graphite composites by P/M routes.
    A.K. Jha, S.V. Prasad, G.S. Upadhyaya.
    Powder Metallurgy, Vol. 32, No. 4, 1989, p. 309.

178. Oxidation behaviour of sintered 316L austenitic stainless steel-yttria composites with various Additions.
    S. Lal, G.S. Upadhyaya.
    Oxidation in Metals, Vol. 32, Nos. ¾, 1989, p. 317-335.

179. Sintering behaviour and properties of 6061 aluminium alloy-titanium carbide particle composites.
    A.K. Jha, S.V. Prasad, G.S. Upadhyaya.
    Science of Sintering, Vol. 21, No, 2, 1989, p. 81-89.

180. Phase stability and sintering of multiphase alloy systems.
    G.S. Upadhyaya.
    In 'Sci. of Sintering', Ed. D.P. Uskokovic, H. Palmour III and R.M. Spriggs, Pergamon Press, N.Y., 1989, p. 215-226.

181. Novel liquid phase sintered high speed steels.
    G.S. Upadhyaya, P.K. Kar.
    In 'Proceedings of the First Int. High Speed Steel Conference',
    Leoben, 26-28th March, 19980 (Ed. G. Hackl and B.
    Hribernik), Montan Universitat, Leoben, 1990, p. 477-486.

182. Effect of microstructure anisotropy on mechanical properties of
    P/M 7091 aluminium alloy.
    H.N. Azari, G.S. Murty, G.S. Upadhyaya.
    In 'Aluminium Alloy 90', Proceedings of 2nd Int. Conference
    on Aluminium Alloy—Their Physical and Mechanical
    Properties, Oct. 9-13, 1990, p. 167.

183. Sintered 6061 aluminium alloy based P/M particulate composites.
    A.K. Jha, S.V. Prasad, G.S. Upadhyaya. ibid, p. 144.

184. Synergetics of sintering of multiphase metal and ceramic alloy
    systems.
    G.S. Upadhyaya.
    In 'Sintering of Multiphase Metal and Ceramic Systems', Ed.
    G.S. Upadhyaya, Sci-Tech. Publications, Vaduz, 1990, p.
    95-106.

185. Sintering of lead bronze containing tin and its based porous bearings.
    S. Kumar, G.S. Upadhyaya, M.L. Vaidya. ibid, p. 259-267.

186. Sintered 6061 Al alloy-graphite particle composites: Sliding war
    and mechanisms of lubrications.
    A.K. Jha, S.V. Prasad, G.S. Upadhyaya. ibid, p. 289-298.

187. Liquid phase assisted sintering of 316L austenitic stainless steel-Al_2O_3
    composites.
    S. Lal, G.S. Upadhyaya. ibid, p. 361-368.

188. Effect of carbide powder type and refractory compound additives
    on properties of sintered WC-10 Co hard metals.
    D. Basu, S.K. Bhaumik, G.S. Upadhyaya. ibid, p. 409-414.

189. Liquid phase sintering of P/M high speed steels.
     P.K. Kar, G.S. Upadhyaya.
     Powder Metallurgy Int., Vol. 22, No. 1, 1990, p. 23.

190. Powder metallurgy in developing countries: Problems and prospects.
     G.S. Upadhyaya.
     Powder Metallurgy Int., Vol. 22, No. 2, 1990, p. 44.

191. Effect of composition and sintering on the densification and microstructure of Tungsten heavy alloys containing Cu and Ni.
     K.N. Ramakrishnan, G.S. Upadhyaya.
     Mat. Sci. Letters, Vol. 9, 1990, p. 456-459.

192. Sintered 6061 Al alloy-particle composites.
     A.K. Jha, S.V. Prasad, G.S. Upadhyaya.
     In 'Metal and Ceramic Matrix Composites: Processing, Modelling and Mechanical Behaviour', Ed. R.B. Bhagat, A.H. Clauer, P. Kumar and A.M. Ritter, The Minerals, Metals and Materials Society, Warrendale, 1990, p. 127.

193. Stereology of some liquid phase sintered metal-metal composites.
     G.S. Upadhyaya. ibid, p. 629.

194. Mechanical behaviour of sintered 6061 Al alloy and its composites containing soft or hard particles.
     A.K. Jha, S.V. Prasad, G.S. Upadhyaya.
     Z. Metallkunde, Vol. 81, 1990, No. 6, p. 457-462.

195. Activated sintered 6061 Al alloy particulate composites containing coated graphite.
     A.K. Jha, S.V. Prasad, G.S. Upadhyaya.
     In 'Controlled Interfaces in Composite Materials' (Ed. H. Ishida), Elsevier Science Publishing Company, New York, 1990, p. 829-840.

196. Trends in advanced materials and processes.
     G.S. Upadhyaya.
     Materials and Design, Vol. 11, No. 4, 1990, p. 171-179.

197. Powder metallurgy in India.
     G.S. Upadhyaya.
     International J. of Powder Metallurgy, Vol. 26, No. 4, 1990, p.
     391-395.

198. Liquid phase sintering and heat treatment of T15 P/M high speed
     steel.
     P.K. Kar, G.S. Upadhyaya.
     Metal Powder Report, Vol. 45, No. 12, 1990, p. 841-843, also
     in Trans. PMAI, Vol. 17, 1990, p. 25-32.

199. Liquid phase sintering of binary Cu alloys.
     G.S. Upadhyaya, A. Bhattacharjee.
     Int. J. of Powder Metallurgy, Vol. 27, No. 1, 1991, p. 23.

200. Powder metallurgy at the Indian Institute of Technology, Kanpur.
     G.S. Upadhyaya.
     Int. J. of Powder Metallurgy, Vol. 27, No. 1, 1991, p. 59.

201. Metallurgy to materials science and engineering.
     G.S. Upadhyaya.
     Tool and Alloy Steels, Jan., 1991, p. 4.

202. Sintered 316L austenitic stainless steels and role of alloy additives.
     S. Lal, G.S. Upadhyaya.
     Tool and Alloy Steels, March-April, 1991, p. 123-127.

203. SEM study of the fracture behaviour of some WC based cemented
     carbides.
     S.K. Bhaumik, G.S. Upadhyaya, M.L. Vaidya.
     Pract. Metallography, Vol. 28, 1991, p. 238.

204. Sintering of WC-10 Co hard metals containing vanadium
     carbonitride and Re, Part I.
     R. Hulyal, G.S. Upadhyaya.
     Int. J. of Refractory and Hard Materials, Vol. 10, No. 1, 1991,
     p. 1-7.

205. Sintering of WC-10 Co hard metals containing vanadium carbonitride and Re, Part II.
R. Hulyal, G.S. Upadhyaya. ibid, p. 9-13.

206. Liquid phase sintering of TiN-enriched T15 grade high speed steels and their mechanical properties.
P.K. Kar, G.S. Upadhyaya.
Steel Research, Vol. 62, No. 8, 1991, p. 352-357.

207. Elevated temperature ductility of rapidly solidified 7091 P/M aluminium alloy.
H.N. Azari, G.S. Murty, G.S. Upadhyaya.
In 'Proceedings of the 2nd Int. Conference on Aluminium: INCAL-91', 31st July-2nd August, 1991, The Aluminium Association of India, Bangalore, Vol. 2, 1991, p. 625-630.

208. Sintering of lead bronze containing tin.
S. Kumar, G.S. Upadhyaya, M.L. Vaidya.
J. Mat. Engg., Vol. 13, 1991, p. 237-242.

209. Mechanical properties and microstructure of carbide and binder modified WC-10 Co cemented carbides.
S.K. Bhaumik, G.S. Upadhyaya, M.L. Vaidya.
In 'Advances in Powder Metallurgy-1991', Vol. 6 (Ed. L.F. Pease III and R.L. Sansoucy), MPIF, Princeton, 1991, p. 435-450.

210. Properties and microstructure of WC-TiC-Co and WC-TiC-Mo$_2$C-Co(Ni) cemented carbides.
S.K. Bhaumik, G.S. Upadhyaya, M.L. Vaidya.
Materials Science and Technology, Vol. 7, August, 1991, p. 723-727.

211. Sintering aspects of nonoxide ceramics.
G.S. Upadhyaya.
In 'Advanced Ceramics' (Ed. G. Ganguly, S.K. Roy and P.R. Roy), Trans.Tech. Publications, Zurich, 1991, p. 205-225.

212. Transient liquid phase sintering of some binary and ternary α-titanium alloy of Ti-Al-Sn system.
M. Sujata, S. Bhargava, G.S. Upadhyaya.
Science of Sintering, Vol. 23, No. 3, 1991, p. 163-181.

213. Alloy design of WC-10 Co hardmetals with modifications in carbide and binder phases.
S.K. Bhaumik, G.S. Upadhyaya, M.L. Vaidya.
Int. J. of Refractory and Hard Materials, Vol. 11, 1991, p. 9-22.

214. Effect of TiN addition on sintering behaviour and mechanical properties of WC-10 Co hard metals containing Mo_2C and Ni.
S.K. Bhaumik, G.S. Upadhyaya, M.L. Vaidya.
J. of Mat. Sci., Vol. 27, 1992, p. 1947-1959.

215. Liquid phase sintering of TiC or TiN enriched T15 grade high speed steels and their mechanical properties.
G.S. Upadhyaya, P.K. Kar.
In 'Sintering 1991' (Ed. A.C.D. Chaklader and J.A. Lund), Trans. Tech. Publication, Zurich, 1992.

216. A transmission electron microscopy study of WC-10 Co cemented carbides with modified hard and binder phases.
S.K. Bhaumik, G.S. Upadhyaya, M.L. Vaidya.
Materials Characterization, Vol. 28, No. 3, 1992, p. 241.

217. Oxidation behaviour of hard and binder phase modified WC-10 Co cemented carbides.
S.K. Bhaumik, R. Balasubramaniam, G.S. Upadhyaya.
J. of Mat. Sci. Letters, Vol. 11, 1992, p. 1457-1459.

218. Liquid phase sintering and heat treatment of T42 high speed steels.
P.K. Kar, G.S. Upadhyaya.
Metal Powder Report, Vol. 47, No. 6, 1992, p. 34-40.

219. SEM study of the fracture behaviour of WC-TiN-Co and WC-TiN-Mo_2C-Co(Ni) cemented carbides.
S.K. Bhaumik, G.S. Upadhyaya, M.L. Vaidya.

Practical Metallography, Vol. 29, No. 7, 1992, p. 366-373.

220. Microstructure and mechanical properties of WC-TiN-Co and WC-TiN-Mo$_2$C-Co(Ni) cemented carbides.
S.K. Bhaumik, G.S. Upadhyaya, M.L. Vaidya.
Ceramics International, Vol. 18, No. 5, 1992, p. 327-336.

221. Sintering aspects of high T$_c$ oxide superconductors—An overview, Part I.
A.C. Vajpei, G.S. Upadhyaya.
Science of Sintering, Vol. 24, No. 2, 1992, p. 77-82.

222. Part II, Bismuth and thallium containing compounds.
A.C. Vajpei, G.S. Upadhyaya
Science of Sintering, Vol. 24, No. 2, 1992, p. 83-88.

223. Part III, Advanced manufacturing methods.
A.C. Vajpei, G.S. Upadhyaya.
Science of Sintering, Vol. 24, No. 2, 1992, p. 89-93.

224. Liquid phase sintering of T15 and T42 high speed steel composites containing Ti(C,N).
B.P. Saha, G.S. Upadhyaya.
Powder Metallurgy International, Vol. 24, No. 6, 1992, p. 345-350.

225. Tungsten spheroid growth in liquid phase sintered heavy alloys.
G.S. Upadhyaya, V. Srikanth.
Grain Growth in Polycrystalline Maerials, Part II (Ed. G. Abbruzzese and P. Brozzo), Trans. Tech. Publications, Zurich, 1992, p. 811-820.

226. Liquid phase sintering of T15 and T42 high speed steel composites containingTiB$_2$.
B.P. Saha, G.S. Upadhyaya.
J. of Materials Processing Technology, Vol. 36, 1993, p. 363-382.

227. Densification of Ti-Al-V powder compacts prepared through premix or prealloyed routes.
     M. Sujata, S. Bhargava, G.S. Upadhyaya.
     Powder Metallurgy International, Vol. 25, No. 2, 1993, p. 70.

228. Properties of sintered T15 and T42 high speed steels.
     P.K. Kar, B.P. Saha, G.S. Upadhyaya.
     Int. J. of Powder Metallurgy, 29, Vol. 2, 1993, p. 135-148.

229. Sintering of 434L ferritic stainless steel-Al_2O_3 particulate composites.
     G.S. Upadhyaya, S.K. Mukherjee.
     Proceedings of 7th Int. Metallurgy and Materials Congress,
     4-8th May 1993, Ankara, Vol. 2, UCTEA Chamber of
     Metallurgical Engineers, Ankara, 1993, p. 1195.

230. Liquid phase sintering of T15 grade high speed steels containing TiN particulates.
     G.S. Upadhyaya, P.K. Kar. ibid, p. 1205.

231. Full density processing of complex WC based cemented carbides.
     S.K. Bhaumik, G.S. Upadhyaya, M.L. Vaidya. ibid, p. 1217.

232. Effect of heat treatment on the microstructure and mechanical properties of rapidly solidified 7091 P/M aluminium alloy.
     H.N. Azari, G.S. Murty, G.S. Upadhyaya.
     Pract. Metallography, Vol. 30, No. 4, 1993, p. 186-199.

233. Liquid phase sintered T15 or T42 high speed steel-TiC particulate composites.
     G.S. Upadhyaya, P.K. Kar.
     Proceedings of 13th Int. Plansee Seminar (Ed. H. Bildstein and R. Eck), Metallwerk Plansee, Reutte, Vol. 2, 1993, p. 328-342.

234. Corrosion behaviour of sintered 6061 Al-alloy graphite particle composites.
     M. Saxena, A.K. Jha, G.S. Upadhyaya.
     J. of Materials Science, Vol. 28, 1993, p. 4053-4058.

235. Elevated temperature deformation behaviour of alumina-dispersed P/M copper.
Govind, R. Balasubramaniam, G.S. Upadhyaya.
Materials Chemistry and Physics, Vol. 36, No. 3-4, 1993, p. 371-376.

236. Effect of hydrogen on ductility of ODS copper.
Govind, R. Balasubramaniam, G.S. Upadhyaya.
Scripta Met. Et Materiala, Vol. 29, 1993, p. 1303.

237. Thermomechanical treatments and recrystallization response of 7091 P/M aluminium alloy.
H.N. Azari, G.S. Murty, G.S. Upadhyaya.
Berg-und Huttenmannische Monatschffts, No. 6, 1993, p. 347.

238. Interface interactions in WC based cemented carbides: A TEM study.
S.K. Bhaumik, G.S. Upadhyaya, M.L. Vaidya.
Composite Interfaces, Vol. 1, No. 4, 1993, p. 357-364.

239. Processing and properties of sintered tool steels and cemented carbides.
G.S. Upadhyaya.
Bull. Mat. Sci., Vol. 16, No. 6, 1993, p. 465-476.

240. High temperature deformation of rapidly solidified 7091 powder metallurgy aluminium alloy.
H.N. Azari, G.S. Murty, G.S. Upadhyaya.
Materials Sci. and Technology, Vol. 9, 1993, p. 686.

241. Elevated temperature strengthening in carbide (Al_4C_3) dispersed aluminium.
M.V. Gurjar, G.S. Murty, G.S. Upadhyaya.
J. of Mat. Sci., Vol. 28, 1993, p. 5054.

242. Anisotropy in the microstructure and mechanical properties of P/M 7091 aluminium alloy.
H.N. Azari, G.S. Murty, G.S. Upadhyaya.

Materials Chemistry and Physics, Vol. 37, 1994, p. 349-354.

243. Refractory compound enriched T42 high speed steels by liquid phase Sintering.
P.K. Kar, G.S. Upadhyaya.
Materials & Design, Vol. 15, No. 2, 1994, p. 99.

244. Effect of Ti(C,N) addition on sintering behaviour and properties of binder modified WC-10 Co cemented carbides.
S.K. Bhaumik, G.S. Upadhyaya, M.L. Vaidya.
J. of Materials Sci., Vol. 29, 1994, p. 54-60.

245. P/M metal matrix composites: Experience at IIT Kanpur.
G.S. Upadhyaya.
Materials & Design, Vol. 15, No. 3, 1994, p. 155.

246. Superplastic behaviour of thermomechanically treated P/M 7091 aluminium alloy.
H.N. Azari, G.S. Murty, G.S. Upadhyaya.
Metallurgical and Materials Trans A, 25A, 1994, p. 2153.

247. Electronic mechanisms of sintering: Some case studies on real systems.
G.S. Upadhyaya.
Bulletin of Materials Science, Vol. 17, No. 6, 1994, p. 921-934.

248. Powder metallurgy high speed steels and their composites.
P.K. Kar, G.S. Upadhyaya.
Tool & Alloy Steels, Vol. 29, No. 1, 1995, p. 1.

249. Molybdenum base TZM alloy as the die material.
G.S. Upadhyaya.
In 'Proceedings of Nationals Conference Forge India, 95', 25-26 April 1995, New Delhi, IIM Delhi Chapter, Delhi, 1995, Paper No. C3.

250. Sintering of real systems.
G.S. Upadhyaya.
Science of Sintering, Vol. 27, No. 2, 1995, p. 49-70.

251. Sintered 6061 Al alloy-Al_2O_3/BN particulate composites.
     D.K. Gaur, G.S. Upadhyaya.
     Trans. IIM, Vol. 48, No. 2, 1995, p. 85-96.

252. Sintering of copper-Al_2O_3 composites through blending and mechanical alloying powder metallurgy routes.
     A. Upadhyaya, G.S. Upadhyaya.
     Materials & Design, Vol. 16, No. 1, 1995, p. 41-45.

253. SEM studies of mullite-ZrO_2 particulate composites.
     N. Kapuri, K.N. Rai, G.S. Upadhyaya, G.K. Warrior, K.G. Satyanarayana.
     Pract. Metallography, Vol. 32, No. 4, 1995, p. 197-206.

254. Thermomechanical treatment and superplastic forming of P/M 7-91 aluminium alloy.
     H.N. Azari, G.S. Murty, G.S. Upadhyaya.
     In 'Proceedings of Heat Treatment & Surface Engineering, IFHT '95', Ed. M. Salehi, Isfahan, Iran, Sept., 1995, p. 289-294.

255. Sintering of real systems—A perspective of my academic research (G.D. Birla Lecture).
     G.S. Upadhyaya.
     Trans. IIM, Vol. 48, No. 4, 1995, p. 275-287.

256. High temperature deformation of rapidly solidified P/M 7091 aluminium alloy.
     H.N. Azari, G.S. Murty, G.S. Upadhyaya.
     Sc. & Tech. Of Rapid Solidification and Processing, Ed. M.A. Otooni, Kluwer Academic Publishers, Dordrecht, 1995, p. 195-203.

257. Sintering of mullite prepared through two routes.
     N. Kapuri, K.N. Rai, G.S. Upadhyaya.
     Trans. Ind. Cer. Soc., Vol. 54, No. 3, 1995, p. 65-73.

258. Sintering of mullite based particulate composites containing zirconia.
N. Kapuri, K.N. Rai, G.S. Upadhyaya.
In 'Fourth Euro Ceramic', Vol. 4, Ed. A. Bellosi, Gruppo Editorial, Faenza Editrice SpA, Faenza (Italy), 1995, p. 45-52.

259. 2014 and 6061 Al-alloy based powder metallurgy composites containing SiC particles/fibres.
C. Srinivasa Rao, G.S. Upadhyaya.
Materials & Design, Vol. 16, No. 6, 1995, p. 359-366.

260. Powder metallurgy processing of aluminide intermetallics.
S. Suwas, G.S. Upadhyaya.
Metals, Materials and Processes, Vol. 7, No. 4, 1995, p. 225-250.

261. Effect of binder phase modification and Cr_3C_2 addition on properties of WC-10 Co cemented carbide.
D. Banerjee, G.K. Lal, G.S. Upadhyaya.
J. of Materials Engg. & Performance, Vol. 4, No. 5, 1995, p. 563-572.

262. Processing of mullite and its composites, Part I.
N. Kapuri, K.N. Rai, G.S. Upadhyaya.
Ceramic Industries International, Vol. 105, December, 1995-Jan., 1996, p. 12-16.

263. Sintering of fused mullite based particulate composites containing zirconia.
N. Kapuri, K.N. Rai, G.S. Upadhyaya.
Mat. & Manufacturing Processes, Vol. 11, No. 1, 1996, p. 137-151.

264. Processing of mullite and its composites, Part II.
N. Kapuri, K.N. Rai, G.S. Upadhyaya.
Ceramic Industries International, Vol. 106, Feb/March, 1996, p. 14-18.

265. Sintering of mullite based particulate composites containing ZrO_2.
N. Kapuri, K.N. Rai, G.S. Upadhyaya.
J. of Mat. Sc., Vol. 31, 1996, p. 1481-1487.

266. Full density processing of complex WC based cemented carbides.
S.K. Bhaumik, G.S. Upadhyaya, M.L. Vaidya.
J. of Mat. Processing Tech., Vol. 58, 1996, p. 45-52.

267. Development of Al-Ti based cast composites containing powder metallurgy inserts.
Sohan Lal, G.S. Upadhyaya.
Tool & Alloy Steels, Vol. 30, No. 12, 1996, p. 44-49.

268. Sintering of binder modified $Mo_2Fe(Ni)B_2$-Fe(Ni) cermets and their properties.
G.S. Upadhyaya, P.K. Bagdi.
Sintering Technology, Ed. R.M. German, G.L. Messing and R.G. Cornwall, Marcel Dekker, New York, 1996, p. 181-188.

269. Sintered mullite-ZrO_2 composites prepared through different routes.
N. Kapuri, K.N. Rai, G.S. Upadhyaya.
Interceram, Vol. 45, No. 6, 1996, p. 427-436.

270. Role of Cr_3C_2 in tungsten carbide based hard composites.
G.S. Upadhyaya, D. Banerjee.
In 'Proceedings of 14th Int. Plansee Seminar', Vol. 2 (Ed. G. Kneringer, Rodhammer and P. Whilhartitz), Plansee AG, Reutte (Austria), 1997, p. 463-476.

271. Effect of sol-gel mullite composition on sintering of zirconia containing composites.
N. Kapuri, K.N. Rai, G.S. Upadhyaya.
Science of Sintering, Vol. 25, No. 2, 1997, p. 77-93.

272. Indian metallurgical engineering education: A challenge.
G.S. Upadhyaya.
Tool & Alloy Steels, Vol. 31, No. 8, 1997, p. 9.

273. Short bar plane-strain fracture toughness testing.
G.S. Upadhyaya.
Tool & Alloy Steels, Vol. 31, No. 12, 1997, p. 8.

274. Sliding wear behaviour of T15-Al$_2$O$_3$ particulate composites with or without 5 wt. % copper addition.
     P. Mazumdar, G.S. Upadhyaya.
     Tool & Alloy Steels, Vol. 32, No. 7, 1998, p. 3-10.

275. Powder metallurgy aluminium alloy-SiC composites.
     C.S. Rao, G.S. Upadhyaya.
     Brazilian J. of Mat. Science & Engg., Vol. 1, No. 1, 1998, p. 40-55.

276. Co-sintering of tungsten alloy slurry coated alumina composites and their properties.
     K. Biswas, G.S. Upadhyaya.
     Materials & Design, Vol. 19, 1998, p. 231-240.

277. WC-Co based cemented carbides with large Cr$_3$C$_2$ additions.
     V. Zeckrissori, D. Jansson, G.S. Upadhyaya, H.O. Andren.
     Int. J. of Refractory Metals & Hard Materials, Vol. 16, 1998, p. 417-422.

278. Sintering of some low alloy steels & their heat treatment.
     A.K. Agrawal, G.S. Upadhyaya.
     Tool & Alloy Steels, Vol. 32, No. 12, 1998, p. 21-27.

279. Copper enhances the sintering of duplex P/M stainless steels.
     P. Datta, G.S. Upadhyaya.
     Metal Powder Report, Vol. 54, No. 1, Jan., 1999, p. 26-29.

280. Effect of sintering variables on the properties of 316L and 434L stainless steels.
     P. Datta, G.S. Upadhyaya.
     Industrial Heating, June, 1999, No. 6, p. 37-41.

281. Shrinkage and sintering of TiB$_2$ and TiB$_2$-TiC composite under high pressure.
     S.K. Bhaumik, C. Divakar, A.K. Singh, G.S. Upadhyaya.
     Mat. Science & Engg. A, Vol. 279, 2000, p. 275-281.

282. Effect of CrB addition on sintering of 316L/434L stainless steels-10 v/o Cr_3C_2 composites.
P. Datta, G.S. Upadhyaya.
Science of Sintering, Vol. 32, No. 1, 2000, p. 109-120.

283. Reactive liquid phase sintering of Mo_2FeB_2-Fe cermets.
G.S. Upadhyaya, P.K. Bagdi
Int. J. of Mat. & Product Technology, Vol. 15, No. 3-5, 2000, p. 275-291.

284. Effect of sintering temperature on densification and properties of T15-5 wt. % Cu steels containing Al_2O_3 particles.
P. Mazumdar, G.S. Upadhyaya.
Indian J. of Engg. & Materials Sciences, Vol. 7, June, 2000, p. 141-149.

285. Sintering bonding of Mo_2FeB_2 based cermet onto steel substrate.
Dhaval Rao, G.S. Upadhyaya.
P/M Science & Technology Briefs, Vol. 2, No. 4, 2000, p. 9-13.

286. Some issues in sintering science and technology.
G.S. Upadhyaya.
Materials Chemistry and Physics, Vol. 67, No. 1-3, 15th January, 2001, 1-5.

287. Liquid phase sintering and microstructure-property relationships of silicon carbide ceramics with oxynitride additives.
K. Biswas, G. Rixecker, I. Wiedmann, M. Schweizer, G.S. Upadhyaya, F. Aldinger.
Materials Chemistry and Physics, Vol. 67, No. 1-3, 2001, p. 180-191.

288. Sintered porous cermets based on TiB_2 and TiB_2-TiC-Mo_2C.
M. Singh, K.N. Rai, G.S. Upadhyaya.
Materials Chemistry and Physics, Vol. 67, No. 1-3, 2001, p. 226-233.

289. Sintered duplex stainless steels from premixes of 316L and 434L powders.
P. Datta, G.S. Upadhyaya.
Materials Chemistry and Physics, Vol. 67, No. 1-3, 2001, p. 234-242.

290. Sintering of Mo_2FeB_2 layered cermet containing SiC fibers.
D. Rao and G.S. Upadhyaya.
Materials Chemistry and Physics, Vol. 70, 2001, p. 336-339.

291. Corrosion behaviour of fully dense P/M Al and Cu alloys.
M. Debata and G.S. Upadhyaya.
Proceedings Global-2000 Corrosion Meet (Corrcon-2000), Mumbai, Vol. 1, Paper No. 1 (CD-ROM).

292. Corrosion behaviour of Mo2FeB2 based cermet in H2So4 and NaCl solutions.
M.Debata and G.S.Upadhyaya
Transactions Ind.Cer.Soc.,Vol.60, No.4, 2001,163-166.

293. Powder Metallurgical processing and metal purity : A case for capacitor grade sintered tantalum.
G.S.Upadhyaya
Bull.Materials Science, Vol. 28, No, 2005, 305-307.

294. Nonferrous Metal Powder based Sintered Products : The Tehnological Challenges.
G.S.Upadhyaya
IIM Metal News, Vol.8, No.4, 2005, 9-12.

295. Structure Centric Education in Materials Engineering
G.S.Upadhyaya
Materials Science Forum, Vol.475-479, 2005, 305-3-7.

296. Basic and Applied Aspects of Tungsten carbide based hardmetals
G.S.Upadhyaya and Anish Upadhyaya

In 'Modern Hardmeatals', Ed. N.V.Novikov, V.N. Bakul Institute for Superhard materials, National Academy of Sciences of Ukraine, Kiev, 2008, 185-196.

297. Powder Metallurgy in India
G.S.Upadhyaya
International Journal of Powder Metallurgy,Vol.44, No.4,2008,37-42.

298. Copper in Powder Metallurgy Iron and Steel
G.S.Upadhyaya
Copper Topics, Vol. 33, No.4, 2008, 20-23.

299. Powder Metallurgy Processing, Structure and properties of Metallic Systems: Identifying the Synergy
G.S.Upadhyaya
Dr.D.Swarup Memorial Lecture, IIM Metal News, Vol.11, No./6, 2008,17-37.

300. Strategy for Metallurgical Manpower Management in Metallurgical Industries
G.S.Upadhyaya
Consulting Ahead, Vo.3, No.1, 2009,37-46.

Membership of Academic bodies, Awards & Honours

Membership of Professional Societies

- Member — International Institute for the Science of Sintering (1983)
- Fellow — Indian Institute of Metals (1993)
- Hon. Fellow — Powder Metallurgy Association of India (2008)
- Life Member — Indian Science Congress (1975)
- Member : American Powder Metallurgy Institute, Princeton (1973)
- Life Member : Indian Ceramic Society (1982)
- Life Member : Powder Metallurgy Association of India (1973)
- Life Member : Magnetics Society of India (1975)
- Life Member : Materials Research Society of India (1989)

Member Organising/Liaison Committees of International Conferences:

- International Plansee Seminar, Austria, 1971
- International Powder Metallurgy Conference, Toronto, 1973
- International School on Sintering, New Delhi, 1983.
- International Powder Metallurgy Conference, Dusseldorf, July 1986.
- International Conference on Sintering, Tokyo, November 1987.
- 3rd International Conference on the Science of Hard Materials, Nassau, November 1987.
- 7th Conference on Powder Metallurgy in Poland, Cracow, October 1988.
- International Conference on Sintering of Multiphase Metal and Ceramic Systems, New Delhi, January/February 1989.
- VII World Round Table Conference on Sintering, Herceg-Novi, August/September 1989.

- International Conference on Advanced Metal and Ceramic Matrix Composites, Interfaces, Cleveland, June 1990.
- International Powder Metallurgy Conference and Exhibition, London, July 1990.
- International Powder Metallurgy Conference and Exhibition (P/M 93), Koyto, 1993.
- International Powder Metallurgy Conference (P/M 94), Paris, 1994.
- Fifth International Conference on the Science of Hard Materials, Maui (Howai), February 1995.
- International Conference on Sintering, Penn State University, U.S.A., November 1995.
- VII World Round Table Conference on Sintering, Belgrade, 1998.
- 9th World Ceramic Congress (Section E), Florence, Italy, June 1998.
- 6th International Conference on the Science of Hard Materials, Lanzarite, Spain, March 1998.
- International Conference on Sintering, Penn State University, U.S.A., 1999.
- Sintering 2000, New Delhi, India, February 2000.
- P/M 2000, Kyoto, Japan, November 2000.
- 7th International Conference on the Science of Hard Materials, Ixtapa, Mexico, March 2001.
- World Congress in Powder Metallurgy, Busan, South Korea, September, 2006.

Member Editorial Board of National and International Journals:

- International Journal of Powder Metallurgy,
- Transactions Powder Metallurgy Association of India (formerly)
- Science of Sintering, Serbia (Regional Editor).
- Materials and Design,
- International Journal of Refractory Metals and Hard Materials, U.K.
- Tool and Alloy Steels, India. (ceased to be published)

- Materials Chemistry & Physics,
- Powder Metallurgy International (ceased to be published)
- Key Engineering Materials, Trans. Tech., Switzerland.
- P/M Science & Technology Briefs.(ceased to be published)
- Internet Journal <RefractoryMetals.com>

Awards & Honour

- Hon. Diploma, International Institute for the Science of Sintering, 1979.
- President, Powder Metallurgy Association of India (1987-88 and 1988-89).
- Niobium Medal by Powder Metallurgy Laboratory, Max Planck Institute for Metals Research, Stuttgart, Germany, 1989.
- MRSI (Materials Research Society of India) Medal, 1993.
- Samsonov Prize of International Institute for the Science of Sintering (IISS), 1993.
- G.D. Birla Gold Medal, The Indian Institute of Metals, 1994.
- Distinguished Aluminus Award, Metallurgical Engineering Departemnt,Banaras Hindu University, 1998.
- Hon.Fellow, Powder Metallurgy Association of India, 2008
- Dr. Daya Swarup Memorial Lecturer (2008), Indian Institute of Metals.
- D.N.Agrawal Memorial Lifetime Achievement Award, Indian Ceramic Society, Kolkata,2009

M. Tech./Ph.D. Theses guided:

Ph.D. (12 in number)

1. P.S. Misra, "Study of carbide dispersed aluminium sintered products", University of Roorkee, Roorkee, August, 1974.
2. P.B. Kadam, "Preparation and mechanical behaviour of powder metallurgical lead-base particulate composites" (co-guide: Prof. G.S. Murty & M.L. Vaidya), IIT, Kanpur, December, 1979.

3. M. Hamiuddin, "Effect of alloying additions on sintering of iron-phosphorus premixes", IIT, Kanpur, September, 1980.

4. S.K. Mukherjee, "Sintering of 434L ferritic stainless steel-Al_2O_3 particulate composites", IIT, Kanpur, March, 1984.

5. V. Srikanth, "Effect of binder composition on sintering of tungsten based heavy alloys", IIT, Kanpur, August, 1985.

6. A.K. Jha, "Sintering of 6061 aluminium alloy based particulate composites and their sliding wear behaviour" (co-guide: Dr. S.V. Prasad), IIT, Kanpur, April, 1988.

7. Sohan Lal, "Sintering of 316L austenitic stainess steel-Y_2O_3 particulate composites", IIT, Kanpur, June, 1988.

8. P.K. Kar, "Sintering of refractory compound enriched high speed steels and their properties", IIT, Kanpur, May, 1991.

9. S.K. Bhaumik, "Processing and properties of modified WC-10 Co cemented carbides" (co-guide: Prof. M.L. Vaidya), IIT, Kanpur, February, 1992.

10. H.N. Azari, "Strength-property relations in the rapidly solidified 7091 P/M aluminium alloy" (co-guide: Prof. G.S. Murty),

11. N. Kapuri, "Pressureless sintering of mullite-ZrO_2 particulate composites and their properties" (co-guide: Prof. K.N. Rai), IIT, Kanpur, March, 1995.

12. P.K. Bagdi, "Processing and properties of $Mo_2Fe(Ni)B_2$-Fe(Ni) cermets", IIT, Kanpur, December, 1995.

M. Tech. (37 in number)

1. S.S. Singh, "Activated sintering of Al-bronze", (co-guide: Mr. P.S. Misra), University of Roorkeee, Roorkee, 1971.

2. Madan Lal, "Thermomechanical treatment of 18, 19, 25% maraging steels, University of Roorkee, Roorkee, 1971.

3. P. Thareja, "Activated sintering of Al-Cu alloys with boron addition", University of Roorkee, Roorkee, 1972.

4. Naushad Khan, "Stability of some intermediate phases in transition metal alloy Systems", University of Roorkee, Roorkee, October, 1972.

5. J.P. Tiwari, "Sintering of low alloy steels", University of Roorkee, Roorkee, 1974.

6. Sushil Kumar Singhal, "Effect of transition metal additions on sintering of Cu-7 Al premix," IIT, Kanpur, July, 1979.
7. Utpal Gangopadhyay, "Phase transformation induced activated sintering of AISI 4600 steels" (co-guide: Prof. M.L. Vaidya), IIT, Kanpur, July, 1980.
8. Edwin Samuel, "Abrasion wear of some wrought heat treated steels during jaw Crushing of an Indian iron ore", IIT, Kanpur, July, 1980.
9. P.K. Kar, "Annealing of cold rolled and coated 300-grade silicon steel and its effect on properties", IIT, Kanpur, October, 1980.
10. Sohan Lal, "Preparation and properties of cast aluminium base composites containing powder metallurgy inserts", IIT, Kanpur, June, 1982.
11. A.K. Jha, "Sintering of 2014 Al-alloy based powder metallurgical particulate composites", IIT, Kanpur, January, 1983.
12. Debabrata Basu, "Sintering of tungsten carbide based hardmetals and their properties", IIT, Kanpur, July, 1984.
13. G. Suresh, "Sintering of steel bonded titanium carbides", IIT, Kanpur, January, 1985.
14. Sanjoy Roy, "Sintering of astrology powder compacts and their composites containing yttria", IIT, Kanpur, December, 1985.
15. S.K. Bhaumik, "Sintering of submicron WC based hardmetals", IIT, Kanpur, April, 1986.
16. S.V.V. Ramanna, "Sintering and heat treatment of low alloy steels" (co-guide: Prof. M.L. Vaidya), IIT, Kanpur, August, 1986.
17. M. Basavaiah, "Stereology of sintering of metal powders" (co-guide: Dr. A.M. Gokhale), IIT, Kanpur, July, 1987.
18. S. Kumar, "Effect of tin addition on sintering of lead bronze powder compacts", IIT, Kanpur, January, 1988.
19. S.I. Majagi, "Binder substitution aspects in WC-10 Co hardmetals", IIT, Kanpur, December, 1988.
20. K.N. Ramakrishnan, "Quantitative metallography of some liquid phase sintered systems", IIT, Kanpur, January, 1989.
21. Rajendra Hulyal, "Sintered properties of WC-10 Co hardmetals containing vanadium carbonitride and rhenium", IIT, Kanpur, May, 1989.
22. M. Sujata, "Sintering behaviour of multicomponent titanium alloys" (co-guide: Prof. S. Bhargava), IIT, Kanpur, January, 1991.

23. B.P. Saha, "Liquid phase sintering of T15 and T42 grade high speed steel composites containing TiB_2 or $Ti(C,N)$ particles", IIT, Kanpur, September, 1991.

24. M.V. Gurjar, "Mechanical behaviour of carbide (Al_4C_3) dispersed aluminium" (co-guide: Prof. G.S. Murty), IIT, Kanpur, March, 1992.

25. Prasanta Panigrahi, "Sintering of alumina-molybdenum composites containing calcium aluminosilicate glass", IIT, Kanpur, August, 1992.

26. Govind, "Recrystallization and hydrogen embrittlement of P/M alumina dispersed copper alloys" (co-guide: Dr. R. Balasubramaniam), IIT, Kanpur, March, 1993.

27. Devarshi Kumar Gaur, "Sintering of 6061 Al-alloy and its based composites", IIT, Kanpur, December, 1993.

28. Amitabh Sinha, "Sintering of manganese and chromium containing low alloy steels", IIT, Kanpur, December, 1993.

29. Debangshu Banerjee, "Sintering of binder phase modified WC-10 Co cemented carbides containing chromium carbide" (co-guide: Prof. G.K. Lal), IIT, Kanpur, August, 1994.

30. C.S. Rao, "Sintering of 2014 and 6061 aluminium alloy based composites containing SiC particles or fibres", IIT, Kanpur, February, 1996.

31. Pallav Mazumdar, "Sintering of T15 high speed steel-alumina particulate composites", IIT, Kanpur, May, 1998.

32. Pradyot Datta, "Sintering of 316L and 434L stainless steels and their based composites", IIT, Kanpur, June, 1998.

33. Koushik Biswas, "Liquid phase assisted sintering of alumina and silicon carbide based ceramics" (co-guide: Prof. F. Aldinger), IIT, Kanpur, May, 1999.

34. M. Singh, "TiB_2 based sintered porous cermets" (co-guide: Prof. K.N. Rai), IIT, Kanpur, May, 1999.

35. Ranjan, "Effect of copper and V(C,N) addition on sintering of low alloy steel", IIT, Kanpur, May, 2000.

36. Dhaval Rao, "Sintering bonding of Mo_2FeB_2 based cermet onto steel substrate and sintering of boride cermet-SiC fiber composites", IIT, Kanpur, May, 2000.

37. Mayadhar Debata, "Corrosion behaviour of sintered metallic alloys", IIT, Kanpur, November, 2000.

B.Tech Projects : Numerous, not accounted

Collaborative Research Work:

'Liquid phase sintering of silicon carbide with oxynitride additives', Max Planck Institute for Metals Research, Stuttgart, Germant, 1999-2000 (Prof F.Aldinger)

'WC-Co based cemented carbides containing Cr3C2 additions', Chalmers University, Goteborg, Sweden, 1997-98 (Prof. H.O. Andren)

'Sintered Ceramic Matrix Composites', National Aerospace Laboratory, Bangalore, 1995-97, (Dr. A.K. Singh Dr. S.K. Bhaumik).

'Microstructural Studies of Mullite-based Ceramic Matrix Composites', Regional Research Laboratory, Trivandrum, 1993-94, (Dr. K.G.K. Warrier).

'Sintered Al-base Particulate Composites', Regional Research Laboratory, Bhopal, 1986-88, (Dr. S.V. Prasad / Dr. A.K. Jha).

'Sliding Wear of P/M Steels', I.I.T., Madras, 1978-80, (Dr. K. Gopinath).

'Abrasion Wear of Low Alloy Steels', Tata Steel, Jamshedpur, 1978-79, (Dr. T. Mukherjee / Mr. Edwin Samuel).

'Soft Magnetic Transformer Steels', Tata Steel, Jamshedpur, 1978-79, (Dr. T. Mukherjee / Mr. P.K. Kar)

APPENDIX II

Acronyms

AICTE	All India Council of Technical Education
ASM	American Society for Metals
AIME	American Institute of Metallurgical Engineers
BARC	Bhabha Atomic Research Centre
BHU	Banaras Hindu University
Caltech	California Institute of Technology
CGCRI	Central Glass and Ceramic Research Institute
CSIR	Council of Scientific and Industrial Research
DMRL	Defence Metallurgical Research laboratory
DRDO	Defence Research and Development Organisation
HNC	Higher National Certificate
HND	Higher National Diploma
ICI	Imperial Chemical Industry
IIM	Indian Institute of Metals
IISc	Indian Institute of Science
IISS	International Institute for the Science of Sintering
IIT	Indian Institute of Technology
ISRO	Indian Space Rsearch Organisation
Hindalco	Hindustan Aluminium Co.

MIT	Massachusetts Institute of Technology
MPIF	Metal Powder Industries Federation
NFC	Nuclear Fuel Complex
NML	National Metallurgical Laboratory
ODS	Oxide Dispersion Strengthened
PM	Powder Metallurgy
PMAI	Powder Metallurgy Association of India
PR	Public Relations
SAIL	Steel Authority of India Limited
Tisco	Tata Iron and Steel Co.
TRA	T.R. Ananthraman
USSR	United States of Soviet Republics
YMCA	Young Men's Christian Association